Current Trends in New Testament Study

Current Trends in New Testament Study

Special Issue Editor

Robert E. Van Voorst

MDPI • Basel • Beijing • Wuhan • Barcelona • Belgrade

MDPI

Special Issue Editor
Robert E. Van Voorst
Western Theological Seminary,
Emeritus Holland, Michigan
USA

Editorial Office
MDPI
St. Alban-Anlage 66
4052 Basel, Switzerland

This is a reprint of articles from the Special Issue published online in the open access journal *Religions* (ISSN 2077-1444) in 2019 (available at: https://www.mdpi.com/journal/religions/special_issues/ New_Testament).

For citation purposes, cite each article independently as indicated on the article page online and as indicated below:

LastName, A.A.; LastName, B.B.; LastName, C.C. Article Title. *Journal Name* **Year**, *Article Number*, Page Range.

ISBN 978-3-03928-026-1 (Pbk)
ISBN 978-3-03928-027-8 (PDF)

Contents

About the Special Issue Editor . . . . **vii**

Robert E. Van Voorst
Introduction to the Special Issue "Current Trends in New Testament Study"
Reprinted from: *Religions* **2019**, *10*, 647, doi:10.3390/rel10120647 . . . . **1**

Michele A. Connolly
Antipodean and Biblical Encounter: Postcolonial Vernacular Hermeneutics in Novel Form
Reprinted from: *Religions* **2019**, *10*, 358, doi:10.3390/rel10060358 . . . . **4**

J. J. Johnson Leese
Ecofaith: Reading Scripture in an Era of Ecological Crisis
Reprinted from: *Religions* **2019**, *10*, 154, doi:10.3390/rel10030154 . . . . **25**

Michael R. Licona
Are the Gospels "Historically Reliable"? A Focused Comparison of Suetonius's *Life of Augustus*
and the Gospel of Mark
Reprinted from: *Religions* **2019**, *10*, 148, doi:10.3390/rel10030148 . . . . **38**

Emilio Matricciani and Liberato De Caro
A Deep-Language Mathematical Analysis of Gospels, Acts and Revelation
Reprinted from: *Religions* **2019**, *10*, 257, doi:10.3390/rel10040257 . . . . **56**

Peter S. Perry
Biblical Performance Criticism: Survey and Prospects
Reprinted from: *Religions* **2019**, *10*, 117, doi:10.3390/rel10020117 . . . . **81**

James L. Resseguie
A Glossary of New Testament Narrative Criticism with Illustrations
Reprinted from: *Religions* **2019**, *10*, 217, doi:10.3390/rel10030217 . . . . **96**

Mitzi J. Smith
Paul, Timothy, and the Respectability Politics of Race: A Womanist Inter(con)textual Reading of
Acts 16:1–5
Reprinted from: *Religions* **2019**, *10*, 190, doi:10.3390/rel10030190 . . . . **135**

About the Special Issue Editor

Robert Van Voorst, Professor Emeritus of New Testament in Western Theological Seminary in Holland, Michigan, is a graduate of Hope College, Western Theological Seminary, and Union Theological Seminary (NY). In 1989, he became a professor of religion at Lycoming College. He was a visiting professor at Westminster College in Oxford, England. He was also a visiting professor at Zhejiang University in China, where he lectured and advised doctoral students. Van Voorst has contributed articles to several reference works, most recently *The New Interpreters Dictionary of the Bible*. He is the author of eleven books, including two best-selling textbooks in world religions, and is also the co-author of two books. His latest book, *Commonly Misunderstood Verses of the Bible*, was published in August of 2017 and was featured on CNN. One of his research monographs, *Jesus Outside the New Testament*, examines traditions about Jesus from pagan, Jewish, and Christian documents before and after the New Testament; it has also been published in Italian. His *Reading the New Testament Today* textbook has also been published in Chinese. For more than twenty years, Dr. Van Voorst has been featured on Marquis' *Who's Who in America* and *Who's Who in the World* for his contributions to the field of religious studies.

religions | MDPI

Editorial

Introduction to the Special Issue "Current Trends in New Testament Study"

Robert E. Van Voorst

Professor Emeritus of New Testament, Western Theological Seminary, 1114 Post Ave, Holland, MI 49424, USA;
bobvv@westernsem.edu

Received: 21 November 2019; Accepted: 22 November 2019; Published: 26 November 2019

check for updates

This special issue of *Religions* focuses on seven of the most important formal methods used to interpret the New Testament today. Several of the articles also touch on Old Testament/Hebrew Bible interpretation. In line with the multiplicity of methods for interpretation of texts in the humanities in general, biblical study has never before seen so many different methods. This situation poses both opportunities and challenges for scholars and students alike.

This issue contains contributions by a mix of established scholars and younger scholars who have recently demonstrated their expertise in a certain method. Some articles will be easily accessible only to biblical scholars, but most will be accessible and instructive for beginning- and intermediate-level students of the Bible. I hope that the free-access essays offered here will become required reading in many universities and seminaries. The readership statistics displayed with each article, with information about how they have been read since their online publication here, show that they already have a wide appeal. I want to thank these authors for their contribution to this issue and for working so well with me and indirectly with the anonymous peer reviewers. Here, adapted from their abstracts, are brief introductions to their articles.

Michele A. Connolly's article, "Antipodean and Biblical Encounter: Postcolonial Vernacular Hermeneutics in Novel Form," gives a post-secular exploration of what the Bible offers to modern-day Australia. She maintains that Australian culture, despite its secularity, has a capacity for spiritual awareness in ways that resonate with the Bible. Connolly employs R. S. Sugirtharajah's concept of "vernacular hermeneutics" to show that a contemporary Australian novel, *The Shepherd's Hut* by Tim Winton, expresses an Australian spirituality saturated with the images and values of the New Testament, but in a non-religious literary form that needs interpretation for a secular audience. Connolly's creative and fascinating article speaks not only to the Australian context but can serve as a model for the intersection of postcolonial biblical criticism and contemporary literature from many parts of the post-Christian world.

J. J. Johnson Leese has contributed a significant article on one of the most important issues of our time. "Ecofaith: Reading Scripture in an Era of Ecological Crisis," outlines the emerging field of ecological theology. Johnson Leese deals especially with the methods of ecological hermeneutics developed by biblical scholars, ethicists, and theologians. This relatively new approach to reading scripture has emerged in tandem with increased awareness of the environmental impact of global warming and climate change. Scholars are now challenged to consider how religious anthropocentric worldviews have influenced past readings of the Bible in ways that have contributed to this crisis and constricted the ecological contours of the ancient text. In the first section, Johnson Leese summarizes the history and trajectory of ecological hermeneutics over the past four decades. In the second section, shegives a concise treatment of the reading strategies being considered among scholars today and includes examples of promising ecocritical readings of biblical texts. These readings are based on a constructive and critical engagement of ancient texts in light of modern environmental challenges.

Michael R. Licona, a rising expert in some of the most important matters of New Testament historicity, entitled "Are the Gospels 'Historically Reliable'? A Focused Comparison of Suetonius's *Life of Augustus* and the Gospel of Mark." The question of the historicalreliability of the Gospels has been a constant issue since the rise of critical scholarship but has gained new interest and urgency recently. Licona shows that ancient writers of history had objectives for writing that differed somewhat from those of modern historians. Consequently, literary conventions also differed. In this essay, a definition for the historical reliability of ancient texts is proposed, whereby such a text provides an accurate gist of events or an essentially faithful representation of what occurred. Four criteria that must be met are then proposed. Licona then assesses Suetonius's *Life of the Divine Augustus* and the Gospel of Mark using these criteria. The result of this focused comparison suggests that the *Life of Augustus* and the Gospel of Mark can be called historically reliable in the qualified sense proposed. Both professors and students will benefit from a close reading of this article.

"A Deep-Language Mathematical Analysis of Gospels, Acts and Revelation," by Emilio Matricciani and Liberato De Caro, offers a different kind of statistical analysis of the New Testament than scholars may be familiar with. It uses mathematical methods developed for studying what the authors call deep-language parameters of literary texts, for example, the number of words per sentence, the number of characters per word, the number of words between interpunctions (punctuation within sentences), and the number of interpunctions per sentence. Matricciani and De Caro consider, in concert with generally-accepted conclusions of New Testament scholarship, the full texts of the canonical Gospels, Acts and Revelation, then the Gospel passages attributable to the triple tradition (Matthew, Mark and Luke), to the double tradition (Matthew and Luke), to the single tradition in Matthew and Luke, and to the Q source. The results confirm and reinforce some common conclusions about the Gospels, Acts, Revelation, and Q source, but the authors show that they cast some new light on the capacity of the short-term memory of the readers/listeners of these texts. The authors posit that these New Testament writings fit very well in the larger Greek literature of the time. For readers unaccustomed to using mathematical models in the study of the New Testament, this article will present some challenges, but will more than repay the work put into it.

Peter S. Perry's "Biblical Performance Criticism: Survey and Prospects," which deals with one of the newest critical methods of understanding the Bible. After discussing four aspects of communication events (a communicator, traditions re-expressed, an audience, and a social situation), Perry surveys the history of biblical performance criticism and its current prospects. He then points to the future work of developing a fine-grained theoretical foundation for its work. Unlike many other methods of biblical criticism, performance criticism has an analytical mode, a heuristic mode, and a practical mode. In the analytical mode, a scholar gathers and examines data from a past performance event to describe it, and its effects, in detail. In the heuristic mode, a performer presents a tradition or passage to an audience in order to discover its dynamics more fully. In the practical mode, a person reflects on the performance of biblical traditions in daily life. In these ways, Perry suggests, performance criticism helps to overcome the critical reduction and fragmentation of current biblical study and also bridges the gap between the academic and popular use of the Bible.

James Resseguie, an expert in narrative criticism of the New Testament, offers both scholars and students a unique and comprehensive "Glossary of New Testament Narrative Criticism with Illustrations."This glossary lists prominent terms, concepts, and techniques of narrative criticism, all in alphabetical order. Commonly used terms that every student of narrative criticism should know are included, including for example character and characterization, double entendre, misunderstanding, implied author, implied reader, irony, narrator, point of view, plot, rhetoric, and more. Lesser-known terms and concepts are also defined and illustrated. Major methods of reading the text—for example, narratology, New Criticism, and reader-response criticism—are explained with references to the prominent literary critics/theorists who developed them. An important part of this glossary is the illustration of each term drawn from the New Testament, and cross-references to other terms increase the value of the definitions. Resseguie states that this is the first stand-alone glossary of New Testament narrative-critical terms in the English language, and one may expect that it will find its way into many classes in New Testament interpretation as well as be used by scholars as a handy reference tool.

The final article is Mitzi J. Smith offers a fresh, thought-provoking reading of the story of the Apostle Paul's circumcision of Timothy, "Paul, Timothy, and the Respectability Politics of Race: A Womanist Inter(con)textual Reading of Acts 16:1–5". Her approach is intersectional and inter-contextual, featuring a dialogue between African American women's experiences of race and racism, respectability politics, and the narrative of Acts 16. Drawing on leading critical race theorists, Smith discusses the intersection of race/racism, gender, geopolitical Diasporic space, and respectability politics. Respectability politics, a critical understanding of which stands at the heart of Smith's essay, claims that when non-white people in predominantly white societies engage in certain "proper" behaviors, they will ameliorate or even overcome the racism they face. Smith concludes that Paul engaged in respectability politics by compelling Timothy to be circumcised because of his Greek father, despite the Jerusalem Council's decision that Gentile believers should not be required to be circumcised. Smith has included a short video introducing her article.

Conflicts of Interest: The author declares no conflict of interest.

religions

MDPI

Article

Antipodean and Biblical Encounter: Postcolonial Vernacular Hermeneutics in Novel Form

Michele A. Connolly †

Catholic Institute of Sydney, Sydney College of Divinity, Strathfield, NSW 2135, Australia;
mconnolly@cis.catholic.edu.au
† Michele A. Connolly, rsj.

Received: 12 March 2019; Accepted: 29 May 2019; Published: 31 May 2019

check for
updates

Abstract: This article argues that in postcolonial and post-secular Australia, a country in which Christianity has been imported from Europe in the process of colonization in the eighteenth century by the British Empire, institutional Christianity is waning in influence. However, the article argues, Australian culture has a capacity for spiritual awareness provided it is expressed in language and idioms arising from the Australian context. R. S. Sugirtharajah's concept of vernacular hermeneutics shows that a contemporary novel, *The Shepherd's Hut* by Tim Winton, expresses Australian spirituality saturated with the images and values of the New Testament, but in a non-religious literary form.

Keywords: vernacular hermeneutics; Australian spirituality; colonial; landscape; crucifixion; mercy; New Testament

1. Introduction

A fundamental question that must be asked by any postcolonial biblical critic thinking about the relationship between the New Testament and Australia is this: What capacity does the postcolonial and post-secular Australian consciousness have in the first quarter of the twenty-first century to receive the message of the New Testament as a guide for living?

My response in this article to this question is that postcolonial and post-secular Australia has that capacity to embrace Christian faith that comes from walking the journey of life fully engaged with the Australian, postcolonial context in its contemporary, post-secular reality. This journey must be expressed in a contemporary idiom that allows authentic, convincing expression of a spirituality that rings true to Australian experience.

Just such an expression of this spiritual journey is made in the recently published Australian novel, *The Shepherd's Hut*, by Tim Winton.[1] Winton was born in 1960 in the rural town of Scarborough, not far from Perth in the State of Western Australia. In his autobiographical writing, Winton describes a childhood spent close to the Australian bush but also close to the coast where he has surfed from childhood. Of growing up in small-town Western Australia, Winton has said, "I write about small places; about people in small situations. If I get a grip on the geography, I can get a grip on the people."[2] He has also written that surfing led him to writing. "The child of a pragmatic, philistine and insular culture, I responded," he writes," to the prospect of something wilder, broader, softer, more fluid and emotional. It sounds unlikely but I suspect surfing unlocked the artist in me."[3] Winton has turned his writing skills to defending Ningaloo Reef, a coral reef on the Northern edge of Western

---

1   Winton 2018.
2   Wilde et al. 1994, p. 822.
3   Winton 2016, p. 132–33.

Australia, working to protect the reef by having the Ningaloo Marine Park and adjacent Cape Range National Park added to the World Heritage Register, in 2011 and beyond that to protest against large multinational mining companies setting up dredging operations in the Park.[4]

Winton has written twenty-nine novels, mostly for adults but some also for children. He has won the major Australian literary prize, the Miles Franklin Award, four times and has been shortlisted for the Book Prize twice.[5] He writes on Australian life, particularly as it is lived in Western Australia, a vast State which is nine times the size of Texas in the USA.[6] Winton writes about family life in rural towns, especially about boys growing to manhood in a culture of toxic masculinity, about the Australian landscape and seascape, and increasingly about the environment. The power of the Australian landscape, and father-son relationships are the focus of *The Shepherd's Hut*, which tells the story of two characters whose encounter with each other in the Australian bush leads each to a new place of promise or rest in his life.

The principal character, Jaxie Clackton, is a fourteen-year-old boy who runs away from a violent father and a fear that the law is pursuing him for murder. He escapes into the bush where his bushmanship helps him to survive until he meets the other main character, Fintan, an old man with a mysterious history living alone in the bush. Surviving together in the beautiful but dangerous Australian landscape, the two overcome mutual suspicion and fear, until they finally share both companionship and love. The crisis point of the novel comes when the contemporary criminal world breaks into Jaxie and Fintan's precarious existence in the form of drug runners whose clandestine operation Jaxie has discovered. In the rupture the criminal world makes, the fate of both Jaxie and Fintan is resolved, the former to freedom in a new life and the latter to his final rest.

In this novel, Tim Winton portrays the profoundly spiritual encounter a young postcolonial child of the Australian culture has with himself, with life and death, with the joys and dark terrors of life, all this provoked by a sojourn of survival through the Australian bush. This writing shows that Australian consciousness has a capacity, even an appetite, for spiritual consciousness. In this paper I will argue that the novel regularly employs the specific spiritual language and imagery that comes from the Christian New Testament and that given the popularity of this novelist in his home country, this reveals that Australians can engage with deep spiritual matters as they are expressed in the New Testament. Before embarking on a necessary explication of Australian postcolonial and post-secular identity, it is necessary to clarify that I do not argue that Tim Winton is making an explicitly biblical, Christian or even religious case in this novel. He is not promoting any particular religious institution or stance. It is not that Winton cites the Bible unconsciously. He himself has written about his religious upbringing as a result of his parents' conversion to Christianity in response to marked kindness from a Christian to Winton's father as he recovered from a severe motor accident. Winton describes his family as "a twice-on-Sundays outfit ... unaccountably and unreasonably churchy."[7] He says that at church he learnt the value of story because "without narrative there is only theological assertion, which is in effect, inert cargo."[8] Even more specifically, he began to discover through the focus on the Bible, the power of language, especially of metaphor. It became food to his adolescent mind. "Language, I was to discover, is nutrition, manna without which we're bereft and forsaken, consigned like Moses and his restive entourage to wander in a sterile wilderness."[9] Lyn McCredden writes that "Winton's publicly declared religious values ha[ve] complicated critical debates."[10] This may be because it seems

---

4   Winton 2018–2019.
5   Tim Winton won the Miles Franklin award for his novels, *Shallows* (1984), *Cloudstreet* (1991), *Dirt Music* (2001) and *Breath* (2008). He was shortlisted for the Booker Prize for *The Riders* (1994) and for *Dirt Music* (2001). See Winton n.d..
6   Western Australia's area of 2,527,013 square km, of which a very large amount is desert is 9.4 times the area of Texas at 695,662 square km. For details on Texas and Western Australia see respectively, McNamee et al. 2019; Area of Australia n.d..
7   Winton 2016, p. 94.
8   Ibid., p. 106.
9   Ibid., p. 108.
10   McCredden and O'Reilly 2014, p. 8.

to pre-empt critical decisions about Winton's intention. I mention Winton's well-known religious background to avoid any suggestion that his use of the Bible is not conscious.

The Shepherd's Hut is saturated with religious sensibility, that is articulated, often with intense irony, in the language of the Bible but particularly of the New Testament. Tim Winton's skill as a novelist ensures that there is no sense of "Bible-bashing" in his novel; his very sure hand with plot and characterization make any expression of spiritual ideas or biblical language sound entirely natural, credible and remote from anything like preaching—while at the same time provoking the reader to thought. For example, in the course of three pages of stream-of-consciousness from the mind of the character Jaxie Clackton, Winton probes the inadequacies of contemporary Christian church and religious ritual; touches on both clericalism and revulsion against clerical sexual abuse; and explores prayer, the need for mercy and the manifold ways in which real people exercise their spirituality.[11] It does not read as a treatise on religion in Australia; it reads as a novelistic exposé of the ideas a teenage boy has about religious matters. Many Australian (and non-Australian) readers would be likely to resonate with Jaxie's concerns, to identify with his rejection of shallow religiosity and to recognize themselves in his reaching for a credible and dignified way to express spiritual desire in his life.

The story itself, the beautifully rendered Australian landscape and the development of the characters in the novel, especially of the young anti-hero Jaxie Clackton, express in an unmistakably Australian vernacular a desire for or awareness of such spiritual values as mercy, gratitude and tenderness. While these values are not the exclusive property of the New Testament, they are unmistakably part of its worldview.

Winton does not set out to provide a systematic exposé of the values of the New Testament. Rather, from his obvious familiarity with its language and images, he selects incidental parts to help him construct his characters by having them express or enact these values. Later in this paper, after listing a sample of Winton's allusion to various New Testament texts, I will focus on ideas or images Winton uses from the Gospel of John. The Johannine Jesus' expression of his purpose in terms of having "food to eat;" his identity expressed in the expression, "I am;" concerns about the truth and above all the power of the Word appear in Winton's characterization. However, it is the image of the body strung up, "lifted up" on the cross, echoing the serpent raised up on a standard of Num 21:9, that Winton uses as a *lietmotif* through his novel on which I will concentrate in the final phase of this paper.

The language of the novel is shot through with an ironic juxtaposition between the language and imagery of the whole Bible but particularly of the Christian New Testament on the one hand, and with Jaxie's Australian speech on the other. Winton shows with pleasure how oddly they sit together at the level of diction, yet how truly they speak in concert of the deep issues of life. This writing shows that Australian sensibility can respond to what Jesus of Nazareth teaches in the New Testament. Jesus' vision of God's intent for the world was hard-edged with realism yet insistent on hope in life; Jaxie's vision is equally as hard-edged, as sharp as the knife he whets on stone, but also committed to life and to a fiercely protective tenderness. An Australian consciousness that can express itself in this way has a capacity to hear the message proclaimed by the New Testament.

A. Postcolonial and Post-secular Australia: A Setting for Encounter with the New Testament

In order to develop this argument, it is necessary to establish the idea of Australia as a postcolonial nation, for which postcolonial biblical criticism is relevant. Second, a few words will be useful to clarify what I mean when I refer to the New Testament and its message. Third, it will be important to lay out the relationship between contemporary postcolonial Australia and Christian faith, as it is practiced in publicly recognized churches in Australia. Finally, postcolonial biblical criticism must be discussed, especially the particular form of it that I will use, called "vernacular criticism."

---

[11] See Winton 2018, pp. 22–24.

1. Postcolonial Australia

Early twenty-first century Australia is properly called "postcolonial" because of its foundation as a colony of the British Empire in the late eighteenth century.[12] Australia is no longer a colony of that Empire but continues in a political relationship with the British Crown. Like Canada, New Zealand, Papua New Guinea and a dozen small island nations of the Caribbean Sea and the Pacific Ocean, Australia conducts its own affairs but with the British Crown as its formal Head of State.[13] A failed attempt by an Australian Republican Movement to move Australia to a republican form of government by national referendum in 1999 means that for the foreseeable future, Australia will remain a constitutional monarchy, a political arrangement that harks back to Australia's colonial origins.[14] On this basis, it is appropriate to consider Australia as a postcolonial nation.

Post-secular Australia

Another dimension of contemporary Australia relevant to this paper is Australia's public attitudes towards religion. It is now widely recognized that in the West, most nations have seen a significant decline in formal public, religious affiliation and practice. Until recently, this reality was ascribed to the influence of secularism, defined by Charles Taylor as involving both "the falling off of religious belief and practice, in people turning away from God, and no longer going to Church," and then "a move from a society where belief in God is unchallenged and indeed, unproblematic, to one in which it is understood to be one option among others, and frequently not the easiest to embrace."[15] However, many theorists now argue that Western nations have moved into what they call "post-secularity," which they identify not as the opposite of secularity but as "a consciousness that develops within a secular society."[16] Elaine Graham cites Graham Tomlin as describing the stance of the West to Christianity as "Not hostile to or uninformed about Christianity, often interested in spiritual questions and prepared to face the difficult issues of mortality and meaning. And yet the Church is the last place they would look for answers."[17] Gary Bouma echoes this assessment, of the place of public religion, writing that, as in other similar secular nations, in Australia "religion and spirituality have seeped out of the monopolistic control of formal organization like church ... [resulting in] vastly increased diversity of both organized religious and private spiritualities."[18]

An expression of this stance that is frequently heard in Australia is the statement that a person is "spiritual but not religious."[19] It is surely not surprising then, that surveys by both government and church agencies in Australia find that regular forms of religious practice have continued to decline over the last half of the twentieth century into the twenty-first. A media release from the Australian Bureau of Statistics (ABS) of 27 July 2017, reporting on the Australian 2016 census, found that "The religious makeup of Australia has changed gradually over the past 50 years. In 1966, Christianity (88 per cent) was the main religion. By 1991, this figure had fallen to 74 per cent, and further to the 2016 figure of 52.1%."[20] More than this, there has been a steady growth in people declaring that they have no religion

---

[12] Standard treatments of the foundation of Australia from its beginning as a penal colony set up on the banks of Sydney Harbor in 1788 can be found in such historical studies as Atkinson 1977; Clark 1950; Hughes 1987; Kociumbas 1992; and various chapters from the study of the British Empire in Louis 1998–1999.

[13] The full list of nations which are constitutional monarchies is: Canada; Bahamas; Grenada; Australia; Tuvalu; Solomon Islands; New Zealand; Jamaica; Antigua & Barbuda; Saint Vincent and the Grenadines; Barbados; Saint Lucia; Belize; Papua New Guinea; Saint Kitts & Nevis. See Galka 2016 for a very helpful series of charts explaining the complex relationships between the United Kingdom and the former colonies of the British Empire.

[14] For a full discussion of the reasons why the referendum failed to support a move to Australia becoming a democratic republic see McKenna and Hudson 2003, esp. pp. 1–9; 249–52; 273–75; McKenna 1996; McKenna 2004.

[15] Taylor 2007, pp. 3, 4.

[16] Dixon 2018, p. 74.

[17] Dixon 2018, p. 57.

[18] Bouma, Gary D. 2006. *Australian Soul: Religion and Spirituality in the 21st Century*. Melbourne: Cambridge University Press, p. 5, cited in Dixon 2018, p. 74.

[19] See Taylor 2007, p. 535; Graham 2018, p. 56 for descriptions of the contexts in which people make this assertion.

[20] See Census Data 2017.

at all. The media release notes that "Those reporting no religion increased noticeably from 19 per cent in 2006 to 30 per cent in 2016."[21] Bob Dixon interprets the 2011 Australian Census' data about Australia's largest religious group, Roman Catholics, examining ten categories ranging from age, ethnic diversity, and changing beliefs of churchgoers through the declining numbers of Australian-born priests and members of religious orders to disillusionment over Catholic Church responses to clergy sexual abuse. He concludes that as one of the largest employers in the country because of its commitment to education, health and social services, the church will continue to be a significant player in the public space, "too big not to engage with." Nevertheless, at the level of private commitment, Dixon argues that "ordinary Australian Catholics are likely to be increasingly diverse in their religious practices, beliefs, spiritualities and attitudes towards the institutional church."[22]

The Message of the New Testament

This article asks whether contemporary postcolonial Australia has the capacity to engage with the message of the New Testament as a way of living. The twenty-seven documents of various literary styles that constitute the New Testament present a message about Jesus of Nazareth and his religious vision. The New Testament message is that God loves human beings to the point of committing God's own son to live and die in earthly, mortal condition and to rise to life beyond the limits of death. Christians believe that this death and resurrection of Jesus restored the relationship between God and human beings that had been destroyed by sin, originating with the primordial disobedience against God's word by the first humans Adam and Eve, but participated in by all human beings. This restoration of relationship by the faithful obedience of Jesus, even to death on a cross, redeemed human beings from the power of Sin and enabled them to participate in the Reign of God, even here and now on earth, that was inaugurated by Jesus' resurrection from death. God initiated this process of redemption out of love, offering mercy, compassion and forgiveness for no reason other than God's love for God's creation. The only price asked to enjoy the benefits of God's generosity is faith and human readiness to live out the implications of being redeemed by, among other things, expressing God's mercy and compassion to one another.

This message, of course, has been presented across two thousand years of Christian history not only in the New Testament documents but in a vast range of cultural perceptions of what the New Testament says and means. This article takes as a test case, the perception in contemporary postcolonial Australia of what that message is and whether it is of any value today. This issue will be addressed by a discussion of the way it is treated in a contemporary Australian novel that I argue shows a particularly strong engagement between Australian culture and biblical, especially New Testament, values. How this will be carried out will be explained in section A.2. Postcolonial Biblical Criticism: The Vernacular Hermeneutic below, which discusses postcolonial biblical criticism.

2. Relationship between Contemporary Postcolonial Australia and Christian Faith

i. Christian Faith

There are issues on both sides of this relationship between Christianity and contemporary, postcolonial Australia. Christianity itself faces a two-part challenge that is intrinsic to its character as an historically-based religion. That is, Christian origins are remote in both time and space from contemporary Australia. With regard to time, as an historically based religious tradition, Christianity originated during the first century C.E. in the life and death and proclaimed resurrection of Jesus of Nazareth and was brought to Australia in the late eighteenth century by the first European settlers, both by ordained clergy of Christian churches and by believers themselves, even if these believers

---

[21] Ibid.
[22] Dixon 2018, p. 91.

were convicts. Both the world of the first century and the world of the eighteenth century are remote in time from contemporary Australia, even the days of the convict settlement of the country.

With regard to space, Jesus of Nazareth lived and the New Testament itself was composed in the ancient Mediterranean. The New Testament was written in the language and literary forms of that place and time. Much more recently those who brought Christianity to Australia came from the Northern hemisphere, from Great Britain, Ireland and to a lesser degree, Europe. The Christianity they brought was inevitably expressed in the language, metaphors, symbolism and worldview of the Northern hemisphere. While the idea of England as "mother" and "home" or of Ireland as "the old country" prevailed in the predominantly Anglo-Saxon settler population of Australia as far as into the early twentieth century, Christian faith experienced in church membership and regular Sunday attendance at worship seemed all of a piece with the larger cultural world view. However, as the nation has grown beyond its bicentenary of the establishment of British culture and as it becomes notably multi-cultural, including peoples who practice religions other than Christianity, and as the post-secular worldview has become normative in Australia, Christianity has ceased to appear to be a natural, unquestioned, necessary part of Australian life.

Rather, Christianity has found it necessary to defend itself as good against accusations that it has historically been the cause of deadly wars and destructive divisions even within itself. In recent times Christianity has been accused of being deeply hypocritical morally as evidenced by the recent exposure of the high degree of sexual abuse perpetrated within churches especially by its clergy. Bob Dixon sums up that on the issue of sexuality in general, in Australia, "For the Church, evil is the deliberate violation of the natural law; for contemporary Australians, especially younger Australians, evil is the deliberate prevention of people from exercising their rights."[23] A third charge laid against Christian practice is that it promotes an unsustainable fantasy world that has been exposed as delusional by the hard empirical sciences.[24]

ii.   Contemporary Postcolonial and Post-secular Australia

Australia's postcolonial situation is not the same as any other nation's reality, even postcolonial nations, because Australia's history is its own. Founded relatively late in the imperialist period by the British Empire for the inglorious purpose of disposing of Great Britain's excess convict population, Australia has had to grow into a nation without a clear, long-term goal or purpose beyond the fact of its mere existence.

As Australians struggle amongst themselves in their political connection to the British crown and the Northern hemisphere, they need to establish their own identity in the world, to take themselves seriously. Australians are still working to find their own voice beyond imitation of the greater economic powers and older Northern hemisphere cultures. Australians need to come to serious terms with Australia: with its geo-political location and relationship to the larger, more powerful economies in its history and geography; with its own ecology which is ancient, rare, beautiful and fragile; and with its cultural history and the religious traditions of both the ancient original peoples and of the more recent Northern hemisphere Western culture founding peoples. Australia could benefit from developing a more mature religious sense that allows not only diversity of faith expressions as already exists but also an ability to express values and consciousness that are larger than the solely empirical. Christianity, practiced in Australia since the beginning of British settlement, is one such religious tradition

What can be done is to bring the Australian context, with its history, cultural practices, language and rituals into a realistic encounter with Christianity. Each needs to be able to declare itself truly; neither can dominate over the other; each needs to hear the other at its truest and best, articulating values that Australians can recognize as desirable, as able to help them realize their own best and

---

[23]   Dixon 2018, p. **89**.
[24]   For prominent discussion of contemporary atheism and its interaction with religion, see Gray 2018; Carroll and Norman 2017; Martin 2007.

credible selves. One way that enables this to happen is distinctly Australian creative work which connects the worldviews and idioms of both Australia and Christianity. The Australian novelist Tim Winton has done this remarkably well in his recent novel, *The Shepherd's Hut*. The biblical critical methodology of postcolonial biblical criticism, especially a form of it called "vernacular hermeneutics," makes it possible to show how Tim Winton engages both the Australian context and the Christian worldview with insight, humor and human integrity. This paper will next provide a brief survey of this methodology before treating Tim Winton's novel in some depth, to show how a non-religious, secular novel can bring both contemporary and ancient biblical cultural issues into suggestive connection with each other.

2. Postcolonial Biblical Criticism: The Vernacular Hermeneutic

Postcolonial Biblical Criticism has been developed since the 1980s in countries which experienced colonization by the imperial powers of Northwest Europe, from the age of exploration to the "new world" on. Nations of the African sub-continent, of India, South and East Asia, the Pacific, the Caribbean and Latin America have all contributed to the development of this methodology which reflects on the way the Bible can be, even must be, interpreted in nations in which biblically based Christianity was imported along with military, political and economic imperial takeover of lands, a takeover that suppressed existing indigenous cultures and their sovereignty.[25]

A scholar who has contributed very strongly to postcolonial biblical criticism is Rasiah S. Sugirtharajah. Born and educated initially in Sri Lanka, Sugirtharajah is Emeritus Professor of Biblical Hermeneutics in the Department of Theology and Religion at the University of Birmingham, UK. He has published widely in the field of postcolonial biblical criticism, shaping the field as he has done so.[26] One very important contribution that he has made is a particular mode of postcolonial biblical criticism that Sugirtharajah calls "vernacular hermeneutics." He defines vernacular hermeneutics as "the indigenization of biblical interpretation."[27] Under this rubric of vernacular hermeneutics, Sugirtharajah has developed a methodology that focuses on culture, beginning with the culture of the interpreter which is therefore valued from the outset of any interpretive process, before moving to read the biblical text for its cultural content. Sugirtharajah has identified three large categories under which first, an interpreter's culture may be analyzed and then, a biblical text may also be understood. In this way, working by analogy, sympathetic cultural resonances between an interpreter and a sacred text may be identified.

These three categories deal with ideas or concepts; with behaviors, especially deeply significant ritual actions of a culture or a text; and the various material manifestations of a culture in which Sugirtharajah includes language and symbolism. In his words, the cultural content of the interpreter may be grouped under three headings, namely "ideational (world views, values and rules), performantial (rituals and roles) and material (language, symbols, food, clothing, etc.)."[28] Once the interpreting culture has been located in this way, it is possible to approach the text to be interpreted by what Sugirtharajah calls "at least three modes of vernacular reading—conceptual correspondence, narratival [sic] enrichments and performantial parallels."[29] The term "conceptual correspondences" refers to conceptual similarities found in both the culture of production of a text and the culture seeking to interpret it. "Narratival enrichments" identify the various story-telling strategies by which a culture makes sense of the world to itself, such as, for example, in Australia the strong tendency to tell the story of the unlikely underdog who succeeds by grit, determination and unorthodox methods. Such story-telling practices in the interpreting culture can be set beside narratives in the biblical text to be

---

[25] For an extensive treatment of the modern British imperialism relevant to this paper, see Louis 1998–1999.
[26] Some recent titles of R. S. Sugirtharajah include Sugirtharajah 1999, 2008, 2012, 2016, 2018.
[27] Sugirtharajah 2001, p. 177.
[28] Ibid., 182.
[29] Ibid. See fuller descriptions of these three modes of reading on pp. 182–90.

interpreted, as a way to access what both cultures have in common. "Performantial parallels" refers to "ritual and behavioral practices which are commonly available in a culture" and which thus provide a cultural commonality between the interpreting culture and that of the text to be interpreted.[30]

B. Tim Winton's *The Shepherd's Hut:* Vernacular Hermeneutics in Novel Form

Winton's novel is a form of narrativel enrichment of contemporary Australian experience. It tells the story of a young' mans' journey through trial to self-discovery and affirmation of himself as a human being and a man. This is a common human story told here in the contemporary Australian context. Vernacular hermeneutics makes it possible to show that this particular novel does the work of vernacular hermeneutics because in its telling of the tale, the novel constantly moves from the interpreting culture to biblical texts to be interpreted—in such a way that new light is shed on them.

In the second half of this article, I will argue that Winton's *The Shepherd's Hut* brings Australian postcolonial vernacular culture into productive, often rueful and sometimes delightful conversation with biblical values, especially those of the New Testament. I do not argue that Winton has in any sense, consciously set out to use what R. S. Sugirtharajah names "vernacular hermeneutics." However, I do assert that what Winton has done is able to be accounted for by the insights of vernacular hermeneutics, which Sugirtharajah himself declares is not a new methodology but has a long history in human interpretation.[31] In the novel, all three categories of the cultural world of the interpreter can be found, that is the performantial (focused on rituals and roles); the material (surfacing in language, symbols, food and clothing and other material manifestations of culture) and the ideational (expressing world view and values). As an interpreter of this novel in its vernacular interpretation of an Australian experience in connection with the worldview of the Bible, especially the New Testament, I will show that all three modes of vernacular hermeneutics operate within the novel.

1. The Wild Colonial Boy

A brief plot survey of the novel is that it is told in the first-person voice of a teenaged Australian boy who reviews recent events, indeed his whole life, in which he survived brutality at home, months in the Australian bush on the barest resources, and finally risked life itself in combat with deadly criminals. Its plot is that of a thriller; its meaning is profoundly spiritual. Much of this meaning emerges in a months-long encounter between the young anti-hero narrator, Jackson (Jaxie) Clackton and the mentor figure of Fintan MacGillis, the failed Irish priest who learned to survive as a civilized man in the Australian wilderness. The novel opens in Jaxie's present moment but then flashes back to the past that has led him to this moment, both the immediate past which creates the plot of the novel and the whole of Jaxie's brief past life. This reveals his origins and the joys and sufferings that have prepared him to engage in the hero's survival and self-discovery journey in the Australian bush.

As the journey of the anti-hero, the novel is very concerned with Jaxie's discovery of his own identity as a young Australian male. As the son of the town butcher who passed off ill-gotten horsemeat as beef, Jaxie is derided in his hometown as "Jaxie Horsemeat."[32] Fintan gives him a new name as "the wild colonial boy," singing to him lines from a famous colonial Australian ballad about an Irish teenaged boy who led a life of crime in Australia and was eventually shot by the police. The lines Fintan sings tell Jaxie's history as a son, prophesy some criminal acts that Jaxie in fact will commit in the course of the novel and sums him up, "*A terror to Australia was the wild colonial boy.*"[33] Here we see Jaxie cast in a distinctly Australian colonial role, a role harking back to Australia's convict origins. The meaning of this colonial ballad in the novel can be accounted for by both the material and the performantial dimensions of vernacular hermeneutics. The material dimension, attentive to

---

[30] Ibid., p. 182.
[31] Ibid.
[32] Winton 2018, p. 43.
[33] Winton 2018, pp. 108–9, italics in the original text.

language and symbols, highlights the resonance this ballad has in Australian ears, who recognize it as a very typical expression of the colonial era. The performantial category of vernacular hermeneutics identifies the role of "the wild colonial boy" as larger in meaning than just a joke nickname from the old man; it reveals that Jaxie is still at risk of being cast in a criminal role of the colonial past. Jaxie's task is precisely to acquire *post*colonial status, to leave his wrecked youth behind, to negotiate what life throws in his path and to achieve a future that is free. The attentive reader will be encouraged that Jaxie might succeed by his assertion in the opening section of the novel, "For the first time in me life I know what I want and I have what it takes to get me there."[34]

2. The Vernacular Hermeneutics of the Wild Colonial Boy

It is important to note that the movement from the culture of postcolonial Australia in the person of Jaxie making sense of the world to the spiritual world expressed by the Bible begins from Jaxie's distinctly Australian speech, his "ocker" vernacular. It is clearly the only language available to him from his up-bringing. It is frequently grammatically incorrect, uses crude, often abbreviated vocabulary, and an abundance of four-letter words to express surprise, consternation but very often fear and loathing. Fiona Morrison cites the Australian postcolonial scholars Ashcroft, Griffiths and Tiffin, arguing that the vernacular language "comprises 'the complex of speech habits which characterize the local tongue, or even the evolving ... local English [sic] of a monolingual society trying to establish its link with place'."[35] Vernacular hermeneutics, under the heading of the "material," recognizes this movement from the interpreting culture to the text to be interpreted as a culturally necessary progression from the known and valued to the unknown, yet to be evaluated.

a. *Jaxie's vernacular speech evokes and interacts with biblical discourse*

Since the novel is narrated in Jaxie's voice, it is filled with examples of his speech. He is given to particularly Australian similes to describe his experiences. Some are perhaps learned expressions; others are Jaxie's own invention. Describing his thirst, Jaxie says he is "dry as a camel's cookie"; water in the swimming hole was so cold it was "brass monkeys"; something that clings "stuck like shit to a blanket"; an unpleasant surprise was "like a kick in the clacker"; and a place riddled with snakes is as "snaky as fuck."[36] While, as we will see, Jaxie can at certain moments express the beauty of the Australian landscape, he also recognizes his isolation in a place that he calls "bumfuck nowhere."[37] When he shoots a bungarra, a goanna, to avoid starvation, he laments the death of the animal in a backhanded, laconic fashion. He asks himself how his culture would interpret the sudden, violent loss of life for an animal supremely at home in its world and answers with an expression he's learned. "What do they say? Rooster Sunday, feather duster Monday."[38]

Yet, Jaxie is open to learn, seen when he turns the word "cogitate" over in his mind and his mouth, a word he learned from Fintan. In this, he is like many Winton characters, for whom, writes Lyn McCredden, "A preoccupation with words—written, spoken storytelling, vernacular, lyrical, humorous, abject, ideological—is central."[39] "Cogitate," Jaxie says "that's a word I didn't even know back at the diggings but I like the sound of it."[40] Jaxie likes the sound of it because he is a poet and he is hungry to learn what is real. The material dimension of vernacular hermeneutics recognizes Jaxie as a poet when he describes the Australian landscape because his language is specific with the perceptions of his eyes, his sense of smell and his feeling of texture. When he encounters the natural world Jaxie is fully alive in his senses. Early on his journey, he describes the Australian landscape at

---

[34] Ibid., p. 5.
[35] Morrison 2014; Rooney 2014, p. 53.
[36] For these expressions in sequence, see pp. 48, 81, 88, 92, 114.
[37] Ibid., p. 63.
[38] Ibid., p. 61.
[39] McCredden 2016, p. 19.
[40] Ibid., p. 62.

night: "That night the stars come out early and clear as I'd ever seen them and I could smell everything in the bush round me. I tasted smoke and gum sap in the air. Moths and bugs heavy as birds bumped and skidded off me."[41]

As he journeys the next day, Jaxie " . . . come[s] into the valley where everything was cool and shadowy and the salmon gums were shivering with birds."[42] The material dimension of vernacular hermeneutics suggests at least two resonances here with the biblical text. First, when the Australian postcolonial subject comes into an open-eyed encounter with the Australian landscape, he talks about it with ease and authority, naming it as Adam did the creatures of God's handiwork.[43] Indeed, as Jaxie describes the valley, it has a hint of Eden about it: just as the man and his wife walk in the Edenic garden at the time of the evening breeze, where they hear the sound of God walking (Gen 3:8), so Jaxie notes the cool of the vegetation and a shivering spiritual presence created by birds in the salmon gums. For Jaxie, being in the bush, a longing to learn and birds create a state of peace. "Weird to be thinking of school" he says, "traipsing through the mulga like that. I guess because of them birds and how peaceful it was."[44]

It is not too far a stretch to remember the wryly humorous injunction of Jesus in the Gospel of Matthew, "Look at the birds of the air; they neither sow nor reap nor gather into barns, and yet your heavenly Father feeds them. Are you not of more value than they?" (Matt 6:26; see also Luke 12:24). Jesus gives this example to tease his audience out of anxiety about the necessities of life. "Do not worry," says Jesus, "about your life, what you will eat or what you will drink, or about your body, what you will wear. Is not life more than food, and the body more than clothing?" (Matt 6:25) In much of this novel, Jaxie is necessarily consumed with protecting his life, with procuring basic food and drink for survival and the bare minimum of clothing. Yet in the midst of his struggle to survive, he also experiences the beauty of the place, the compassion of Fintan, the reality of small mercies poured on him in the provision of food, drink, clean water, fire, human comfort and conversation, what amounts to civilization.

There are numerous examples where Jaxie's vernacular and the biblical language interact with each other. Very early in their encounter, when Fintan knows Jaxie is spying on him from the bush, but hasn't declared himself, Fintan announces out loud, "To everything a season." To this Jaxie replies, but only to himself, "And I'm thinking what the fuck."[45] Fintan's first phrase is a direct biblical quotation, from Ecclesiastes 3:1; Jaxie's bewildered reply is a pure vernacular response. This is one of many exchanges in which the biblical text or imagery is juxtaposed sharply with postcolonial Australian vernacular language in a deceivingly simple but effective way. The interchange between the two characters works very credibly in the novel at the matter-of-fact level, revealing the character of the speakers and their worldviews. Yet for the biblically-alert audience, there is an enjoyable play of irony as we hear the two dictions, that of the Scriptures and that of the biblically innocent postcolonial Australian, playing back and forth with each other. Only in this contemporary Australian environment is this interchange credible, but here, as Winton constructs it, it teases the mind with the possibility that the ancient biblical text speaks into this context that is so remote from it in both place and time.

---

[41] Ibid., p. 68.
[42] Ibid., p. 75.
[43] See Gen 2:19–20, "So out of the ground the LORD God formed every animal of the field and every bird of the air, and brought them to the man to see what he would call them; and whatever the man called every living creature, that was its name. The man gave names to all cattle, and to the birds of the air, and to every animal of the field; but for the man there was not found a helper as his partner." [emphasis mine]. Biblical translation here and elsewhere in the paper is taken from the New Revised Standard Version.
[44] Ibid., p. 46.
[45] Ibid., p. 102.

b. Jaxie, the Hero Explorer "On the Way"

As he steps out through the mulga scrub, Jaxie follows every Australian explorer of the inland desert, such as the ill-fated Burke and Wills, the somewhat more fortunate Ludwig Leichhardt, and the first European man to cross the Nullarbor Plain, Edward John Eyre. At the same time, much of Winton's description of Jaxie's travel echoes the biblical story of journey. Early in the novel Jaxie faces the agony of choice between the road back to regular society which offers comfort but probably also legal trouble and the rough road of a path through the inland, beyond human habitation. It was, he says, "the highway or the wildywoods."[46]

The large biblical story evoked by this choice is that of the ancient Israelite people's forty-year trek through the wilderness, told in the Old Testament Books of Exodus through Deuteronomy. In the New Testament, Jesus' preaching journey to proclaim the "reign of God" is called being "on the way," on the *hodos*. Both are journeys of self-discovery through trials of endurance and deprivation, the first for the people of Israel and the latter for Jesus. This certainly is also the case with Jaxie. The plot of the entire novel traces his journey from an abusive home to being within striking distance of his brief life's goal, namely untrammeled freedom with the girl he loves. Within this larger journey there are smaller journeys: having discovered the prospector's hut, Jaxie makes a trip to collect salt, in the course of which he discovers the shepherd's hut. From there he makes several shorter trips to hunt wild game but then a final series of explorations to locate the mysterious noise that tells him he and Fintan are not alone and safe in the bush. The final journey back to the shepherd's hut to protect Fintan when he could simply have run away brings all Jaxie's search for self-identity and moral integrity to fulfilment so that he is truly free afterwards to continue on the journey he had begun months before.

These journeys are satisfying as the content of a novel; for the postcolonial biblical scholar, alerted by the performantial dimension of vernacular hermeneutics to the role of explorer and the ritual of journeying, these journeys become symbolic of the human search for meaning and life. For the Biblically-literate reader, the background of both the Old and New Testament uses of the journey theme adds great richness to this symbolism. For the purposes of this paper, this close connection between a contemporary Australian story in the distinctly Australian landscape and the ancient biblical narratives shows that there is a capacity in Australian consciousness to hear the deeply human account of encounter between God and human beings that the Scriptures express.

In the final section of this paper, I will treat some of the most outstanding features of the novel as themes exploring the experiences of the postcolonial subject in the Australian environment that can be seen as related to the Bible. Where relevant I will continue to point out which of the three dimensions of vernacular hermeneutics most clearly identifies the cultural features being expressed.

C. Themes of Tim Winton's *The Shepherd's Hut* in Relation to the New Testament

The novel is shot through with quotations from and allusions to the Bible, especially the New Testament. Lest the reader doubt the presence of the biblical word, Winton has Jaxie remark, well into his time at the shepherd's hut, that Fintan regularly recited texts he knew by heart, "Poems and bits of the Bible and that and he said them to me pretty often by the fire after dark."[47] One of these biblical snatches turns up when Jaxie reminisces that Fintan compares himself and Jaxie to the biblical figures of "the original odd couple, a veritable David and Jonathan."[48] Part of the pleasurable irony of Winton's construction of these characters is that Jaxie has no idea what Fintan's reference means. Vernacular hermeneutics notes that a distinctly Australian scenario can be accounted for, even if ironically, by allusion to a famous biblical image, that of the deep bond between David and his friend Jonathan.[49]

---

[46] Ibid., p. 49.
[47] Ibid., p. 175.
[48] Ibid., p. 181.
[49] See 1 Sam 18:1–20:42 for the tale of the brief but intense and politically fraught relationship between the young warrior David and the Jonathan, the son of King Saul against whom David was engaged in conflict.

1. Old Testament Themes in *The Shepherd's Hut*

We have already seen that the novel presents Jaxie's journey in terms of walking through the biblical Eden, but also in a way that echoes the wilderness journey portrayed in the book of Exodus. Winton does not, however, romanticize this allusion to biblical scenes. While Jaxie and his girlfriend Lee sometimes get away by themselves to swim at the reservoir or to patches of bush around town, theirs was no idyllic Adam and Eve relationship. The natural world was not in fact enough for them: they needed civilized privacy. As Jaxie said, "When all you get is dead grass and asbestos roofs and the stinky shade of the grandstand, the idea of a proper room is deadset luxury."[50] Fintan can describe aspects of the landscape, such as the moon rising over the salt lake in religious terms such as "Behold," (used in the Scriptures to, among other things, announce a momentous event), asking if the moon's presence "Doesn't [make] some small part of you shrivel in awe," saying it is "Like the wafer," (the Eucharistic bread).[51] Nevertheless, in less transported moments, he can use other biblical language to name their place of isolation as a "forsaken wilderness," echoing the language of Isa 27:10, "For the fortified city is solitary, a habitation deserted and forsaken, like the wilderness." Thus, place or material setting is a very important theme in the novel, being presented in a way that evokes biblical traditions of the capacity of place and material reality to provide occasions for encounter with divinity.

A second important and resonant theme in the novel is food. At the shepherd's hut the work of hunting it, shooting or killing, preparing it and preserving it is a never-ending round of survival. The food that keeps the body alive is hard to come by. However, Jaxie is fed by another kind of food which sustains him emotionally, psychologically and spiritually. This food is the motivation that keeps him moving beyond the shepherd's hut. Instead of settling at the edge of the desert for the rest of his life as Fintan appears to have done, Jaxie always remains determined to move on to a goal beyond that place. The reason he is able to do this is his relationship with Lee, who he trusts is waiting for him if he can only reach Mt. Magnet where she lives. Even when he can no longer look at pictures of her on his phone, Jaxie finds that he has her image in his memory. "I had the light of her in me," he says. In an image recalling the gift of the manna the Israelite people received in the wilderness (see Exod 16:11–16) Jaxie says her presence in his memory "was like food falling from the sky."[52] The allusion is obvious to anyone with a small familiarity with the Bible; Winton has put it credibly on the lips of a boy who has foresworn church and is wary of praying. The postcolonial subject who rejects organized religion can nevertheless be heard speaking tenderly and with gratitude in biblical terms of a gift from the heavens. This is vernacular biblical hermeneutics in novelistic action. It expresses in the contemporary Australian vernacular a credible experience that is open to the encounter with a spiritual experience of gifts from God, of which the Bible speaks.

A third major theme in the novel that echoes both the Old and New Testaments is that of fleshliness with its potential of death, especially as expressed in the slaughter of animals for food. This theme ranges on a sliding scale from a focus on sheer materiality to a spiritually rich perception of bodies. An awareness of the performational aspect of vernacular hermeneutics, focusing on roles and rituals, highlights the significance of this novel's treatment of bodies.

An early scene in the novel shows Jaxie working in his father's butchery where his father has assaulted him, knocking him unconscious and into the container in which rejected meat parts are thrown. Jaxie says he "come to in the bone crate. Woke up arse over and half stupid in the slimy pile of shins and knuckles and chook frames."[53] Jaxie is physically immersed in the refuse of butchered animals, feeling reduced to mere animality. From the dead bodies of animals, Jaxie's memory takes

---

50 Winton 2018, p. 85.
51 Ibid., pp. 223, 228.
52 Ibid., p. 199.
53 Ibid., p. 7.

us to the dead bodies of his father, mother and grandmother (Nanna).[54] His memory of the death of Nanna, the first corpse he saw in his life, is triggered by a highly significant scene in the novel to which I will turn next.

Jaxie's reflection on Nanna's death registers the deep human sense that death confronts us with something disjointed, a body at one moment living but in the next, completely vacant. From seeing his Nanna's dead body, Jaxie says he learned that "She was meat. That's what dead things are. She was gone but not gone."[55] This memory is evoked for Jaxie by seeing the old man Fintan kill a goat. The goat goes from being alive to being "suddenly floppy as a bathmat."[56] At the prospector's hut Jaxie has already killed a number of animals in order to survive: a bungarra (a goanna), a euro (like a small kangaroo) and two large kangaroos. [57] While these scenes explain how Jaxie survives in the wilderness of the Australian bush, each also plants images in the mind of the reader that have spiritual and theological potential. As the size of his kill grows, Jaxie begins to need a gambrel, a device for elevating slaughtered game so that it can be gutted and skinned. When he butchers the first kangaroo Jaxie makes do with bits of rope and wire he has found. He says "I strung that doe up from a dead tree."[58] By the time the second kangaroo is described, it has become a body "hanging from a gum tree, a body twisting in the wind like some poor bastard's had enough of this prospecting caper ..."[59] Already, for any biblically-alert person, these scenes evoke the crucifixion of Jesus, which I will discuss in the final section of the paper.

First, however, it is important to note an Old Testament image that is evoked in the scene where Fintan kills the goat. Jaxie's killing of four animals has prepared us to appreciate Fintan's efficiency and skill in trapping, killing and butchering the goat. Observing Fintan, Jaxie remarks, "Bloke's got it all figured out. But he's quick as a snake."[60] Fintan kills the goats that run feral in outback Australia but his action also alludes to the ancient Jewish practice of slaughtering a goat annually for the forgiveness of the sins of the people. Lev 16:1–34 details the instructions God gave to Moses, to be followed by Aaron, the Jewish High Priest. On a set annual date, the tenth day of the seventh month (Lev 16:29) the High Priest is to take "two male goats for a sin offering and one ram for a burnt offering." (Lev 16:5) One of the goats is to become the scapegoat onto whom the sins of the people will be symbolically transferred and banished into the wilderness (Lev 16:20–22). The other goat is to be a sin offering, slaughtered, its blood sprinkled on the mercy seat of the sanctuary and its entire body burned outside the camp because of "the uncleannesses of the people of Israel, and because of their transgressions, all their sins (Lev 16:15–16, 27)."

Fintan has a civilized situation with not only shelter, water, vegetables growing, a yard in which to trap animals and a sharp knife for slaughtering, but also "a gambrel that twisted a bit in the wind."[61] On this, he strings up the goat and butchers it cleanly in what is clearly a practiced ritual. The detailed description of this process embeds the image in the mind of the reader; it will not be until later in the novel that the reader will realize that it is highly appropriate that Fintan can do this so well because he is a priest, someone whose role in ancient times was to slaughter animals in ritual sacrifice. At the same time, Jaxie slowly uncovers that Fintan is in the wilderness as a punishment for a crime he has committed as a priest. The crime has to do with money, not the sexual abuse of children that Jaxie fears.[62] It is as though Fintan, still alive and a priest, not only slaughters goats but is a kind of

---

54 See Ibid., pp. 11–13, 23 for the death of Jaxie's father; pp. 23, 38 for the death of his mother and pp. 98–99 for the death of Nanna.
55 Ibid., p. 98.
56 Ibid., p. 97.
57 See Ibid., pp. 61 for the bungarra; 67–68 for the euro; 69–70 for a grey kangaroo and 73–74 for a red kangaroo.
58 Ibid., p. 69.
59 Ibid., pp. 73–74.
60 Ibid., p. 97.
61 See Ibid., p. 95 for a description of Fintan's hut.
62 See Ibid., pp. 230–31 for Fintan's description of his criminal behaviour.

scapegoat himself, carrying away into the wilderness, the sins of the people. Nevertheless, the primary, abiding image is of the slaughtered body strung up on high. Here we see both the material and the performational aspects of culture operating together as language constructs an intense image that expresses the ritual of slaughter by someone in the role of a priest. Australian capacity to envisage a goat or a native animal slaughtered in the ritual process portrayed very credibly in this novel is the kind of capacity that could begin to grasp and value a relationship with the divine transacted through animal sacrifice and even human sacrificial death that becomes spiritual food. This image of the body elevated on high carries the biblically alert reader's mind from the world of the Old Testament into that of the Christian scriptures.

2. New Testament Themes in *The Shepherd's Hut*

In the New Testament, the image of the body raised up on high is that of Jesus of Nazareth crucified. This image is central to everything the New Testament has to say, whether narrated in all four canonical Gospels, or reflected on in the letters, or treated symbolically in the Book of Revelation. In *The Shepherd's Hut*, Tim Winton cites or alludes to many of these New Testament documents. As Jaxie grows to self-awareness, particularly in his reflections on mercy and thankfulness there are echoes of the Gospel of Matthew. When both Jaxie and Fintan both mistake first trees and then rocks for men, there seem to be strong but reverse allusions to Jesus' two-part healing of the blind man of Bethsaida who saw men but thought they looked like trees, in the Gospel of Mark (Mark 8:22–26).[63] Jaxie's wonderful yet also highly ironic discovery and acceptance that he is indeed, "an instrument of God," cites both 2Tim 2:20–21 and Acts 9:15–16. Similarly ironic but profoundly true is Jaxie's identity as "the end of the world" or "the end of days" as Fintan thinks he must be, which picks up the apocalyptic language of Dan 7:13, Mark 13:7 and 2 Pet 3:10 and the Book of Revelation as a whole.[64] These allusions and others saturate the novel, articulating its themes, providing its characters with language and behaviors that are rich in their power to evoke spiritual reality. Each of these images or concepts is well worth exploring but cannot be treated in the present paper.

a. Johannine Themes in The Shepherd's Hut

The image of the body raised up on high, however, is developed in a quite specific way in the Gospel of John and will be the focus for the remainder of this paper. Brigid Rooney notes that the Gospel of John is one of Winton's two favorite Gospels, the other being the Gospel of Luke. Rooney cites Winton saying that "Luke and John, doctor and mystic respectively, correspond to the 'two halves of my upbringing.'"[65] Even before turning to this image it is worth noting that this novel is shot through with Johannine ideas and symbols.[66] Just to mention some of the most obvious, Jaxie says that a euro he shot "was meat tasted like nothing you ever had in your life."[67] This invites the memory of the Johannine Jesus telling his disciples "I have food to eat that you do not know about" (John 4:32). Ultimately, despite initial denial, Jaxie agrees with Fintan that he was "sent . . . destined."[68] This echoes an important aspect of Johannine Christology that is based on Jesus calling himself the one who was sent by his Father, who is often named as "the one sending me."[69] Worthy of a paper by itself is the lengthy discussion between Jaxie and Fintan when they have just met each other and each is trying

---

63 See Ibid., pp. 90–91 for Jaxie mistaking rocks for people and pp. 225–28 for Fintan's perception of the stones walking and dancing in the sunlight.

64 See Ibid., p. 4 for the "end of the world" citation and p. 134 for the "end of days."

65 Rooney 2014, p. 242.

66 For two fine works on symbolism in the Gospel of John, see Koester 1995; Lee 2002.

67 Ibid., p. 68.

68 Ibid., pp. 72–73.

69 See the following references in the Gospel of John where the Father of Jesus is referred to by use of the participial phrase, "the one (or the Father) sending me." It is declined grammatically in the four most frequently occurring cases: the nominative, accusative, genitive and dative. See John 1:33; 4:34; 5:23, 24, 30, 37; 6:38–39, 44; 7:16, 18, 28, 33; 8:16, 18, 26, 29; 9:4; 12:44–45, 49; 13:16, 20; 14:24; 15:21; 16:5.

to discover the identity of the other, to know whether or not he is a threat. It is effectively a trial as each one probes, feints, and attempts to avoid giving himself away. At the outset, when Fintan has suggested a likely scenario for Jaxie's sudden unexplained appearance in the bush, Jaxie responds "If you say so," which he then repeats.[70] Ears attuned to the Johannine Gospel hear behind Jaxie's dismissive remark, Jesus' reply in his interrogation by the Roman procurator Pontius Pilate, "You say that I am a king." (John 18:37). Jesus goes on to say that he has come to proclaim the truth, to which Pilate famously replied "What is truth? (John 18:38). Fintan presses Jaxie with the questions "Is that the truth?" and " . . . does the truth mean something to you?"[71]

Because it is a novel built from words, but also because the novel explores human relationships, it is appropriate that in their first conversation Fintan and Jaxie finally agree that they have no option but to take each other at their word (p. 133). Fintan's final word in this encounter between them is "There you are in your beginning and here am I near my end."[72] Here we hear echoed not only the Johannine Prologue which opens "In the beginning was the Word" (John 1:1), but also the Johannine narrator's comment about Jesus that having loved his disciples "in the world, he loved them to the end" (John 13:1). Of course, sitting behind the terms "beginning" and "end" is a concept of God's own self as the beginning and end of all that there is. Typical of the way language and thought operate in this novel, Fintan's summation is true at a simple, matter-of-fact level in the lives of both characters. This truth then lends authenticity to the other, spiritual level of meaning that brings biblical ideas into consciousness through ordinary Australian speech.

Later in Winton's novel, a most distinctive Johannine idiom appears, when Fintan explains that the ancient Australian landscape says to him: "Here I am, son, still here. I was here before the likes of you and yours were born. Before you even drew breath, I am."[73] For the biblically-literate reader, this is quite a stunning statement. The assertion, "I am" is used in at least three different grammatical modes in the Gospel of John.[74] Its power in that Gospel stems from an ancient self-declaration of God who replied to Moses' request for a name for him, "I am who I am" (Exod 3:14). Its power in Winton's novel stems from the sense of sacrilege Jesus created when he used this name for God to identify himself, when he asserted provocatively to his fellow Jews, "Very truly, I tell you, before Abraham was, I am" (John 8:58). Fintan's speech recalling Jesus' self-declaration brings into powerful exchange, an ancient biblical name for God and the presence of God that can be felt in the Australian context, by someone who takes the time to feel its presence and to see that it is "a rare and beautiful place . . . With a memory."[75] This is vernacular hermeneutics in practice, the material aspect of culture in the texture of its location conversing with the biblical text, enriching its ancient meaning by expanding its frame of reference. This is precisely the work that the postcolonial vernacular hermeneut of the biblical text must do. Through the medium of Fintan MacGillis, Winton achieves this in the narratival enrichment of contemporary Australian consciousness that his novel makes.

Alerted by these allusions to the Gospel of John, the biblically-conscious reader sees the regularly recurring image of the slaughtered animal strung up on a gambrel as an evocation of the image of "one lifted up" found only in the Gospel of John. As with the name, "I am," this phrase in the Gospel of John carries forward into Christian interpretation of the execution of Jesus of Nazareth, a powerful symbolic ancient Jewish image. In this case, the image is of a serpent lifted up on a standard. The story behind this symbol is told in Num 21:5–9, about serpents biting and killing the people of Israel in the

---

[70] Winton 2018, p. 127.
[71] Ibid., pp 132, 133.
[72] Ibid., p. 135.
[73] Ibid., p. 152.
[74] See Brown 1966, pp. 533–38 for "Appendix IV: *EGŌ EIMI*—"I AM," which lists John 8:24, 28, 58 and 13:19 as places where "I am" is used without a predicate; 6:20 and 18:5 as instances where a predicate may be understood even if not expressed; and 6:35, 51; 8:12 (9:5); 10:7, 9, 11, 14; 11:25; 14:6 and 15:1, 5 as examples of the phrase being used with a predicate in the nominative case.
[75] Winton 2018, p. 152.

wilderness. The solution God offered Moses was that if the people gazed on a brazen serpent set up on a standard, they would be healed of any snake bite.[76] Uniquely in the Gospel of John, Jesus refers to his impending crucifixion as being "lifted up." In the three places where this expression is used (see John 3:14; 8:28; 12:32–34), Jesus is identified as the Son of Man, the ancient Jewish figure associated with triumph through suffering and to whom sovereignty over all peoples is granted by God (see Dan 7:13–14). As this Jewish symbolism is used in the Gospel of John, the ghastly image of the crucified Jesus is reframed as a figure raised up on high to be enthroned and invested with power, especially the power to heal all those who will contemplate it. Winton's steady construction of the image of the animal raised up on the gambrel already listed above (see C.1 Old Testament Themes in *The Shepherd's Hut*) builds a high sense of ritual that expresses in the language of the colonial hunter, a sensitivity to a deeper meaning. This deeper meaning touches on the value of each life that is taken. When he has to leave a large red kangaroo carcass in order to fetch salt with which to preserve it, Jaxie says "I guess it's a rotten thing to do, bowl a roo over and just leave him there." [77] At the same time, the novel presents very plainly, the reality of hunger that legitimates taking life. Jaxie says that when he shot his first animal he was "gagging for a feed," and that when he shot the euro he "cored a loin out of him and ... et it raw.[78] It is because killing the game is so necessary that Jaxie can observe the contradiction that while a bullet can "do that kind of damage. It was beautiful."[79]

Invitations to hear a Johannine theology speaking through these scenes come first when Jaxie describes the challenge of butchering his first kangaroo with only a sharpened butter knife. Because it was too difficult to do the task fully, he says he "left the legs whole. Used a rusty iron bar to bust the shins. Wasn't pretty but it done the job."[80] This description brings to mind the Johannine depiction of the death of Jesus where, to hasten the deaths of the two criminals crucified either side of Jesus, the soldiers break their legs, but do not break the legs of Jesus because he is already dead (John 19:32–33). Given that Jesus died at the time of the Jewish Passover feast, this unique Johannine detail accesses the stipulation in Exod 12:46 and Num 9:12 that when the lamb was prepared for this feast, none of its bones were to be broken. As Francis Moloney explains, "Scripture is fulfilled as the Passover Lamb is slain without a bone being broken (cf. Ps 34:20–21; Exod 12:10, 46; Num 9:12)."[81] Winton takes the fulfilment of this text one step further, bringing it into conversation with the Australian postcolonial vernacular. This makes it possible for Australian consciousness to hear the gospel story as something spoken in a language that contemporary Australia knows.

Late in the novel, Winton begins to apply this language of stringing up to both Jaxie and Fintan. First, Jaxie recounts his sadness at killing a big red kangaroo. He says he "felt kind of sick" when the animal fell and that there was always "this sad feeling" when he had to kill any animal that like the 'roo, had "a big round cow eye" that seemed to accuse him of his violent act.[82] Jaxie says that when he had this roo strung up, "I looked at his big brown eye and saw meself, a reflection of me ... and I had this mad idea, like there it is, Death, that's me, that's what I am."[83] Here, in the picture of himself reflected back in the mirror of the kangaroo's eye, Jaxie is confronted with the idea of himself as an agent of Death, which he finds depressing. Jaxie's depressed mood issues in a dream a little later where he realizes that an animal that is strung up is not a goat or a kangaroo but himself, as "a beast with all the wildness bled out of him."[84] Perhaps this scene registers Jaxie's subconscious awareness that he must move on from the shepherd's hut lest he stagnate. For the purposes of this paper, we note

---

[76] See Budd 1984, pp. 232–34 for a full historical-critical exposition of this story in the Book of Numbers.
[77] Winton 2018, p. 73.
[78] Ibid., pp. 61, 68.
[79] Ibid., p. 67.
[80] Ibid., p. 70.
[81] Moloney 1998, p. 505.
[82] Winton 2018, pp. 183–84.
[83] Ibid., p. 185.
[84] Ibid., p. 236.

that it shows this novel exploring a deeply resonant cultural symbol, that of the dead animal strung up for slaughter in a way that invites conversation with the similarly deep imagery of bodies lifted up in the Bible. The "material" practices of culture in the form of language, symbols and food and the "performantial" in the form of the ritual practice of slaughtering express the capacity contemporary Australian consciousness has to engage with the biblical story.

Second, Fintan himself introduces the idea that he is a man strung up. In the final, profound conversation that he and Jaxie have, watching the moon rise over the salt lake, Fintan describes his truly priestly concern to communicate who God is to Jaxie as "the rusty hook I dangle from. In some pain, I might add."[85] Dangling from this hook, Fintan makes two wonderful statements, one about God and the other about Jaxie. About God, Fintan speculates that "God is what you do, not what or who you believe in."[86] His reasoning is that when a person does what is right, brings about the good and makes life better for other people, then he is "an instrument of God, ... joined to the divine, to the life force, to life itself."[87] From this, Fintan thanks Jaxie for coming to the shepherd's hut and making his life better. Because Jaxie has done this, Fintan declares, "Jaxie Clackton, you are an instrument of God."[88] Here, as noted already, Fintan speaks the word of God (cf. 2Tim 2:20–21 and Acts 9:15–16), to which Jaxie replies "Get fucked, I said still laughing." This is another example of vernacular hermeneutics at work in the novel, where Jaxie's vernacular appears insulting but is, in fact, full of deep gratitude to Fintan, for Fintan's biblically versed affirmation of him as good, so good that his actions are the very actions of God.

Jaxie's comment here may seem dismissive of Fintan. It is internally contradictory: a laugh that expresses his delight at Fintan's affirmation of him as an "instrument of God," combined with a vulgar insult. The insult is so habitual in Jaxie's speech that its meaning is determined by the tenor of the conversation in which it happens. Thus, it is possible for Jaxie's apparent rejection of Fintan's compliment to him to be a backhanded expression of gratitude. Jaxie is still making sense of himself, the world and his role in it. He is still weighing up the inconsistent behaviour of the frail, life-battered adults that he knows, such as his father and Fintan. In this scene and those that follow immediately upon it, we hear the apparently contradictory reflections of a still-teenaged, emotionally stressed boy, confronting raw issues of survival largely alone.

The novel at this point is close to the culmination of its plot. Briefly, a moment's absent-mindedness by Jaxie exposed the existence of himself and Fintan to two drug-growing criminals who have a clandestine operation in the area. Jaxie arrives back at the shepherd's hut to find that the two criminals have found it and are interrogating Fintan violently. Winton creates dramatic irony that bonds the viewpoints of Fintan, Jaxie and the reader as all three know from their perspectives, how cleverly evasive Fintan is in his responses to the criminals. We can hear Jaxie's affection for the old man as he describes him "nattering away like butter wouldn't melt in his mouth," with "that rolled-gold look of surprise on" and describing himself more truly than the drug-dealers know, as having been in the game of "pastoral concerns ... fifty years, give or take."[89]

The criminals torture Fintan by poking him with a knife to find who his accomplice is, the one who left telltale binoculars at their drug-growing site, but Fintan will not tell them anything. They tie Fintan to the gambrel but do not string him up, because as Jaxie reckons "they didn't know how." Winton stops short of scripting a human crucifixion but the scene opens with a goat on the gambrel, half-skinned, so the imagery is as present as it can be. Because Fintan can feel Jaxie hiding in the bush nearby, he sings a verse of the ballad "The Wild Colonial Boy," to warn Jaxie that if he shoots, he will reveal himself and be captured, as was the young man in the song.

---

[85] Ibid., pp. 232–33.
[86] Ibid., p. 233.
[87] Ibid.
[88] Ibid.
[89] Ibid., pp. 256–57.

However, while these external events have been happening, other processes have been going on within Jaxie. When faced with the choice, he had decided not simply to run away and leave Fintan alone, as he could have done. Jaxie has grown into the ethical position expressed by Fintan that a person who does what is kind and thus "enlarges" another person's life, is "an instrument of God."[90] This keeps Jaxie determined to rescue Fintan because he decides, "whatever was gunna happen was my fault. It was me responsible."[91] In this moment, Jaxie acts like a mature adult, prepared to sacrifice his own life for someone else. The reader knows for sure who Jaxie is and what he is: a young man who has experienced being known and loved by someone who then wishes to respond in gratitude. Jaxie has experienced love, what he calls the "dangerous feeling [of] getting noticed, being wanted. Getting seen deep and proper, it's shit hot but terrible too. It's like being took over."[92]

However, Jaxie is still a teenaged boy. He needs his identity and value confirmed for him by someone who knows him well. He sees Fintan for who he is: "... old and lost and sorry and fucked up and still [able to] see so clear and far."[93] Jaxie yearns to hear from Fintan who he is and what he is. These are precisely the questions the criminals ask of Fintan, stabbing him with a knife that stabs Jaxie also with exquisite remorse because it is sharp precisely because it is "... the blade you [i.e., Jaxie] stoned up sharp as a motherfucker to show you're grateful."[94] As Fintan endures the torture, becoming in Jaxie's eyes "fuller and firmer and prouder" and as the criminals persist, probing Fintan with Jaxie's own questions about himself, a moment of revelation happens for Jaxie. "All the decent things in him [Fintan] landed. On me. On my head. And I knew where I was and who I was, and what I was."[95]

Emboldened by this knowledge, Jaxie moves to conclusive action. He shoots the two criminals torturing Fintan, knowing that as an "instrument of God," this was the right thing to do. He lets Fintan down from the gambrel and there is between them a moment of communion where Jaxie does speak to Fintan but the most important thing is that Jaxie knows "He felt me. He always knew what I was. And now I saw him too."[96] It takes only another couple of paragraphs to complete the plot: the burial of the two dead criminals and of Fintan and of Jaxie's departure from the shepherd's hut, driving the drug-growers' vehicle, carrying their petrol, their money and Fintan's food. For him "peace is on its way. It fucking better be."[97] And we have caught up to the present moment with which the novel began, with Jaxie on his way North to what he hopes will be the rest of his life.

3. Conclusions

The point concluding our analysis need only be made briefly. In its culmination and denouement, the novel embodies in its two principal characters Jaxie and Fintan, the values of truth, love and compassion preached by Jesus in the New Testament, values which he underwrote with his own life. The novel affirms that human beings who act with self-forgetting integrity and love towards their fellow human being are indeed, instruments of God. The meaning of being an instrument of God is told in a regular novel, set in a quintessentially contemporary postcolonial Australian setting. Significant parts of the story, especially those parts that lead to its meaning, are told either in explicit citation of or in allusion to the Bible. Especially in the enduring theme of the creature strung up on a gambrel, the central story of the New Testament, the crucifixion of Jesus, is brought into conversation with the postcolonial reality of Australia. The interchange of values between the ancient biblical text and contemporary life in Australia rings utterly true to both cultural worlds. The vernacular hermeneutical methodology of postcolonial biblical criticism is able to show that in his novel, *The Shepherd's Hut*,

90   Ibid., p. 233.
91   Ibid., p. 251.
92   Ibid., p. 235.
93   Ibid., p. 234.
94   Ibid., p. 262.
95   Ibid., pp. 264–65.
96   Ibid, p. 266.
97   Ibid., p. 267.

Tim Winton has actually effected a cultural interchange that demonstrates the capacity that postcolonial Australia has for the spirituality expressed by the New Testament. It is that capacity that can hear its own search for satisfying spiritual life in its own context experience told in language that is authentic to Australia and at the same time open to the Bible's ancient wisdom.

Sugirtharajah defines vernacular hermeneutics as " . . . a call to self-awareness, aimed at creating an awakening among people to their indigenous literary, cultural and religious heritage."[98] As Australians engage more fully with their own context, with the joys and challenges, the benefits and limitations of life in the postcolonial antipodean world, they will have more access to their own spiritual awareness and a greater capacity to articulate it. Whether this leads to a higher commitment to organized religion in the traditional mainstream denominations is another question. But it is surely a necessary feature of Australian growth to be able to name in the terms of the Australian context—its environment, its seasons, its ancient indigenous as well as its contemporary multi-cultural society with their value systems—Australian experience, Australian identity and Australian ideals.

In *The Shepherd's Hut,* where all pretense is stripped away, what emerges is the anti-hero, Jaxie Clackton, who can be admired for his courage, intelligence, endurance, perceptiveness and tenderness as he articulates a spiritual view of the world utterly in the Australian vernacular. Some may ask if Jaxie is "redeemed" in the classic sense of Christian theology. The novel presents Jaxie as a work in progress: he has been through a wilderness trial in which he learned not only to survive but to care for another person, to the point where he could risk his own life for him, because it was a responsibility that Jaxie had learned to accept. Jaxie learned this responsibility in the course of daily living and through reflection about life shared with Fintan in the almost palpable presence of the Australian landscape. After all his struggles and to his own amazement, Jaxie describes himself as subject to an "angel feeling. Like you're just one arrow of light."[99]

If Jaxie can be taken as a personification of postcolonial and post-secular Australia, his trajectory in this novel suggests a pathway into spiritual maturation for the nation. As Jaxie came to self-discovery in the Australian wilderness, learning to discern the essential from the superficial, choosing the compassion, mercy and wisdom of Fintan over the bullying, murderous violence of a pair of drug-runners, so postcolonial and post-secular Australia needs to engage with Australia, its history, its place in the world, its very distinct physical landscape whose austere and challenging beauty offers spiritual encounter. Tim Winton's novel, *The Shepherd's Hut,* shows contemporary postcolonial and post-secular Australians that it is possible in this land to be one, focused arrow of light. It is an experience long overdue for this country, one which Winton's novel strongly suggests is truly possible.

Funding: This research received no external funding.

Conflicts of Interest: The author declares no conflict of interest.

References

Area of Australia—States and Territories. n.d. Available online: https://www.ga.gov.au/scientific-topics/national-location-information/dimensions/area-of-australia-states-and-territories (accessed on 26 May 2019).

Atkinson, Alan. 1977. The Beginning. In *The Europeans in Australia: A History*. Oxford and Melbourne: Oxford University Press Australia, vol. 1.

Brown, Raymond E. 1966. The Gospel According to John. In *The Gospel According to John I–XII*. Garden City: Doubleday, vol. 1.

Budd, Philip J. 1984. *Numbers*. Waco: Word Books.

Carroll, Anthony, and Richard Norman, eds. 2017. *Religion and Atheism: Beyond the Divide*. London; New York: Routledge/Taylor & Francis Group.

---

[98] Ibid. p. 177.
[99] Ibid., p. 3.

Census Data Reveals "No Religion" Is Rising Fast. 2017. Available online: http://www.abs.gov.au/AUSSTATS/abs@.nsf/mediareleasesbyReleaseDate/7E65A144540551D7CA258148000E2B85 (accessed on 07 February 2019).

Clark, C.M.H., ed. 1950. *Select Documents in Australian History, 1788–1850*. Sydney: Angus and Robertson, 1973 reprint.

Dixon, Bob. 2018. Post-secularity and Australian Catholics. In *Faith and the Political in the Post-Secular Age*. Edited by Anthony Maher. Bayswater: Coventry Press, pp. 50–71.

Galka, Max. 2016. The Absurdly Confusing Lands of the British Crown, Explained in 1 Chart. Available online: http://metrocosm.com/british-crown-explained/ (accessed on 27 January 2019).

Graham, Elaine. 2018. Post-Secularity. In *Faith and the Political in the Post-Secular Age*. Edited by Anthony Maher. Bayswater: Coventry Press, pp. 72–91.

Gray, John. 2018. *Seven Types of Atheism*. London: Penguin.

Hughes, Robert. 1987. *The Fatal Shore*. London: Collins Harvill.

Kociumbas, Jan. 1992. 1788–1860: Possessions. In *The Oxford History of Australia*. Oxford and Melbourne: Oxford University Press Australia, vol. 2.

Koester, Craig R. 1995. *Symbolism in the Fourth Gospel: Meaning, Mystery, Community*. Minneapolis: Fortress Press.

Lee, Dorothy. 2002. *Flesh and Glory: Symbol, Gender, and Theology in the Gospel of John*. New York: Crossroad.

Louis, Roger. 1998–1999. *The Oxford History of the British Empire: Five Volumes*. Oxford and New York: Oxford University Press.

Martin, Michael, ed. 2007. *The Cambridge Companion to Atheism*. Cambridge: Cambridge University Press.

McCredden, Lyn. 2016. *The Fiction of Tim Winton*. Sydney: Sydney University Press.

McCredden, Lyn, and Nathanael O'Reilly. 2014. Introduction: Tim Winton, Literature and the Field of Literary Criticism. In *Tim Winton: Critical Essays*. Edited by Lyn McCredden and Nathanael O'Reilly. Crawley: University of Western Australia Publishing, pp. 1–15.

McKenna, Mark. 1996. *The Captive Republic: A History of Republicanism in Australia 1788–1996*. Cambridge: Cambridge University Press.

McKenna, Mark. 2004. *This Country: A Reconciled Republic?* Sydney: The University of new South Wales Press.

McKenna, Mark, and Wayne Hudson. 2003. *Australian Republicanism: A Reader*. Carlton: Melbourne University Press.

McNamee, Gregory Lewis, DeWitt C. Reddick, and Ralph A. Wooster. 2019. Texas, State, United States. Available online: https://www.britannica.com/place/Texas-state (accessed on 25 May 2019).

Moloney, Francis J. 1998. *The Gospel of John*. Collegeville: Liturgical Press.

Morrison, Fiona. 2014. 'Bursting with Voice and Doubleness:' Vernacular Presence and Visions of Inclusiveness in Tim Winton's Cloudstreet. In *Tim Winton: Critical Essays*. Edited by Lyn McCredden and Nathanael O'Reilly. Crawley: University of Western Australia Publishing, pp. 49–74.

Rooney, Brigid. 2014. From the Sublime to the Uncanny in Tim Winton's Breath. In *Tim Winton: Critical Essays*. Edited by Lyn McCredden and Nathanael O'Reilly. Crawley: University of Western Australia Publishing, pp. 241–62.

Sugirtharajah, Rasiah S., ed. 1999. *Vernacular Hermeneutics*. Sheffield: Sheffield Academic Press.

Sugirtharajah, Rasiah S. 2001. *The Bible and the Third World: Precolonial, Colonial, and Postcolonial Encounters*. Cambridge and New York: Cambridge University Press.

Sugirtharajah, Rasiah S. 2008. *Troublesome Texts: The Bible in Colonial and Contemporary Culture*. Sheffield: Sheffield Phoenix Press.

Sugirtharajah, Rasiah S. 2012. *Exploring Postcolonial Biblical Criticism: History, Method, Practice*. Chichester and Malden: Wiley-Blackwell.

Sugirtharajah, Rasiah S., ed. 2016. *Voices from the Margin: Interpreting the Bible in the Third World*, 25th Anniversary ed. Maryknoll: Orbis Books.

Sugirtharajah, Rasiah S. 2018. *Jesus in Asia*. Cambridge: Harvard University Press.

Taylor, Charles. 2007. *A Secular Age*. Cambridge: Belknap Press of Harvard University Press.

Wilde, William H., Joy Hooton, and Barry Andrews. 1994. *The Oxford Companion to Australian Literature*, 2nd ed. Oxford: Oxford University Press, Australia.

Winton, Tim. 2016. *The Boy Behind the Curtain*. Melbourne: Penguin Random House.

Winton, Tim. 2018. *The Shepherd's Hut*. Melbourne, Australia: Penguin Random House.

Winton, Tim. 2018–2019. Saving Ningaloo Again. *The Monthly*. December 2018–January 2019. Available online: https: //www.themonthly.com.au/issue/2018/december/1543582800/tim-winton/saving-ningaloo-again (accessed on 26 May 2019).

Winton, Tim. n.d. Available online: https://www.penguin.com.au/authors/tim-winton (accessed on 26 May 2019).

Article

Ecofaith: Reading Scripture in an Era of Ecological Crisis

J. J. Johnson Leese

School of Theology, Seattle Pacific University and Seminary, Seattle, WA 98119, USA; leesej@spu.edu

Received: 4 February 2019; Accepted: 1 March 2019; Published: 4 March 2019

Abstract: This essay outlines the emerging field of ecological theology (ecotheology) with a primary focus on the methods of ecological hermeneutics developed by biblical scholars, ethicists, and theologians. This relatively new approach to reading ancient sacred texts has emerged in tandem with, and partially as a result of, increased public, political, and scientific consensus on the impacts of anthropogenic global warming and the ranging environmentally related effects (e.g., reduction of biodiversity and ecosystems, deforestation, loss of fertile lands, and so forth). The demands of our current context have challenged scholars to consider how religious anthropocentric worldviews have influenced historical readings of the Bible in ways that have contributed to the crisis and constricted the ecological contours of the ancient text. In order to place these developments within a broader historical context, the first section summarizes the history and trajectory of ecological hermeneutics over the past four decades. The main section of this work outlines and summarizes the different types of reading strategies being considered and debated among scholars today and includes promising examples of ecocritical readings of biblical texts. These readings are based on a constructive and critical engagement of ancient texts in light of the modern environmental challenges.

Keywords: Bible; New Testament; ecotheology; hermeneutics; anthropocentric; hierarchical dualism; environment; nature; creation

---

1. Introduction

How are Christians to read Scripture in an era where the earth is "groaning in travail" (Rom. 8:22)? What is the relationship of the triune God to the cosmos that humans call home? Is the Spirit of God breathing life into the natural world? These types of questions reflect recent trends in the related disciplines of theology, biblical interpretation, and ethics, trends that attest to the attraction of reframing theological frameworks and biblical interpretation in light of environmental and ecological considerations. Because of the introductory nature of this article and the complexity of each discipline, I use the terms *ecotheology* and *ecological hermeneutics* broadly, acknowledging that ecotheologians and biblical scholars utilize distinct methods and engage Scripture to varying degrees. Ecotheology has quickly arisen as a respected discipline of theological inquiry, while fresh hermeneutical methods have concurrently been employed by biblical scholars, demonstrating the interrelated nature of these trends.[1] Evidence of the ecumenical appeal for such readings is reflected in the expanding scholarship and the growing praxis among Christians to care for the creation. This trend is present in all the major branches of Christianity and ecumenical organizations: examples include statements by the World Council of Churches (WCC) and the Evangelical Environment Network, initiatives by most

---

1   Attempting such a broad methodology will inevitably collapse some of the complexity of these distinct fields and perhaps create tension for some readers. The intent is to establish overarching developments that have impacted, to varying degrees, theology and biblical studies.

mainline Protestant traditions, and the emergence of faith-based NGO's with environmental concerns.[2] Of recent note is the highly acclaimed 2015 encyclical by Pope Francis, *Laudato Si': On Care for Our Common Home*.[3]

In order to situate this relatively new development within a broader historical context, this essay will first provide a brief overview of the trajectory of ecological hermeneutics over the past four decades.[4] This is followed by the main section of this work, which summarizes a variety of ecocritical reading strategies and hermeneutical approaches to Scripture. The categories outlined below are neither exhaustive, nor preferential to any one approach, but alternatively are representative of various strategies employed by a majority of ecotheological readings of Scripture. Although the focus of this journal issue is on New Testament trends, included throughout the discussion are examples of key creation texts from the Hebrew Bible as well. This is due in part to the intertextual nature of scriptural writings and the models of interpretation that these key texts illustrate.

2. Historical Factors Contributing to Ecological Hermeneutics

Clearly the most significant development contributing to a reorientation of reading Scripture with ecological sensitivities results from increased scientific findings highlighting the environmental crisis facing the planet earth. Increased public, political, and scientific consensus on the impacts of global warming and the ranging environmentally related effects (e.g., reduction of biodiversity and ecosystems, deforestation, loss of fertile lands, and so forth) have contributed toward environmental issues becoming a central priority for the international community. The crisis, considered to be overwhelmingly caused by human patterns and habits, has led scientists to coin the term *Anthropocene* as a technical descriptor for the current geological epoch. These sobering developments become even more disturbing when findings affirm that the impact of climate change patterns disproportionately affect the most underprivileged and vulnerable in the world. The culmination of these factors and others highlights the complexity of this global challenge. In response many religious communities are reassessing historical teachings and praxis and collaborating together, making ecology a topic of religious urgency.[5]

This reassessment was thrust upon Christians by a now famous article, "The Historical Roots of Our Ecologic Crisis", by historian Lynn White Jr., in 1967. His assessment focuses primarily on how anthropocentric interpretations of Genesis 1 have given priority to humanity as uniquely made in God's image and the endorsement "to have dominion over" all the earth (Gen. 1:26–28), a reading he claims exacerbated and accelerated exploitation of nature. White's underlying thesis is that for most of the history of Christian interpretation, Christians have read Scripture in such a way that "not only established a dualism of man and nature but also insisted that it is God's will that man exploit nature for his proper ends" (White 1967, p. 1205). He further draws a direct correlation between the conquests of nature characteristic of technological advancements of the industrial era and domineering patterns of Christian existence such as during the period of colonialization: "Both our present science and our present technology are so tinctured with orthodox Christian arrogance toward nature that no solution for our ecological crisis can be expected from them alone" (White 1967, p. 1205–6). White's

---

[2] See, for example, the list of Christian Environmental Activism organizations in Deane-Drummond (Deane-Drummond 2017, pp. 131–34). For an example of a voluminous collection of articles resulting from a series of conferences in 1996 through 1998 on the world and ecology see *Christianity and Ecology: Seeing the Well-Being of Earth and Humans* (Hessel and Ruether 2000).

[3] Eastern Orthodox theology has been more attentive to the spiritual connections with the material realm than Western and Protestant traditions. Due to the different trajectory of the Orthodox traditions, they will not be addressed in this article. For an overview, see the recent contribution of Elizabeth Theokritoff (Theokritoff 2017).

[4] This brief overview is neither comprehensive nor complete. For a lengthy and critical discussion of a historical genealogy, see *Ecotheology and the Practice of Hope* (Dalton and Simmons 2010, pp. 19–38).

[5] Within the literature, a variety of terms are employed. The terms *nature* or *environment* more generally refer to our surroundings, whereas the term *ecology* suggests all living organisms that find their home in the earth, inclusive of humanity. In order to highlight the interconnection of humanity with all living organisms, I primarily use the term *ecology* in this essay. For a discussion of the importance of terminology in this field see Wirzba (2015).

stinging critique of Christianity generated a proliferation of responses, ranging from sharp derision to reflective consideration. In spite of this range of critique, White's generative thesis remains a historically significant point of reference that set the trajectory for biblical and theological re-readings of Christian Scripture.[6]

One common consideration of any reading of Scripture is that biblical interpretation is an act of re-appropriation that considers the ancient text in light of the context of the human reader. Therefore, an ecological hermeneutic must consciously establish a link between the biblical narrative and the pressing ecological questions of our current context. Such an approach requires a paradigmatic shift establishing ecology and the ecocrisis as a bona fide hermeneutical lens for reading Scripture, a lens that ideally enables interpretation to inform praxis. The need for this shift is succinctly expressed by author Wendell Berry: "Our predicament now, I believe, requires us to learn to read and understand the Bible in the light of the present fact of Creation" (Berry 2002, p. 306).

Employing eco-sensitive lenses to the interpretive process has shaped emerging reading strategies in ecotheology. What have resulted are studies that concentrate primarily on identifying texts that include themes or teachings about nature or alternatively have an explicit theology of creation (e.g., Gen. 1–2; 6–9; Lev. 25; Job 37–39; Pss. 8; 19; 24; 98; 104; Isa. 9–11; Matt. 6:28–30; Rom. 8:18–23; Col. 1; and Rev. 21–22). Demonstrating a more comprehensive approach, *The Green Bible* represents attempts to highlight every biblical reference to other-than-human creation (e.g., soil, earth, plants, air, mountains, rivers, trees, etc.). In helpful ways, such hermeneutical approaches affirm that creation themes and motifs are not limited to the early chapters of the Bible and reflect a growing sensitivity to the degree to which the agrarian context of the ancient world influenced biblical writers, writers who reflect a keen sense of their place. Although the evangelical Christian community has been relatively late in contributing toward ecotheological readings of the Bible, Calvin DeWitt represents one of the exceptions. Trained as an ecologist and environmentalist scientist, he has focused primarily on outlining a biblically grounded stewardship ethic of caring for the earth. For those advocating for such a framework, his more recent works provide a robust set of principles for consideration (DeWitt 2000, pp. 65–67).

In subsequent years, these earlier approaches to biblical exegesis, theology, and praxis have been critiqued from at least three perspectives. One critique is that these approaches are too narrowly focused, with the effect of relegating ecological motifs to marginal themes of the biblical narrative or as isolated within key texts. In keeping with historical readings, non-human elements of the text effectively function as a backdrop or stage for the more important divine-human drama to unfold (Watson 2010, pp. 127–30). A second and formidable critique follows the lead of both liberation and feminist interpretive traditions. In both instances, their struggle with the ancient text has led them to acknowledge that the Bible is not unbiased, nor does it speak in a univocal voice. Although some texts side with the economically disadvantaged, oppressed, and women, other texts reflect the ruling class and/or the patriarchal interests of the authors, who themselves were shaped by the historical realities of their settings. When these inherent limitations of Scripture are taken into consideration, it is judged as insufficient to simply gather relevant texts or summarize "what the Bible says" about ecology. A final critique considers certain aspects of stewardship models as inadequate. Central to stewardship models is the responsibility placed on humans as those granted by God to care for the creation. In this framework humans retain a position of being the "subject" while all created matter is relegated to "object", a framework considered deficient by many (Bauckham 2010, pp. 1–10; Berry 2006). An alternative model called *ecojustice* rejects the notion of earth as the object of human discipleship, emphasizing rather the full integrity and value of creation completely apart from

---

[6] The significance of White's article is demonstrated by the numerous times it is referenced in articles (e.g., Horrell et al. 2010). In light of the 50th anniversary of its publication, other more detailed responses have emerged (e.g., Jenkins 2009).

humanity. This model is often considered as having been first articulated by the Earth Bible project, discussed further below.

In light of these critiques and realities, a new era of engaged discussion about what constitutes a more robust form of ecological hermeneutics and praxis has emerged, represented in part by the burgeoning corpus of ecotheological readings of Scripture. The expanding field of resources attests to the appeal and relevance of ecological hermeneutics for our day. Our unique challenges and questions demand a more sophisticated and nuanced constructive process of biblical interpretation, readings that are predicated on the ancient text yet shaped by various factors, including the modern context, traditions of reading, personal experience, reason, and other relevant epistemological sources. It seems inevitable that thoughtful encounters between modern reader and Scripture will determine that some texts are objectionable in light of modern insights on the current state of the earth community.

For example, the *Earth Bible project*, based in Australia, has advocated for a reconstructive approach that goes beyond simply retrieving eco-friendly texts. Central to this paradigmatic shift is the insistence that a posture of recovery, suspicion, and even resistance is necessary in the interpretive process. To appeal to a broad ecumenical audience and in dialogue with ecologists, the Earth Bible team crafted a set of *ecojustice principles* that approach the interpretive practices from the perspective of the earth: *intrinsic worth of all creatures, interconnectedness of all things, creation's capacity of voice, purpose in each component of creation, role of humans as mutual custodianship,* and *resistance of earth to injustices* (Habel and Wurst 2000). These principles establish earth as subject and are set forth as a normative guide for theological and biblical interpretation, pioneering a new era for fresh dialogue and discussion.[7] Although more limited in scope, the *Exeter project*, funded by the Arts and Humanities Research Council of the UK (AHRC), established an interdisciplinary research group that through focused collaboration produced important scholarship. One particularly valuable contribution is a 2010 publication, *Ecological Hermeneutics: Biblical, Historical and Theological Perspectives*, which is the culmination of a multi-year project by over twenty scholars (Horrell et al. 2010). Scholars associated with both of these organizations have also been active contributors to the initiatives and papers presented at the *Seminar on Ecological Hermeneutics* hosted by the Society for Biblical Literature. Just as Lynn White's article helped to shape the contours of the earliest interpretive considerations, the Earth Bible project and the Exeter project in tandem with liberation and ecofeminist hermeneutical perspectives have fostered a setting fertile for the growth of eco-scholarship. Although the limitations of a journal article do not allow for a comprehensive analysis of all ecotheological trends, what follows is a representative listing of strategies and principles present in the majority of ecotheological scholarship.[8]

3. Representative Strategies and Approaches to Ecological Hermeneutics

3.1. Identifying Anthropocentrism

One fundamental consideration for ecocritical readers of the text is to acknowledge and reassess anthropocentric bias in biblical texts, biblical interpretation, and praxis, a bias that is particularly evident in the Western Christian tradition. This recognition does not deny that the biblical text, by its very nature, is to some degree both *anthropotopic* (a text having humanity as the central theme or topos) and *androcentric* (a text having a male person as the central theme or topos). Scriptural texts were written by male persons for the Israelite and early Christian communities, reflecting topics of human interest from the ancient world. In relationship to this, Paul J. Schutz reflects, "Theology must continue to wrestle with ideas like the *imago Dei* and with the priority of God's self-communication to human creatures in the tradition" (Schutz 2018, p. 15). Ancient texts do not directly address modern epistemology, concerns, and/or questions on any number of topics, including the ecocrisis.

---

[7] For contributions from this perspective, see particularly the Earth Bible Series and the Earth Bible Commentaries (Habel 2000, 2001; Habel and Wurst 2000, 2001; Habel and Balabanski 2002).

[8] Other categories are identified with various emphasis (e.g., Horrell 2010; Habel 2009).

Therefore, to critically evaluate Scripture with criteria of modern questions and concerns is simplistic and anachronistic. Nevertheless, acknowledging that anthropocentric habits of thought are present, and at times problematic, remains an essential step in biblical interpretation. Bias presupposes that humans are the most important part of creation and has clearly influenced historical readings of Scripture. This *de facto* results, either consciously or not, in a devaluation of the other-than-human created matter and/or the eclipse of non-human characters in biblical interpretation.

Readers who are sensitive to these considerations approach biblical exegesis anticipating that the text contains hidden ecological themes and/or novel theological insight. One step in the process is ascertaining to what degree any given text may have a history of misreadings. In these cases, interpreters attempt to recover the text from incomplete or inadequate readings while simultaneously identifying contours of the text formerly neglected or completely overlooked. One example of such an approach is the basis for the book *Behold the Lilies: Jesus and the Contemplation of Nature*, written by veteran ecotheologian Paul Santmire. His thesis is that the command of Jesus "Behold the lilies" in the Sermon on the Mount (Matt. 6:28) is no less an imperative for disciples than, for example, "Follow me" (e.g., Matt. 4:19). Former interpretive traditions almost exclusively focus on the words that announce God's provision of clothing for *humans* in the wider context of direction about not worrying. Santmire's careful exegetical work highlights the intensity of Jesus' use of the imperative and the lexical background to the Greek term *merimnaō* (μεριμνάω), a word used only here in the Bible that has the common meaning of "examine closely", or "scrutinize", in other literature. This usage becomes the basis for Santmire's preference for the translation "behold." In the phrase "behold the lilies", followers of Jesus are called to contemplate the glorious, beautiful flowers in the fields, for as the text further explains, "Even Solomon, in all his glory, was not arrayed like one of these" (Matt. 6:29). Santmire suggests that this command is an invitation to readers "to behold nature more generally or to contemplate nature. This implies ... to celebrate the integrity of nature, apart from human-centered values" (Santmire 2017, p. 6). This approach is sometimes identified as uncovering an "eternal truth" of a text. In this case, a flower is identified as mysterious and captivating, evoking wonder and delight in the one who contemplates. Another way to approach this text is by focusing on the eternal truth of the interdependence of all life. From this perspective Richard Bauckham writes,

> What we have in common with the lilies of the field is not just that we are creatures of God, but that we are fellow-members of the community of God's creation, sharing the same Earth, affected by the processes of the Earth, affecting the processes that affect each other, with common interests at least in life and flourishing, with the common end of glorifying the creator. (Bauckham 2010, p. 88)

3.2. Awareness of Spirit-Nature Dualism

Awareness of anthropocentric bias has also heightened attention given to the prevalence of a Spirit-nature dualism and the degree to which it has plagued Western worldviews from antiquity to the modern day. Early Gnostic dualistic frameworks were based on a hierarchy that reinforced opposing spheres of reality as separate and unequal; spiritual elements were considered sacred, and created matter was relegated to the sphere of the profane. Although Gnostic theology was eventually determined unorthodox, remnants of this thinking remain in philosophical and theological frameworks in modernity.[9] Ecofeminists have contributed significantly to our understanding of how interlocking dualisms prevalent in patriarchal Western culture and thought have functioned to legitimize forms of domination in the name of differences of gender, race, class, education, culture, and species. Elizabeth

---

[9] For a more extensive overview of the Gnostic hierarchical dualism as it relates to the Spirit and created matter, see *Christ, Creation and the Cosmic Goal of Redemption: A Study of Pauline Creation Theology as Read by Irenaeus and Applied to Ecotheology* (Leese 2018, pp. 131–88).

Johnson suggests that the feminist insights of Rosemary Radford Ruether, Sallie McFague, and others provide a critical link between the exploitation of the earth and the exploitation of women:

> In terms of the three basic relationships that shape an ecological ethic, this results in a view in which humanity is detached from and more important than nature; man is separate from and more valuable than woman; God is disconnected from the world, utterly and simply transcendent over it, as well as more significant than it. Hierarchical dualism delivers a two-tiered vision of reality that privileges the elite half of a pair and subordinates the other, which is thought to have little or no intrinsic value of its own but exists only to be of use to the higher. (Johnson 1993, pp. 10–11)

The socially constructed reality of hierarchical dualism is deconstructed further by the study of ecology, which is concerned with the dynamic interrelationship of diverse organisms and their ability to coexist within a given environment. The study of ecology affirms that human beings are but one species in the ecosystem, share the earth as home with all other living organisms, and are completely dependent on the ongoing health of the ecosystem for survival. Linking the scientific study of ecology with theological constructs, it is helpful to see how the term *ecology* is etymologically derived from the Greek term *oikos*, meaning "house" or household", which is related to the term *oikonomia*, understood as "stewardship" or "management" (Conradie 2007). Theologically these terms describe the divine economy of the triune God as encompassing the creation (e.g., Eph. 1:10), with Christians as members of the household of God (Eph. 2:19–22). Biblical terms such as *earth (gē)*, *nature (physis)*, and *creation (ktisis)* reference different elements of creation, depending on the broader context, often inclusive of all living organisms, including humanity.

Readers attentive to anthropocentric bias and sensitive to the function of hierarchical dualism in ancient texts and historical interpretations of Scripture are in a position to retrieve and construct a new ecological vision from the text. For example, historical readings of texts such as Genesis 1:26–28 and Psalm 8 assume a hierarchy of relationships, with God as the transcendent Creator of all things, humanity as subject/ruler of all things, and the earth as an object of conquest or, more recently, as a commodity for consumption. Such approaches contribute to a sense of alienation between human beings and the rest of creation and in some contexts have justified unfettered human domination over the creation.

Ecotheological readings of these same texts have significantly challenged such readings by clarifying the meaning of Hebrew terms typically translated as "to rule" and "to have dominion" (e.g., *radah, kabash*) identifying features of the text formerly missed, and reading Genesis 2 as a complementary creation narrative. For example, the seven repetitions of the phrase "And God saw that it was good (*tob*)" (Gen. 1:4, 10, 12, 18, 21, 25, 31) affirm the integrity, value, and beauty of creation completely apart from humanity. This supports one of the six principles of the Earth Bible project while fostering an awareness of the ecocentric and theocentric consciousness in these texts. Along with many other Old Testament scholars, Ellen Davis reads the priestly creation account as poetry understanding the charge given to humanity "Be fruitful and multiply, and fill the earth and subdue it; and have dominion over ... " (Gen. 1:28) as a directive for humans to practice skilled *mastery* within the broader context of the blessing of animals (Gen. 1:22) and the divine gift of land provided to all creatures by a loving Creator God (Gen. 1:29–30). This language functions to establish a unique role for humanity while affirming a sense of communal membership with all creatures. The overall literary structure is theocentric, with the earth as the primary subject and co-creator with God (Davis 2009, pp. 53–65). When this creation narrative (Gen. 1) is read alongside the second creation narrative (Gen. 2:4b–3:24), these themes become even more prominent. Both Adam (*'adam*) and the living animals and birds have their source of being from the earth/soil (*ha'adam*; Gen. 2:7, 19). The Hebrew wordplay between Adam and the earth/soil highlights the kinship connection of humanity with created matter. These readings align with the study of ecology and agrarian experience of the land. Both perspectives affirm the interconnectedness that humanity shares with other organisms and ecosystems. Richard

Bauckham laments that humanity "somewhere forgot their own creatureliness, their embeddedness within creation, their interdependence with other creatures" (Bauckham 2010, p. 11).

Another method to highlight ecological contours of a text is to identify a feature of the creation narrative formerly downplayed or ignored. In contrast to traditional readings of Genesis 1 that identify humanity as the climax of creation, Jürgen Moltmann correctly identifies Sabbath as the crown of creation. In this text, Sabbath functions in at least four specific ways: to decenter both humanity and work, to become the point of orientation for all creation, to undercut the utilitarian economic valuation of resources, and to embody sacred time, anticipating the final eschatological indwelling of God in creation (Moltmann 1985).[10] Norman Wirzba is one of many scholars who have followed the lead of Moltmann by developing Sabbath theology as one key principle of the ecology of the Bible (Wirzba 2006).

3.3. Listening to the Voice of Creation and the Experts Who Speak on Its Behalf

Another major principle developing from the earliest eco-readings is the need to listen carefully to the *voice* of creation in the text. This component of ecological hermeneutics is a foundational principle promoted by the Earth Bible project, resulting in a number of scholarly works. This practice approaches all other-than-human components of the universe as a "subject" affirming creation's intrinsic integrity and worth apart from any relationship with humanity. Unlike former readings that relegated nature to an object or theme, the earth here is "capable of raising its voice in celebration and against injustice" (Habel 2008, p. 2). The theme of the earth rejoicing toward the Creator and mourning, typically in response to human wrongdoing, is frequent in the Psalms and Prophets (e.g., Pss. 19:1–3; 97:6; 98:7–8; Isa. 24:4; Jer. 4:28; 12:4) and appears in the New Testament as well (e.g., Phil. 2:10; Rom. 8:21–23; Rev. 5:13). Such expressions have typically been considered purely metaphorical or poetic since humans stand as uniquely able to express praise consciously through words. The human inability to comprehend should not detract, however, from the possibilities of other-than-human creatures' capacity to also give glory to God, even if that capacity depends on their unique created capacities of expression. Richard Bauckham's suggestion captures something of this mystery: "The Bible has de-divinized nature, but it has not de-sacralized nature. Nature remains sacred in the sense that it belongs to God, exists for the glory of God, even reflects the glory of God, as humans also do" (Bauckham 2011, p. 13).

The acknowledgment of creation's capacity to reflect God's glory has contributed to a renewed interest in approaching creation as a revelation of the triune God, historically referred to as *natural theology*.[11] The connection of nature to revelation of God has informed doctrinal and moral considerations for much of Christian history. The sentiment of Basil of Caesarea reflects common theological reflections on texts such as Psalm 19:1 and Romans 1:20: "I want creation to awaken such a profound admiration in you, that in every place, whatever plants you may contemplate, you are overcome by a living remembrance of the Creator."[12] Texts such as Job 12:7–9 invite the human to turn to animals, birds, plants, and fish for instruction; a text that prompts the interest of ecotheologians. In Proverbs 6:6–9 humans are exhorted to consider "the ways of the ant", and the New Testament affirms that "all things" come through Jesus Christ (John 1:1–3; Col. 1:15–20). These assertions provide glimpses of how the creation itself, when properly viewed, direct humans toward God.

In attempts to discern a process to *hear* the voice of creation, biblical and theological scholars have increasingly valued and encouraged interdisciplinary collaboration with those who speak on its behalf, particularly experts in relevant scientific disciplines. For example, in *Ask the Beasts: Darwin and the God*

---

[10] For a succinct summary of Moltmann's contribution to ecological hermeneutics, see Jürgen Moltmann's Ecological Hermeneutic. *Ecological Hermeneutics: Biblical, Historical and Theological Perspectives* (Law 2010).

[11] I am not addressing the broad topic of natural theology in this discussion. For a collection of important historical, philosophical, and scientific perspectives on natural theology, see *The Oxford Handbook of Natural Theology* (Manning 2013).

[12] Basil, *Hexaemeron* 5.2 (SC 26:284).

of Love, Elizabeth Johnson methodologically places two classic works in dialogue, Charles Darwin's account of the origin of species and the Christian confession found in the Nicene Creed (Johnson 2014). What results is an excellent example of an enriched and expanded reading of Scripture in light of the contours of scientific inquiry. Drawing more narrowly upon collaboration with agrarian practitioners, in *Scripture, Culture and Agriculture: An Agrarian Reading of the Bible*, Ellen Davis demonstrates not only how the land and agrarian practices are a major topic throughout the Hebrew Bible but also how the relationship with the land makes up an essential aspect of the Israelites' faith and relationship with God (Davis 2009). Ecological themes such as kinship with the land and the interconnectedness of all creation come into sharper focus when one reads Scripture from an agrarian perspective. In a similar vein, recent explorations of critical animal studies within the Bible have resulted in fascinating scholarship identifying new insights of otherwise overlooked texts.[13] A final example of the fruit of interdisciplinary collaboration is *Seven Pillars of Creation: The Bible, Science and the Ecology of Wonder* by William Brown. In the introduction, Brown outlines his approach: "I propose a tour of the biblical contours of creation conducted in conversation with science ... to recapture something of the awe that fostered the spirit of inquiry among the ancients and today ignites the vital spark of wonder that drives the best science" (Brown 2010, p. 5). His exegetical and theological work on key Old Testament texts masterfully demonstrates how scientific findings infuse new exegetical and theological insights.

3.4. Reconceptualization of Theological Frameworks

A notable development emerging as a result of ecotheological approaches to Scripture is a reconceptualization of traditional theological frameworks such as soteriology, pneumatology, and eschatology. The work of Ernst M. Conradie helpfully outlines how doctrinal formulation, in a way similar to the interpretation of any individual text, is a constructive exercise shaped by multiple factors. The selection of a cluster of texts read from within a given historical context and tradition of interpretation shapes doctrinal constructs that play a crucial role in shaping faith traditions. Within times of rapid historical, social, economic, and scientific change, received doctrinal constructions may naturally be considered inadequate to address a new context. We have seen this transpire as the efficacy of the received doctrinal categories of soteriology, pneumatology, and eschatology have been called into question in light of the contemporary environmental crisis (Conradie 2006).

As general awareness of environmental concerns has grown within society, Old Testament theologians have become more cognizant of the priority given to the doctrine of redemption over the doctrine of creation; this awareness has prompted consideration for new constructions. For example, in his Old Testament theology, R. Knierim identifies a paradigmatic shift of emphasis: "Yahweh is not the God of creation because God is the God of the humans or of human history. The most universal aspect of Yahweh's dominion is not human history. It is the creation and sustenance of the world." (Knierim 1995, p. 40). Likewise, Terence Fretheim suggests: "God's work in the world must be viewed in and through a universal frame of reference. That the Bible begins with Genesis, not Exodus, with creation, not redemption, is of immeasurable importance for understanding all that follows" (Fretheim 2005, p. xiv).

Similarly, New Testament scholars have begun to question the adequacy of dominant soteriological constructs that focus almost entirely on individual human salvation from sin. These frameworks were inherited in part from the preoccupation among Reformation scholars on issues of human salvation and exasperated by the tendency in the modern world to relegate nature to the sphere of science. This bifurcation led to reducing theology's compass to issues of human faith. Through a critical assessment of narrowly focused soteriological models, scholars have rediscovered premodern readings of Scripture characterized more by a vision of the whole creation, what Paul Santmire refers

---

[13] See for example, the fascinating work of Ken Stone (Stone 2017).

to as a "universalizing interpretive frame of reference" (Santmire 2000, p. 30).[14] By identifying anthropocentric bias, New Testament scholars are expanding the central doctrine of soteriology by exploring the variety of ways that salvation (*sōtēria, sōzo*) is conceived in the New Testament. In addition to human reconciliation to God, *sōtēria* means to "heal, bring peace, rescue, reconcile, and restore" (Snyder and Scandrett 2011).

It is true that one cannot go to any one set of texts in the Gospels to identify a clear theology of creation as it relates to the theology of redemption, yet the teachings of Jesus presuppose many components of creation theology of the Hebrew Bible. God is understood as Creator of all things (Matt. 19:9; Mark 10:6), cares for creation (Matt. 6:26, 28–30; 10:29–31; cf. Luke 12:6–7; 12:24, 27–28), and is declared the "Lord of heaven and earth" (Matt. 11:25; Luke 10:21). Of special relevance is how the Gospels portray the kingdom of God by drawing upon Old Testament prophetic anticipations of the reign of God, a reign inaugurated in Jesus and one that extends beyond the saving of human souls. The healing miracles of Jesus of Nazareth provide a testimony to physical restoration as a sign of the kingdom. Some of Jesus' interactions with or in nature anticipate prophetic visions for a full restoration of humanity with the other-than-human world: chaotic waters stilled (Mark 4:35-41; cf. Job 26:12; Isa. 27:1; Rev. 21:1) and wild animals at peace (Mark 1:13; cf. Isa. 11:6–9; see Bauckham 2011, pp. 70–78). In both Matthew and Luke, the words of Jesus referencing the healing of humans alludes to Isaiah 35, which links the transformation of nature with the healing of the deaf, lame, and dumb. The teaching of Jesus brings physical, spiritual, and social healing to broken people and anticipates an eschatological wholeness to a broken creation (Bauckham 2011, pp. 63–132).

Kingdom of God language prominent in the Gospels is paralleled by Paul's understanding of the cosmic work of God in the risen Christ as the inauguration of the *new creation* (Gal. 6:15; 2 Cor. 5:17). This terminology is unique to Paul and has ignited a lengthy debate about the scope of what Paul intends with this phrase. Scholars disagree on whether Paul intends new creation to be a reference to individual humans, the Christian community, or the cosmos.[15] Today, the majority of Pauline scholars conclude that based on Isaianic influences, the presence of key apocalyptic themes, and key linguistic considerations, Paul intends new creation to reference a universal dimension of redemption. Such a universal scope of Christ in both creation and redemption comes together in texts such as Colossians 1:15–20. This dense text establishes Christ as the "firstborn before all creation" (Col. 1:15) and Christ as the "firstborn from the dead" (Col. 1:18). Such claims identify Christ as the source and end of the totality of creation. Between these two strophes the church is identified as a new community (Col. 1:17–18a) empowered to continue the reconciling work of God within the creation (Col. 1:12–14 and 1:21–23). Romans 8 has been highlighted as perhaps the most explicit New Testament text linking the reconciling and redemptive work of Christ with not only humanity but all of creation. In this text the groaning, enslavement, hope for redemption, and freedom of the creation are linked to the fate of humanity: "for the creation was subjected to futility . . . in hope that the creation itself will be set free from its bondage to decay and will obtain the glory of the children of God. We know that the whole creation has been groaning in labor pains until now; and not only the creation, but we ourselves, who have the first fruits of the Spirit, groan inwardly while we wait for adoption, the redemption of our bodies" (Rom. 8:20–23). Howard A. Snyder captures the ecological implications from texts such as these:

> God's economy is more than salvation as commonly understood, more than creation healed. It is creation flourishing unendingly to God's glory. God's work is not just restorative; it is creative, generative, beautifully bountiful. Salvation is not just reversing the direction, not

---

[14] For an insightful overview of premodern readings that inform ecotheology, see *The Travail of Nature: The Ambiguous Ecological Promise of Christian Theology* (Santmire 1985).

[15] For a thorough review of the interpretive options, see *Christ, Creation and the Cosmic Goal of Redemption: A Study of Pauline Creation Theology as Read by Irenaeus and Applied to Ecotheology* (Leese 2018, pp. 23–60).

just returning to the starting point. The plan is to liberate all creation for God's original and unending project. (Snyder and Scandrett 2011, p. 108)

As with the reconstruction of soteriological models, considerable energy has been given to eschatological texts that are widely regarded as envisioning a cataclysmic destruction of the cosmos in the future (e.g., Mark 13:8, 24–25; 2 Pet. 3) or depict the elect as lifted out of the earthly realm to meet the Lord (1 Thess. 4:16–17). Second Peter is perhaps considered the most difficult text (2 Pet. 3–13); it seemingly casts a vision for the final destruction of the earth: "But the day of the Lord will come like a thief, and then the heavens will pass away with a loud noise, and the element will be dissolved with fire, and the earth and the works that are upon it will be burned up" (3:10). Texts such as these have contributed toward indifference among some evangelical groups within Christianity. One example of this critique is articulated by David Orr: "Belief in the imminence of the end times tends to make evangelicals careless stewards of our forests, soils, wildlife, air, water, seas and climate" (Orr 2005, p. 291). Yet, when these texts are viewed from within a broader biblical context with exegetical and lexical clarification, many scholars conclude that the heat and fire referenced here indicate not destruction but rather cleansing, refining, or revealing (e.g., Lucas 1999; Moo 2006). The theme of God's refining as a means for transformation runs throughout Scripture (e.g., Mal. 3:2; Zech. 13:9), and fire symbolizes God's holiness and power (e.g., Deut. 4:24, 9:3; Heb. 12:29). While cataclysmic end-time texts have tended to pose a challenge for theologians who seek to instill motivation to care for the earth, other texts, most notably Revelation 21–22, envision a continuity of the present earthly realm into a heaven-like future, readings that focus on earthly restoration or transformation. Barbara Rossing has contributed significantly toward ecocritical readings of eschatological texts in Revelation (Rossing 2005, 2010). The reality of such tension between texts is succinctly summarized by D. Horrell: "The ambivalence of the texts and their openness to diverse interpretations means that various construals of 'biblical teaching' are possible" (Horrell 2010, p. 119). These tensions also affirm why simply reading biblical texts is not sufficient for creating a responsible ecotheology; drawing upon ecclesiastical tradition, interdisciplinary insight, personal experience, and reason is essential to inform how ancient sacred texts can speak a life-giving message into our context.

Within the field of pneumatology recent progress has been made when considering how science can inform traditional theological frameworks. This strategy has induced stimulating new questions about the relationship of God with creation. Particularly within the Western evangelical tradition, Christians and professional theologians have often conceptualized the Spirit as primarily engaged in human transformation and building the Christian community. Influenced, in part, by a dualism between Spirit and matter, this perspective views the Spirit as less involved with or even completely detached from the other-than-human created order. The combination of ecology with Spirit, *ecopneumatology*, prompts questions such as the following, which are paving the way for groundbreaking work on the relationship of the Spirit with ecology: Where is the Spirit of God in an evolving universe? In what ways might scientific explanations of life expand the theological understanding of general divine action through the Spirit? As theologian and biochemist C. Southgate uses the language of evolutionary biology to conceptualize the Trinitarian function of God in creation, "The Father in creation both draws onward the ever-shifting distribution of peaks in the fitness landscape, through the unfolding creative work of the Logos, and encourages organisms, through the power of the Spirit, in their exploration of that landscape, giving rise to new possibilities of being a self" (Southgate 2008, p. 61). Similarly D. Edwards utilizes evolutionary science to affirm a form of Trinitarian panentheism. Here the Spirit makes space for the processes of the emerging and evolving universe to take place and move forward toward the eschatological new creation (Edwards 2004, pp. 130–42). This approach provides a point of discussion of the mutual relations and communion within the Divine while exploring what constitutes the relationship of the Spirit's cooperative work with the laws of nature, drawing creatures and the universe toward communion with God so that "God may be all in all" (1 Cor. 15:28). These analogies give a new level of understanding to texts such as Romans 8 that present the Spirit as one who in self-limiting love and compassion comes alongside the creation that is waiting and groaning as in birth pangs, anticipating an eschatological freedom from bondage and death (Rom. 8:19–23). Each of these examples demonstrates how theological categories, when viewed from an ecologically sensitive vantage, has potential for revealing rich contours of ecological wisdom otherwise unnoticed in sacred texts.

4. Conclusions

In a time when the evidence of growing environmental degradation exasperated by human neglect and consumer patterns seems both undeniable and daunting, people of faith are revisiting the multi-textured resources of ancient texts, traditions, and doctrine seeking a fresh and relevant message. In this brief article, I have surveyed a few of the key reading strategies and ecological hermeneutical approaches within the expanding and important field of ecotheology. Such resources enable scholars, clergy, lay men and women to read ancient texts with ecological lenses which result in fresh biblical insights that inform environmental praxis. Recent theological work considers how key doctrinal constructs such as soteriology, eschatology and pneumatology can be reformulated to reflect the biblical themes of the universal, cosmic scope of God's love and redemptive purposes. Each of these trajectories provide encouragement for readers of Scripture to contemplate new ways of thinking about the earth and the human relationship to it and to discern, value, and listen to the entire earth community as the household of God and God's good creation.

Funding: This research received no external funding.

Conflicts of Interest: The author declares no conflict of interest.

References

Bauckham, Richard. 2010. *The Bible and Ecology: Rediscovering the Community of Creation.* Waco: Baylor University Press.

Bauckham, Richard. 2011. *Living with Other Creatures: Green Exegesis and Theology.* Waco: Baylor University Press.

Berry, Wendell. 2002. Christianity and the Survival of Creation. In *The Art of the Commonplace.* Edited by Norman Wirzba. Berkeley: Counterpoint, pp. 305–20.

Berry, R. J., ed. 2006. *Environmental Stewardship: Critical Perspectives—Past and Present.* New York: T&T Clark.

Brown, William. 2010. *The Seven Pillars of Creation: The Bible, Science, and the Ecology of Wonder.* Oxford: Oxford University Press.

Conradie, Ernst M. 2006. *Christianity and Ecological Theology: Resources for Further Research.* Study Guides in Religion and Theology 11. Stellenbosch: SUN Press.

Conradie, Ernst M. 2007. The Whole Household of God (*oikos*) Some Ecclesiological Perspectives: Part 1 & 2. *Scriptura* 94: 1–28.

Dalton, Ann Marie, and Henry Simmons. 2010. *Ecotheology and the Practice of Hope.* New York: SUNY.

Davis, Ellen F. 2009. *Scripture, Culture and Agriculture: An Agrarian Reading of the Bible.* Cambridge: Cambridge University Press.

Deane-Drummond, Celia. 2017. *A Primer in Ecotheology: Theology for a Fragile Earth.* Oregon: Cascade Books.

DeWitt, Calvin B. 2000. Creation's Environmental Challenge to Evangelical Christianity. In *The Care of Creation: Focusing Concern and Action.* Edited by R. J. Berry. Leicester: InterVarsity, pp. 60–73.

Edwards, Denis. 2004. *Breath of Life: A Theology of the Creator Spirit.* New York: Orbis.

Fretheim, Terence. 2005. *God and World in the Old Testament: A Relational Theology of Creation.* Nashville: Abingdon.

Habel, Norman C. 2001. *The Earth Story in the Psalms and Prophets.* The Earth Bible Series 4; Sheffield: Sheffield Academic Press.

Habel, Norman C. 2008. Introducing Ecological Hermeneutics. In *Exploring Ecological Hermeneutics.* Edited by Norman C. Habel and Peter Trudinger. Atlanta: Society of Biblical Literature, pp. 1–8.

Habel, Norman C. 2009. *An Inconvenient Text: Is A Green Reading of the Bible Possible.* Adalaide: ATF Press.

Habel, Norman C., and Vicki Balabanski, eds. 2002. *The Earth Story in the New Testament.* The Earth Bible 5. Sheffield: Sheffield Academic Press.

Habel, Norman C., and Shirley Wurst, eds. 2000. *The Earth Story in Genesis*. The Earth Bible Series 2; Sheffield: Sheffield Academic Press.

Habel, Norman C., and Shirley Wurst, eds. 2001. *The Earth Story in Wisdom Traditions*. The Earth Bible 3. Sheffield: Sheffield Academic Press.

Habel, Norman C., ed. 2000. *Readings from the Perspective of the Earth*. The Earth Bible Series 1; Sheffield: Sheffield Academic Press.

Hessel, Dieter T., and Rosemary Radford Ruether, eds. 2000. *Christianity and Ecology: Seeking the Well-Being of Earth and Humans*. Cambridge: Harvard University Center for the Study of World Religions Publications.

Horrell, David G. 2010. *The Bible and the Environment: Towards a Critical Ecological Biblical Theology*. London: Equinox.

Horrell, David G., Cherryl Hunt, Christopher Southgate, and Francesca Stavrakopoulou, eds. 2010. *Ecological Hermeneutics: Biblical, Historical and Theological Perspectives*. London and New York: T&T Clark.

Jenkins, Willis. 2009. After Lynn White: Religious Ethics and Environmental Problems. *JRE* 37: 283–309. [CrossRef]

Johnson, Elizabeth A. 1993. *Women, Earth, and Creator Spirit*. Mahwah: Paulist Press.

Johnson, Elizabeth A. 2014. *Ask the Beasts: Darwin and the God of Love*. New York: Bloomsbury.

Knierim, Rolf P. 1995. *The Task of Old Testament Theology: Substance, Method and Cases*. Grand Rapids: Eerdmans.

Law, Jeremy. 2010. Jürgen Moltmann's Ecological Hermeneutic. In *Ecological Hermeneutics: Biblical, Historical and Theological Perspectives*. Edited by David G. Horrell, Cherryl Hunt, Christopher Southgate and Francesca Stavrakopoulou. New York: T&T Clark.

Leese, J. J. Johnson. 2018. *Christ, Creation and the Cosmic Goal of Redemption: A Study of Pauline Creation Theology as Read by Irenaeus and Applied to Ecotheology*. New York: T&T Clark.

Lucas, Ernest. 1999. The New Testament Teaching on the Environment. *Transformation* 6: 93–99. [CrossRef]

Manning, Russell R., ed. 2013. *The Oxford Handbook of Natural Theology*. Oxford: Oxford University Press.

Moltmann, Jürgen. 1985. *God in Creation: The Gifford Lectures 1984–1985: An Ecological Doctrine of Creation*. Translated by M. Kohl. London: SCM.

Moo, Douglas J. 2006. Nature in the New Creation: New Testament Eschatology and the Environment. *JETS* 49: 449–88.

Orr, David W. 2005. Armageddon versus Extinction. *Conservation Biology* 19: 290–92. [CrossRef]

Rossing, Barbara. 2005. For the Healing of the World: Reading Revelation Ecologically. In *From Every Tribe, Tongue, People, and Nation: The Book of Revelation in Intercultural Perspective*. Edited by David Rhoads. Minneapolis: Fortress.

Rossing, Barbara. 2010. God Laments with Us: Climate Change, Apocalypse and the Urgent Kairos Moment. *Ecumenical Review* 62: 119–30. [CrossRef]

Santmire, Paul. 1985. *The Travail of Nature: The Ambiguous Ecological Promise of Christian Theology*. Theology and the Sciences. Philadelphia: Fortress.

Santmire, Paul. 2000. *Nature Reborn: The Ecological and Cosmic Promise of Christian Theology*. Minneapolis: Fortress.

Santmire, Paul. 2017. *Behold the Lilies: Jesus and the Contemplation of Nature*. Eugene: Cascade Books.

Schutz, Paul J. 2018. From Creatureliness to a Creation Imagination. *The Other Journal: An Intersection of Theology and Culture* 28: 10–19.

Snyder, Howard A., and Joel Scandrett. 2011. *Salvation Means Creation Healed: The Ecology of Sin and Grace, Overcoming the Divorce between Earth and Heaven*. Eugene: Cascade Books.

Southgate, Christopher. 2008. *The Groaning of Creation: God, Evolution, and the Problem of Evil*. Louisville: Westminster John Knox.

Stone, Ken. 2017. *Reading the Hebrew Bible with Animal Studies*. Stanford: Stanford University Press.

Theokritoff, Elizabeth. 2017. Green Patriarch, Green Patristics: Reclaiming the Deep Ecology of Christian Tradition. *Religions* 8: 116. [CrossRef]

Watson, Francis. 2010. In the Beginning: Irenaeus, Creation and the Environment. In *Ecological Hermeneutics: Biblical, Historical and Theological Perspectives*. Edited by David G. Horrell, Cherryl Hunt, Christopher Southgate and Francesca Stavrakopoulou. London and New York: T&T Clark, pp. 127–39.

White, Lynn, Jr. 1967. The Historical Roots of Our Ecologic Crisis. *Science* 155: 1203–7. [CrossRef] [PubMed]

Wirzba, Norman. 2006. *Living the Sabbath: Discovering the Rhythms of Rest and Delight*. Grand Rapids: Brazos.

Wirzba, Norman. 2015. *From Nature to Creation: A Christian Vision for Understanding and Loving Our World*. The Church and Modern Culture. Grand Rapids: Baker Academic.

MDPI

Article

Are the Gospels "Historically Reliable"? A Focused Comparison of Suetonius's *Life of Augustus* and the Gospel of Mark

Michael R. Licona

Department of Theology, Houston Baptist University, Houston, TX 77074, USA; mlicona@hbu.edu

Received: 2 February 2019; Accepted: 22 February 2019; Published: 28 February 2019

check for updates

Abstract: Are the Gospels historically reliable? Authors of ancient historical literature had objectives for writing that differed somewhat from those of modern historians. Consequently, the literary conventions that were in play also differed. Therefore, it is difficult to speak of the historical reliability of ancient texts without certain qualifications. In this essay, a definition for the historical reliability of ancient texts is proposed, whereby such a text provides an accurate gist, or an essentially faithful representation of what occurred. Four criteria that must be met are then proposed. Suetonius's *Life of the Divine Augustus* and the Gospel of Mark, are then assessed by using the criteria. Suetonius was chosen because he wrote more closely than his peers to how modern biographers write, and the *Augustus* was chosen because it is the finest of Suetonius's *Lives*. The Gospel of Mark from the Bible was chosen because it is probably the earliest extant account of the "Life of Jesus." The result of this focused comparison suggests that the *Life of Augustus* and the Gospel of Mark can be said to be historically reliable in the qualified sense proposed. However, an additional factor challenging this conclusion is described, and further discussion is needed and encouraged.

Keywords: Gospels; Gospel of Mark; Suetonius; *Life of Augustus*; historical reliability

1. Introduction

Are the New Testament Gospels historically reliable?[1] In this essay, I will approach the question from a foundational level. Before we can answer the question, it will be necessary for us to define what we mean by the term "historically reliable".

We must first acknowledge that historical investigation has many limitations, of which only a few can be briefly mentioned here. Many events in ancient literature, including the Gospels, cannot be verified, due to a lack of data. Moreover, the metanarrative in the Gospels is beyond the reach of historians. This metanarrative is the overarching sequence of events in which God's uniquely divine Son has come into the world to save us and has since returned to Heaven, where he shares a throne with his Father, and will return in the future to judge the world. This metanarrative, of course, cannot be confirmed by historians, who simply do not have the tools capable of confirming such events. This does not mean that the metanarrative is false. However, it does mean it cannot be historically confirmed.

When speaking of ancient history writing, the finest ancient historians—Greek, Roman, and Jewish alike—were committed to accurate reporting, and to writing a good story with literary artistry for the reader's benefit and enjoyment. That almost always meant that authors of ancient historical literature

---

[1]　Perhaps the finest single volume addressing this question is Craig L. Blomberg's *The Historical Reliability of the Gospels* (Blomberg 2007).

reported in a manner which was less concerned with precision than with the standards held by modern historians. Yet, even modern historiography often involves artistic license.

The movie *Apollo 13* (Howard 1995) was praised for its commitment to historical accuracy. Notwithstanding, director Ron Howard exercised some artistic license.[2] For example, when the actual Apollo 13 spacecraft ran into multiple life-threatening difficulties, flight director Gene Kranz and his team at Mission Control never gave up and produced solutions that brought the astronauts home safely. Kranz's firm assertion, "Failure is not an option", became the unforgettable tagline for the movie. However, the "historical Kranz", you might say, never uttered those words. Instead, they were assigned to him by the scriptwriters, who had learned from Kranz and others that this was a creed at NASA's Mission Control.[3] Those scriptwriters had less than two-and-a-half hours to tell the story of events that spanned six days. Now, this is good writing, and it is an accurate portrayal of Kranz and his team, though not in a precise sense.

The first book, written by my late friend Nabeel Qureshi, was a New York Times best seller: *Seeking Allah, Finding Jesus* (Qureshi 2014). It is an autobiography of his journey from Islam to Christianity. Here is what Nabeel wrote in the introduction:

> By its very nature, a narrative biography must take certain liberties with the story it shares. Please do not expect camera-like accuracy. That is not the intent of this book, and to meet such a standard, it would have to be a twenty-two-year-long video, most of which would bore even my mother to tears.

> The words I have in quotations are rough approximations. A few of the conversations represent multiple meetings condensed into one. In some instances, stories are displaced in the timeline to fit the topical categorization. In other instances, people who were present in the conversation were left out of the narrative for the sake of clarity. All of these devices are normal for narrative biographies ... Please read accordingly. (Qureshi 2014, p. 19)

This is a biography written in the 21st century by a meticulous academic.[4] Biographers in antiquity used those types of devices and others. In my view, this does not undermine the overall reliability of the literature, as long as we have the understanding that what we are reading was intended to convey an accurate gist, or an essentially faithful representation of what occurred. Ancient historical literature rarely ever intended to describe events with the precision of a legal transcript.[5]

Sallust commanded one of Caesar's legions, and he would become one of Rome's finest historians. Tacitus referred to Sallust as "that most admirable Roman historian" (*Annales* 3.30), while the famous rhetorician Quintilian said Sallust was a greater historian than Livy and that "one needs to be well-advanced in one's studies to appreciate him properly" (*Institutio oratoria* 2.5.19). So, it is noteworthy that Sallust occasionally displaced statements and speeches from their original context, and transplanted them in a different one, in order to highlight the true intensity, and even the true nature of those events. The finest ancient historians commonly used this technique, and others. In my

---

[2] See the *Apollo 13* DVD special features on Disc 1, "Lost Moon: The Triumph of Apollo 13," including feature commentary with director Ron Howard and feature commentary with Jim and Marilyn Lovell (Howard 1995). The 1995 motion picture is based on the book *Lost Moon: The Perilous Voyage of Apollo 13* by Jim Lovell and Jeffrey Kluger (Lovell and Kluger 1994).

[3] In his autobiography, Kranz (2000, p. 12) describes the Mission Control team's efforts to formulate "workaround" options during the Apollo 13 flight: "These three astronauts were beyond our physical reach. But not beyond the reach of human imagination, inventiveness, and a creed that we all lived by: 'Failure is not an option.'" Several years ago, one of the NASA engineers who was on Kranz's team approached me after a lecture and told me something to the same effect. Moreover, Jerry C. Bostick, who was NASA's flight dynamics officer for Apollo 13, offers a similar explanation for how the saying became the tagline of the film, which had to do with something he said in passing to the same effect while he was being interviewed by the scriptwriters (Woodfill 2019).

[4] Although *Seeking Allah, Finding Jesus* was a book written for a popular audience, Qureshi earned an MPhil in Judaism and Christianity in the Greco-Roman World from Christ Church, University of Oxford. He had just been accepted into the DPhil in New Testament program when he learned he had stage four stomach cancer. Nabeel died in 2017 at the age of thirty-four.

[5] Of course, artistic license has its limits. And some authors went so far that what they wrote could not be considered "historically reliable" apart from dying the death of a thousand qualifications.

view, that does not undermine the overall reliability of the literature in which they appear, as long as we have the understanding that what we are reading was most often intended to convey an accurate gist of the people and events described, rather than preserving details with the precision of a court transcript.

We may think about historical reliability in two ways: specifically and broadly. Many of us have chosen to get our news from a particular network. Those who live in the United States and have political leanings to the right, usually view FOX, while those with political leanings to the left are inclined to view CNN or the other mainstream media. One can focus on specific stories reported by their preferred news agency and assess whether a story is true, false, mostly true, or mostly false. Alternatively, one can assess that news agency on a broader basis. Regardless of the news agency that one chooses, viewers know that every agency is biased and is select in its reporting. Despite these deficiencies, viewers may still assess their preferred news agency as being generally reliable.

Classicists who understand the objectives of ancient historians do not usually speak of a text as being "historically reliable" in the broad sense. For example, though Tacitus is regarded as being among the most accurate of Roman historians, it would be rare to find a classicist saying that the literature that Tacitus wrote is "historically reliable". Instead, classicists focus on the specific reports of an author, such as whether it was Curio or Antony who presented Caesar's counterproposal to the senate in December 50 BCE, over the actual day on which the counterproposal was delivered. In contrast, while historians of Jesus debate over the reliability of specific reports in the Gospels, such as whether Jesus actually claimed to be divine or had predicted his resurrection, it is also the case that some of them speak in the broader sense of the Gospels being historically reliable. It is also in this broader sense that this essay is concerned.

I will begin by proposing a tentative definition for the term 'historically reliable', as follows: A text may be regarded as historically reliable when it provides an accurate gist or an essentially faithful representation of what occurred. In what follows, I will offer four criteria, all of which must be met before one is justified in claiming that a text is historically reliable in a broad sense. Some of these criteria may need to be nuanced or abandoned, and additional criteria may be required. What follows in this essay is simply an initial attempt.

In proceeding, I will employ these criteria to assess Suetonius's *Life of the Divine Augustus* and the Gospel of Mark. I chose Suetonius because he wrote more closely to how modern biographers write. than did others in his day. Others relied on their use of rhetoric to impress and persuade as they told a good story. Suetonius did not, at least not in the same manner and to the same degree. Andrew Wallace-Hadrill (Wallace-Hadrill 1995, p. 19; cf. 18, 23–24) writes,

> He is mundane: has no poetry, no pathos, no persuasion, no epigram. Stylistically he has no pretensions. No writer who sees himself as an artist, one of the elect, could tolerate the pervasive rubric; the repetitiveness of the headings, the monotony of the items that follow, the predictable ending "such he did; and such he did; and such he did". Suetonius is not sloppy or casual; he is clear and concise, but unadorned. His sentences seek to inform, with a minimum of extraneous detail ... The style is neither conversational nor elevated. It is the businesslike style of the ancient scholar.[6]

Mellor (1999, p. 149) similarly comments, "Unlike the historians of antiquity, Suetonius is not primarily a literary artist; he is the ancestor of the modern scholar".[7]

I have chosen to focus on Suetonius's *Life of Augustus*, because it is his finest biography. Suetonius was most interested in the transitional period of the late Republic to the early Empire. This is

---

[6] Wallace-Hadrill (Wallace-Hadrill 1995) is cited by almost all subsequent literature on Suetonius, and is regarded as one of the most valuable treatments of Suetonius. See also Bradley (1998, p. 12), Hurley (2001, p. 19), and Tatum (2014, pp. 163–64). Wallace-Hadrill (Wallace-Hadrill 1995, p. 10) adds, "Suetonius establishes the independence of his genre by distancing himself from history the further".

[7] See also Power (2014, p. 13).

understandable, since that period is not only the most interesting time for Rome, it is also one of the most interesting times in human history. Suetonius shows knowledge of many sources for his work, *Julius* and *Augustus*. However, his use of sources in his twelve *Lives of the Divine Caesars* tapers off significantly afterwards, as does the length and quality of those *Lives*. After Nero, Suetonius shows little interest (Wallace-Hadrill 1995, pp. 61–62). This creates a challenge in speaking of the historical reliability of Suetonius's *Lives* as a collection, and prompts us instead to speak of the historical reliability of each Life.

I have chosen the Gospel of Mark from the Bible, since it is very likely the earliest of the four canonical Gospels, with the other Synoptics using him as their primary source, and because John's Gospel presents unique challenges that require a separate discussion. Thus, it is easier to speak on the historical reliability of Mark, rather than the historical reliability of the Gospels as a collection.

I will now turn to four provisional criteria for assessing the historical reliability of ancient historical literature and employ them for assessing Suetonius's *Life of Augustus* and Mark's Gospel.

2. The Author Chose Sources Judiciously

Gaius Suetonius Tranquillus was born around 70 CE.[8] His date of death is unknown.[9] Suetonius wrote the *Lives of Illustrious Men*,[10] *Lives of the Caesars*, and some other works that have since been lost.[11] It is his *Lives of the Caesars* for which he is best known. Since Suetonius dedicated his *Lives of the Caesars* to the praetorian prefect Septicius Clarus, some scholars date them to the period in which Septicius held that post: 119–122 CE.[12] However, several other scholars think that Suetonius was still writing those *Lives* in the 130s.[13]

For his *Julius*, and especially his *Augustus* in Lives of the Caesars, Suetonius outdid other historians of his day in terms of naming his sources. He held three important posts in the emperor's administration: cultural and literary advisor to the emperor (*a studiis*), director of the imperial libraries of Rome (*a bibliothecis*), and supervisor of the emperor's correspondence (*ab epistulis*). While serving in these posts, he would have enjoyed access to many valuable sources. Although those positions afforded Suetonius unique access to some sources, scholars are not certain about which of his sources would not have likewise been available to others (Wallace-Hadrill 1995, pp. 91, 95; Hurley 2001, pp. 8–9).[14]

When Suetonius wrote about emperors that were closer to his own time, he did not name many sources, if any at all. Scholars do not know why this is the case, but have often suggested that, since his

---

[8]   For the dating of Suetonius's birth, see Bradley (Bradley 2012, p. 1409), Edwards (2000a, p. viii), Keener (2016, p. 146), Keener, *Christobiography* (Keener forthcoming), who says from c. 69 CE to c. 130–140 CE; and Hurley (2001, p. 1): "he wrote in the first quarter of the second century".

[9]   Regarding the date of Suetonius's death, Edwards (2000a, p. viii) says, "There are no further references to his career, though from a passage in *Titus* (chp. 10), it seems he was probably still writing after 130". Hurley (2001, p. 4) reports much the same: "No more is known of him after he left the court. He may have lived on for some time". Hurley (2001, p. 4n16) notes further, "Suetonius seems to have written of Domitia Longina as though she had died, perhaps in the 130s (*Tit.* 10.2[)]". Likewise, Van Voorst (2000, p. 29) says, "ca. 70–ca. 140" (29).

[10]   Hurley (2001, p. 6) notes that *Lives of Illustrious Men* contains more than 100 biographies of Roman poets, orators, historians, philosophers, grammarians, and rhetoricians.

[11]   Bradley (Bradley 2012).

[12]   For the dating of Suetonius's *Lives of the Caesars*, see Bradley (1998, p. 26); Edwards (2000a, p. viii); Keener (2016, p. 146); Keener, *Christobiography* (Keener forthcoming); and Van Voorst (2000, p. 30).

[13]   See Hurley (2001, pp. 4, 4n16) cited earlier in note above; see also Wardle (Wardle 2014, p. 4). Therefore, the dates and the span of time during which *Lives of the Caesars* was composed, is uncertain. It is certain that Suetonius's *Life of the Divine Julius* was the first written of the twelve *Lives*. However, the order in which the other eleven were composed is not known (Hurley (2014, pp. 25–26); Edwards (2000a, p. viii)). There is also uncertainty pertaining to whether Suetonius composed the *Lives of Illustrious Men* before his *Lives of the Caesars*. However, there is a tendency among today's scholars for thinking that his *Lives of Illustrious Men* was written first, perhaps as "a practice run for the *Caesares*" (Hurley (2001, p. 6)) and that *Lives of the Caesars* was his final writing project (Bradley (1998, p. 6)).

[14]   Hurley (2001, p. 9) adds, "This does not mean, however, that he had found a cache of correspondence in a private palace archive which only he and a select few were privileged to see. Wider access was available because earlier, in the second half of the first century, the elder Pliny and Quintilian had seen the correspondence or parts of it, perhaps in an imperial library. Never-published papers of Julius Caesar could be found in Augustus' libraries (*Iul.* 56.7)".

primary interest was the late Republic and its transition to Empire, his curiosities waned after the time of Augustus. It may also be that he relied much more on oral testimony for the later emperors, since eyewitnesses would have been alive, and there would have been much common knowledge about those emperors. It may also be that Suetonius lacked access to the same sources after Hadrian dismissed him from supervising his correspondences, or for any combination of these reasons.

The most valuable sources that Suetonius consulted for his *Augustus* are some of Augustus's letters, from which there are as many as twelve quotes, Augustus's will, and the *Res Gestae*, Augustus's personal account of his accomplishments, which were written to serve as his funerary inscription. He also consulted the proceedings of the senate. Still, Suetonius does not mention his sources for much of the *Augustus*. He was most likely relying on annalistic sources for most of the time.

However, not all of Suetonius's sources were of this quality. A large percentage of those he mentions by name in the *Augustus* are either otherwise unknown, or are not the type of sources that historians typically use (Wallace-Hadrill 1995, pp. 63–64). Also, scholars, such as Wardle (Wardle 2014, p. 20) suspect that most of the sources that he names actually contribute little to the portrait that Suetonius paints of Augustus. Thus, although the *Augustus* is Suetonius's Life that is the richest in named sources, the majority of that Life is not based on those sources. In addition, as Wardle (Wardle 2014, p. 28) notes, Suetonius chose to use questionable anecdotes, so much so, that the *Augustus* may be said to be based on a combination of pristine historical sources and tabloid rumors.

Gascou (1984) performed the most extensive project pertaining to Suetonius's sources for the *Augustus*. After nearly 900 pages, Gascou concludes with a general observation: Suetonius consulted numerous sources, yet in an indiscriminate manner. Thus, although Suetonius was more generous in naming his sources than most other historians of his era, Plutarch was more discriminate in his choice of sources. Did Suetonius use good judgment when choosing sources? Yes and no.

Turning to Mark's Gospel, little is known about its author. We observe that it is an anonymous work, and that it mentions no sources. Neither should come as a surprise, however, though some scholars have made much over these observations. In a recent article, Gathercole (2018, p. 454) takes a different view to those scholars, and argues that the absence of the author's name in the title and preface is "entirely irrelevant to the question of the Gospels' anonymity". In this impressive article, Gathercole lists more than a dozen ancient historians and biographers who do not include their name in the title or preface, in at least some of their writings.[15] Of even more interest (with only two exceptions, one of which is fictitious), no ancient biographers whose writings have survived identified themselves in the title or preface.[16] We can go even further than Gathercole and note that Julius Caesar does not identify himself as the author of his *Commentaries on the Civil War*, and he writes entirely in the third person, as the author of John's Gospel may have done. Also, some of the most highly regarded historians of that era—Sallust, Livy, and Plutarch—chose not to include their names anywhere in the literature that they wrote!

Notwithstanding the common practice of anonymity in a technical sense, the ancients appeared to have known the identity of the authors who wrote these works, although in many instances, we are left to speculate as to how they knew it. The best source attesting Plutarch's authorship is the Lamprias Catalogue, written more than a century and perhaps more than two centuries after Plutarch's death. Additionally, it is falsely attributed to Plutarch's son. Still, no one questions Plutarchan authorship.

The traditional authorship of Mark's Gospel is that it was written by John Mark, who was an associate of Peter, who was one of Jesus's three closest disciples. Evidence for the traditional

---

[15] Gathercole (2018) lists Xenophon's *Hellenica* and *Anabasis*, Josephus's *Jewish Antiquities* and *The Life*, Polybius, Diodorus Siculus, Arrian, Sallust, Livy, Tacitus, Florus, Philo, Plutarch, Lucian's biographical writings, Philostratus's *Life of Apollonius* and *Lives of the Sophists*, and Cornelius Nepos.

[16] Gathercole (2018) identifies Lucian, *Passing of Peregrinus*, and the *Life of Aelius* in the *Historia Augusta*. We do not know if Suetonius included his name in the title or preface of his *Life of the Divine Julius*, the first of the twelve *Lives*, because the first portion of that Life has been lost.

authorship of Mark is much better than we have for Plutarch's *Lives*. Our earliest source is Papias, whose five-volume work, titled *Expositions of the Sayings of the Lord*, has survived only in fragments preserved in the writings of others. Eusebius preserves Papias's comments pertaining to his sources, provided below in Greek, with an English translation:

Οὐκ ὀκνήσω δέ σοι καὶ ὅσα ποτὲ παρὰ τῶν πρεσβυτέρων καλῶς ἔμαθον καὶ καλῶς ἐμνημόνευσα, ⌐συγκατατάξαι ταῖς ἑρμηνείαις, διαβεβαιούμενος ὑπὲρ αὐτῶν ἀλήθειαν. οὐ γὰρ τοῖς τὰ πολλὰ λέγουσιν ἔχαιρον ὥσπερ οἱ πολλοί, ἀλλὰ τοῖς τἀληθῆ διδάσκουσιν, οὐδὲ τοῖς τὰς ἀλλοτρίας ἐντολὰς μνημονεύουσιν, ἀλλὰ τοῖς τὰς παρὰ τοῦ κυρίου τῇ πίστει δεδομένας καὶ ἀπ' αὐτῆς παραγινομένας τῆς ἀληθείας. εἰ δέ που καὶ παρηκολουθηκώς τις τοῖς πρεσβυτέροις ἔλθοι, τοὺς τῶν πρεσβυτέρων ἀνέκρινον λόγους· τί Ἀνδρέας ἢ τί Πέτρος εἶπεν ἢ τί Φίλιππος ἢ τί Θωμᾶς ἢ Ἰάκωβος ἢ τί Ἰωάννης ἢ Ματθαῖος ἢ τις ἕτερος τῶν τοῦ κυρίου μαθητῶν, ἅ τε Ἀριστίων καὶ ὁ πρεσβύτερος Ἰωάννης, οἱ τοῦ κυρίου μαθηταί, λέγουσιν. οὐ γὰρ τὰ ἐκ τῶν βιβλίων τοσοῦτόν με ὠφελεῖν ὑπελάμβανον, ὅσον τὰ παρὰ ζώσης φωνῆς καὶ μενούσης.

3 "I will not hesitate to set down for you, along with my interpretations, everything I carefully learned then from the elders and carefully remembered, guaranteeing their truth. For unlike most people I did not enjoy those who have a great deal to say, but those who teach the truth. Nor did I enjoy those who recall someone else's commandments, but those who remember the commandments given by the Lord to the faith and proceeding from the truth itself. 4 And if by chance someone who had been a follower of the elders should come my way, I inquired about the words of the elders—what Andrew or Peter said, or Philip or Thomas or James or John or Matthew or any other of the Lord's disciples, and whatever Aristion and the elder John, the Lord's disciples, were saying. For I did not think that information from books would profit me as much as information from a living and abiding voice".[17] (Pap., *Frag.* 3.3–4 in Euseb., *Hist. eccl.* 3.39)

It appears that Papias is claiming to have received information from a disciple of the Elder John, pertaining to what the Elder John was presently teaching. Scholars differ on whether Papias was claiming that the "Elder John" is John the son of Zebedee, or a minor disciple named John who had traveled with Jesus.[18] They also differ on the dating of Papias's writings: from the late 90s to 150 CE, with the majority opinion of c. 130 CE.[19] Even if the majority opinion is correct that Papias wrote c.

---

[17] Reference numbers and English translation are as given in Holmes (2007, pp. 734–35).

[18] Irenaeus thought that Papias heard John the son of Zebedee directly, whereas Eusebius—perhaps correctly—thinks that Papias was claiming to have received information from those who had known the apostles (Euseb., *Hist. eccl.* 3.39).

[19] For the range and relative consensus of scholarly opinion on the dating of Papias's writings, see Bauckham (2017, p. 14): "We cannot therefore date his writing to before the very end of the first century, but it could be as early as the turn of the century"; Holmes (2007, p. 722): "within a decade or so of AD 130"; Jefford (2006, p. 37): "ca. 130"; Körtner (2010, p. 176): "The majority of scholarship points to the date of writing as 125/130", but Körtner (2010, pp. 176–77) notes that "little attention has been paid to Eusebius' note in Liber Chronicorum II (frag. 2)" in which Eusebius makes statements suggesting that Papias wrote around 110 CE; Yarbrough (1983, p. 190): "In summary, considerable evidence points to an early date for Papias' writings. The generally accepted date of 130 or later has little to commend it. We conclude that Papias wrote his five treatises ca. 95–110"; Hill (2007, pp. 42, 48): "He wrote perhaps as early as about 110 and probably no later than the early 130s ... Since Papias learned it from the elder, this tradition about Mark goes back at least another generation, to about the end of the first century if not earlier"; Drobner (2007, p. 55): "[T]he attempts at dating the work ... range from 90 to 140; more recent commentators tend to favor a later date of ca. 130/140"; Gundry (1994, p. 610): "Modern handbooks usually put the date of his writing at ca. A.D. 135. Early though it is, this date is not early enough. The only hard evidence in its favor comes in a statement of Philip of Side, who makes Papias refer to the reign of Hadrian (pp. 117–38 ...). But we have good reasons to distrust Philip's statement. He is notoriously unreliable and wrote approximately a century later than Eusebius did (Philip—ca. 430; Eusebius—ca. 324). Hence, if Eusebius leads us to an earlier date for Papias's writing, we should probably prefer the earlier", and thus Gundry (1994, pp. 610–11) goes on to argue that Papias wrote prior to 110 CE; Schoedel (1992, p. 140): "[A]lthough later dates (e.g., a.d. 130–140) have often been suggested by modern scholars, Bartlet's date for Papias' literary activity of about A.D. 110 has recently gained support (Schoedel 1967, pp. 91–92; Körtner 1983, pp. 89–94, 167–72, 225–26)"; and Koester (2000, pp. 68, 171): "early second century ... ca. 100–150".

130 CE, Papias claims that he had heard what John the Elder taught while that John was still teaching. Thus, this situates the time that Papias received the tradition to be during the late first century.

Papias goes on to say that he had information deriving from the Elder John that Mark had written what he remembered Peter saying.

Καὶ τοῦτο ὁ πρεσβύτερος ἔλεγε· Μάρκος μὲν ἑρμηνευτὴς Πέτρου γενόμενος, ὅσα ἐμνημόνευσεν, ἀκριβῶς ἔγραψεν, οὐ μέντοι τάξει, τὰ ὑπὸ τοῦ ⌜Χριστοῦ ἢ λεχθέντα ἢ πραχθέντα. οὔτε γὰρ ἤκουσε τοῦ κυρίου, οὔτε παρηκολούθησεν αὐτῷ, ὕστερον δέ, ὡς ἔφην, Πέτρῳ, ὃς πρὸς τὰς χρείας ἐποιεῖτο τὰς διδασκαλίας, ἀλλ᾽ οὐχ ὥσπερ σύνταξιν τῶν κυριακῶν ποιούμενος ⌜λογίων, ὥστε οὐδὲν ἥμαρτε Μάρκος, οὕτως ἔνια γράψας ὡς ἀπεμνημόνευσεν. ἑνὸς γὰρ ἐποιήσατο πρόνοιαν, τοῦ μηδὲν ὧν ἤκουσε παραλιπεῖν ἢ ψεύσασθαί τι ἐν αὐτοῖς.

Ταῦτα μὲν οὖν ἱστόρηται τῷ Παπίᾳ περὶ τοῦ Μάρκου.

15 And the elder used to say this: "Mark, having become Peter's interpreter, wrote down accurately everything he remembered, though not in order, of the things either said or done by Christ. For he neither heard the Lord nor followed him, but afterward, as I said, followed Peter, who adapted his teachings as needed but had no intention of giving an ordered account of the Lord's sayings. Consequently Mark did nothing wrong in writing down some things as he remembered them, for he made it his one concern not to omit anything that he heard or to make any false statement in them".

Such, then, is the account given by Papias with respect to Mark.[20] (Pap. *Frag.* 3.15 in Euseb., *Hist. eccl.* 3.39.15)

To summarize, sometime in the late first century, Papias learned that Mark had been a follower of Jesus's lead disciple, Peter, and that Mark had written what he remembered Peter saying. Papias learned this from someone who had accompanied one of Jesus's disciples, and had heard it while that disciple was still alive and teaching. Even if Papias had written c. 130 CE, which itself may be too late, that is far less than a century after Mark had been written, and only a century after the events that it purports to describe. Also, it is a report that Papias had heard of, within only a few decades of Mark composing his Gospel.

Despite lingering questions about Papias, such as his report that Matthew recorded the teachings of Jesus in Aramaic (Pap. *Frag.* 3.16 in Euseb., *Hist. eccl.* 3.39.16; see Holmes (2007, pp. 740–41)), and the bizarre report of Judas's death, which was attributed to Papias in the fourth century by Apollinaris of Laodicea (Pap. *Frag.* 18.1–7 in Apollinaris of Laodicea), the testimony of Papias pertaining to the authorship of Mark's Gospel is far superior to the Lamprias Catalogue for Plutarch. Even Irenaeus, who names the authors of all four Gospels, writes just under a century after the final Gospel had been composed.[21] That Irenaeus wrote the report is not in question. Therefore, even Irenaeus is a better source for the authorship of the Gospels than the Lamprias Catalogue is for Plutarch. If Mark wrote what he remembered Peter saying, as Papias claims, Mark's source is remarkable.

There are additional reasons for thinking that Peter was Mark's primary source on Jesus. First, in addition to Papias and Irenaeus, there are numerous other ancient sources who attest to the Markian authorship of the Gospel that is attributed to him: Justin, Tertullian, Clement of Alexandria, Origen, Jerome, Muratorian Canon, Eusebius (who relies on Papias and Irenaeus), and the Anti-Marcionite Prologue to Mark's Gospel.[22] It is difficult to determine which, if any of these sources, are independent

---

[20] Reference numbers and the English translation are as given in Holmes (2007, pp. 738–39).

[21] According to Gathercole (2018, p. 466n68), Irenaeus wrote between 174 and 189 CE, and Gathercole also cites Irenaeus's naming Eleutherius as presently holding the episcopate in the twelfth place from the apostles (Irenaeus, *Against Heresies* 3.3.3). This episcopate began in 174 CE, and lasted until Eleutherius's death in 189 CE.

[22] Specifically, see Justin, *Dialogue with Trypho* 106 (where Justin mentions the "memoirs of the apostles" and "memoirs of him" when referring to Mark 3:16–17); Tertullian, *Against Marcion*, 4.2, 5; Clement of Alexandria (in Euseb., *Hist. eccl.* 6.14.5–7a);

of Papias and Irenaeus. What can be concluded is that the tradition affirming that Mark wrote the Gospel attributed to him, began early, was widespread, and lacks any evidence suggesting that another author was ever posited.

Secondly, 1 Peter 5:13 mentions "Mark, my son", which is consistent with Papias's claim that Mark knew Peter, one of Jesus's twelve disciples. Even if Peter is not the author of 1 Peter, the text at the minimum reveals a very warm association between the apostle Peter and a man named Mark; although there is no guarantee that it is the same Mark posited as the Gospel's author, Bauckham (2017, pp. 538–40) has addressed this concern.[23] Third, that Matthew and Luke stick so closely to Mark when using it as their source may suggest that they highly regarded Mark, which is consistent with reports that Mark's primary source was Peter. These internal reasons suggest that the apostle Peter was Mark's primary source for much of the content in his Gospel. When combined with the early and unanimous testimony of others, the case for Mark containing Peter's eyewitness testimony is quite strong.

Over the past fifty years, a slight majority of critical scholars agree with the traditional authorship of Mark; that is, someone named Mark or John Mark wrote what he remembered the apostle Peter said.[24] Also, a larger majority of critical scholars during that same period date Mark's Gospel as 50–70 CE,[25] which situates Mark's composition to approximately seventeen to forty years after Jesus's death. As stated earlier, great uncertainty exists as to when Suetonius wrote his *Lives of the Divine Caesars*. Most scholars assign a date of c. 119–130 CE, and perhaps even later.[26] Even if we consider the earlier date of 119 CE, that situates Suetonius's composition of *Augustus* 105 years after Augustus's death.

Did Mark use good judgment in his choice of sources? If the traditional view is correct that Mark wrote what he remembered hearing Peter say, as the data suggest, we may answer this with a resounding yes.

3. The Author Used His Sources Reliably

Surviving copies of Augustus's *Res Gestae* assist historians in reconstructing the entire text. As Wardle (Wardle 2014, p. 24n104) notes, "Authors such as Velleius, Seneca, and Tacitus echo the wording of *Res Gestae* so closely as to demonstrate that the text was well known and readily accessible". Thus, we can compare Suetonius's use of *Res Gestae*, and observe his adaptations. He feels free to paraphrase Augustus's words, even expanding on them, in order to provide further information (Wardle 2014, p. 24).[27] Moreover, corresponding details in a few stories mentioned by Josephus, Plutarch, Tacitus, Suetonius, and Dio render it almost certain that these authors often drew from the same sources (Wallace-Hadrill 1995, p. 64; Hurley 2001, pp. 14–15). Targeted comparisons by

---

Origen, *Commentary on Matthew* 1 (in Euseb., *Hist. eccl.* 6.25.5); Jerome, *De viris illustribus*, 8; Muratorian Canon; Eusebius, *Hist. eccl.* 2.15.1; and the Anti-Marcionite Prologue to Mark.

[23] Bauckham (2017, pp. 539–40) acknowledges that Mark was a "very common Roman praenomen, the first of the three names borne by every male Roman citizen in this period. In fact, all praenomina were common. But no Roman citizen would be known by his praenomen alone . . . If Cicero or Brutus or Marcus Aurelius or Mark Antony (Marcus Antonius) had written a Gospel, it would most certainly not have been called 'the Gospel according to Mark.' On the evidence of name usage alone, the author of the Gospel is very unlikely to have been a Roman citizen. He must have been a slave or a non-Roman, and the only relevant evidence will be for the frequency of the name among those who, not being Roman citizens, bore the name Marcus as their only Latin name, and as a name that could be used alone to identify them".

[24] With the assistance of my son-in-law, Nick Peters, I gathered the opinions of seventy-five critical scholars on the matters of the authorship and dating of Mark's Gospel, written between 1965 and 2018. As such, our sampling is by no means exhaustive and considers only literature written in English. Nevertheless, our sampling is large enough to be suggestive. The results have not been published.

[25] It is common to see 65–70 CE as the majority position of critical scholars for the date within which Mark was composed. I suspect many scholars use those dates without giving much thought to the matter, or they check what the majority actually think. I too was guilty of such.

[26] See notes 12–13 above.

[27] One can perform a similar exercise on Plutarch's *Life of Coriolanus*. Classicists believe that Plutarch's lone source for that Life was *Roman Antiquities* by Dionysius of Halicarnassus. By comparing Plutarch's account with that by Dionysius, we can decrypt what Plutarch did with his source when writing his *Life of Coriolanus* (see Russell (1963)). One can observe Plutarch doing what every educated youth of the elite in that day had been taught in their teenage years, and what every historian of that era did: paraphrase their sources rather than quoting them verbatim.

Keener (2016) and Goh (2016) are especially revealing. They conclude that while those historians certainly edit and adapt their source material, they do not engage in wholesale invention.[28] On a few occasions, mostly in his *Augustus*, Suetonius quotes his sources verbatim, or nearly so. Sometimes the Latin writer even quoted the source in its original Greek (Edwards 2000a, p. xxviii; Mellor 1999, p. 151). Accordingly, as Wardle (Wardle 2014, p. 25) notes, Suetonius "proves able to convey [a text's] meaning accurately, but also carefully manipulates the material to suit the temper of his times".[29] Suetonius appears to use his sources reliably.

Since Mark was the first Gospel and does not name his sources, at least directly,[30] and Jesus is not known to have written any literature, we cannot directly compare how Mark used his source(s). However, we can identify a few items in Mark that have parallel details reported in sources independent of Mark, such as Paul, John, and the Q material. Also, we observe that the agreement is quite good. Eve (2014, pp. 160–61) notes several parallel points pertaining to Jesus appearing in Mark and Paul: Jesus descended from David, is the Messiah, and is the Son of God. The "kingdom of God" and "inheriting" the kingdom of God are known by Mark and Paul. Jesus's prohibition of divorce and the centrality of loving others are likewise known by Mark and Paul. Eve (2014, pp. 164–66) further observes that Mark and Paul agree that Jesus instituted the Eucharist, that he did so on the evening/night he was betrayed, that he died by crucifixion, and that the Jewish leadership was responsible for having him executed.

We may go further than Eve and note the close similarities in the wording used by Paul and Mark pertaining to Jesus's Eucharist logia:

Paul (1 Cor. 11:24–25)

²⁴ καὶ εὐχαριστήσας ἔκλασεν καὶ εἶπεν· τοῦτό μού ἐστιν τὸ σῶμα τὸ ὑπὲρ ὑμῶν· τοῦτο ποιεῖτε εἰς τὴν ἐμὴν ἀνάμνησιν. ²⁵ ὡσαύτως καὶ τὸ ποτήριον μετὰ τὸ δειπνῆσαι λέγων· τοῦτο τὸ ποτήριον ἡ καινὴ διαθήκη ἐστὶν ἐν τῷ ἐμῷ αἵματι· τοῦτο ποιεῖτε, ὁσάκις ἐὰν πίνητε, εἰς τὴν ἐμὴν ἀνάμνησιν.

²⁴ And having given thanks, he broke [the bread] and said, "This is my body, which is for you. Do this in remembrance of me". ²⁵ Likewise, also the cup, after supper, saying, "This cup is the new covenant in my blood. Do this as often as you drink it in remembrance of me".

Mark (Mark 14:22–25)

²² Καὶ ἐσθιόντων αὐτῶν λαβὼν ἄρτον εὐλογήσας ἔκλασεν καὶ ἔδωκεν αὐτοῖς καὶ εἶπεν· λάβετε, τοῦτό ἐστιν τὸ σῶμά μου. ²³ καὶ λαβὼν ποτήριον εὐχαριστήσας ἔδωκεν αὐτοῖς, καὶ ἔπιον ἐξ αὐτοῦ πάντες. ²⁴ καὶ εἶπεν αὐτοῖς· τοῦτό ἐστιν τὸ αἷμά μου τῆς διαθήκης τὸ ἐκχυννόμενον ὑπὲρ πολλῶν. ²⁵ ἀμὴν λέγω ὑμῖν ὅτι οὐκέτι οὐ μὴ πίω ἐκ τοῦ γενήματος τῆς ἀμπέλου ἕως τῆς ἡμέρας ἐκείνης ὅταν αὐτὸ πίνω καινὸν ἐν τῇ βασιλείᾳ τοῦ θεοῦ.

²² And while they were eating, taking bread, having blessed it, he broke it and gave it to them and said, "Take. This is my body". ²³ And taking a cup, having given thanks, he gave it to them and all drank from it. ²⁴ And he said to them, "This is my blood of the covenant, which is poured out for many. ²⁵ Truly I say to you, I will never again drink from the fruit of the vine until that day when I drink it new in the kingdom of God".

---

[28] See also Keener, *Christobiography* (Keener forthcoming): "Suetonius's understanding of biography involved not free composition but dependence on prior information; where we can test him, this biographer mostly edited and adapted historical information rather than inventing new stories".

[29] Moreover, when authors such as Plutarch, Dio, Velleius, Seneca, Suetonius, and Tacitus contain numerous corresponding details, even in similar wording, we rightly conclude that they drew on the same sources. Although this does little or nothing to suggest multiple attestation, it allows us to measure the accuracy to which an author used his sources (Wardle 2014, p. 24n104; Wallace-Hadrill 1995, p. 64).

[30] Not naming one's sources was not at all untypical of ancient historical writing. See (Wallace-Hadrill 1995, p. 64).

Although not a verbatim similarity, Jesus's Eucharist logia in Mark and Paul are a close match. Though possible, it is not likely that one or more of those present at the Last Supper were taking notes of Jesus's words as would a stenographer during a deposition or trial. Yet, it is quite plausible that the gist of Jesus's Eucharist logia was recalled by several of those present at the Last Supper, and who continued to proclaim Jesus's message in the years that followed his death.

Eve (2014, p. 167) offers the following conclusions pertaining to Mark and Paul:

This brief survey suggests several things. First, it indicates that where Paul can be used as a check on Mark, Paul tends to support the existence of a tradition similar (but by no means identical) to that reflected in Mark. This in turn suggests that, where we have been able to check it, the tradition seems to have been reasonably stable between Paul's time and Mark's, and also that Mark has been reasonably conservative in his employment of it . . .

Second, Paul's own use of the tradition suggests that it was far from uncontrolled. It is something that he cites as being authoritative on more than one occasion, suggesting that he is, to some extent, constrained by it, and that he expects his audience to also be so. The tradition matters to Paul, because it conveys what he takes to be true (at least in the sense of authoritative); it would be surprising if Paul were alone in this attitude.

Third, although Paul never explicitly states precisely where he obtained his tradition from, his letters, particularly that to the Galatians, do provide some possible clues.

Eve (2014, pp. 167–68) then mentions Paul's two visits to Jerusalem, during which he spent time with no less than Peter (primarily), Jesus's brother James, and John (Gal. 1:18–19; 2:1–10).

This puts Paul in touch with some form of Christian tradition at least as early as 34 CE (within four years of the most likely date of the crucifixion) and with a form of the tradition provided by Peter and James, two men who had known Jesus in the flesh, three years later. (Eve 2014, p. 167)

Since Peter was one of Paul's major sources for Jesus, if Mark's primary source was Peter, it should not surprise us to find so many points of agreement on Jesus between Paul and Mark.[31]

It may also be valuable to observe how Matthew and Luke use Mark. Although they often paraphrase and adapt Mark, their changes are minimal in comparison to how other ancient authors paraphrase and adapt their sources. In my work pertaining to how Plutarch reports the same events in the different *Lives* he wrote (Licona 2017), I was surprised to observe the number and the extent of the differences between the accounts. Plutarch does not copy and paste texts when describing the same event in multiple Lives, but paraphrases and employs numerous compositional devices, such as compression, conflation, transferal, chronological displacement, and others. It is interesting to observe the same author relying on the same sources and reporting the same events, yet with differences (Licona 2017, pp. 23–111). As a rule, although Matthew and Luke edit and adapt Mark, their redactions are minor in comparison to those of Plutarch (Licona 2017, pp. 199–200). Downing (2011, pp. 529, 531; see also pp. 523–45) writes,

It is because people were taught to "say the same thing in other words" that close repetition of the same words among our sources [i.e., the Gospels] . . . appears so striking and so much in need of comment . . . With so much pressure in favour of paraphrase, and so common a conviction of its validity, it really does seem very strange that we find so much identical wording among our Synoptic Gospels.

---

[31] Eve (2014, p. 147) is skeptical of Papias's report. However, in my opinion, his reasons require too much of Papias. If one applies the same burden of proof to other ancient sources, perhaps even many modern ones, we could be confident about very little of the reported past. Moreover, it is apparent that Eve is a metaphysical naturalist who eschews the possibility of miracles. Therefore, it does not surprise us to find that he thinks that the stories of Jesus's miracles could not have occurred, and that they are very loosely based on far lesser events, if any at all. See Eve (2017, pp. 66–85, esp. p. 80) The cumulative case that Peter was Mark's primary source is fairly strong.

Elsewhere, having compared Josephus's use of his sources with how the authors of the Synoptic Gospels use theirs, Downing (1980, p. 33) writes,

> It is not the divergencies among the synoptists (or even between them and John), in parallel contexts, that are remarkable: it is the extraordinary extent of verbal similarities. The question is, why were they content to copy so much? rather than, why did they bother to change this or that? The procedure is not however mechanical, and there *are* considerable divergencies. But it has to be recognized that the relationship may betoken a much greater respect, one for the other, even than Josephus' for Scripture.

Although one can only speculate, the respect that the Gospels of Matthew and Luke appear to have had for Mark makes sense if Peter is the source behind much of that Gospel, and if Mark was thought to report what he had heard from Peter accurately.

Just as Suetonius, who wrote in Latin, will occasionally quote his source in the original Greek, there are three occasions when Mark, who wrote in Greek, quotes Jesus in the original Aramaic. For example, in the story of Jesus raising Jairus's daughter from the dead, Mark reports that Jesus came into the house, "and, having taken the hand of the child, he said to her, '*Talitha Koum*,' which translated is 'Little girl, I say to you, "Get up"'" (Mark 5:41; see also 7:34 and 15:34).

The data suggest that Suetonius and Mark used their sources reliably.

4. We can Verify Numerous Items Reported

Despite his shortcomings mentioned thus far, most of what Suetonius reported is trustworthy. Suetonian scholar Donna Hurley (Hurley 2001, pp. 1–2) writes,

> [The *Caesares*] contain an abundance of factual material to be mined by historians and social historians. Suetonius could be guilty of common error, and some of his information is distorted by misleading generalizations and inappropriate segmentation, but much is trustworthy and often unique ... Suetonius did not make things up. His catholic reportage did indeed include gossip—but it was not his own ...

There are numerous items reported in Mark that have been verified by historians of Jesus. A universal consensus of scholars agrees that the data are sufficient for concluding that Jesus of Nazareth lived in Judea in the first century and believed that God had chosen him to usher in his kingdom, that he had brothers, and that he was baptized by John the Baptist. He performed feats that both he and his followers interpreted as miracles and exorcisms. He challenged the reigning Jewish leadership, who ended up arresting him and bringing him before the Roman governor Pontius Pilate, who crucified him in April of 30 or 33. It is rare to find a historian of Jesus who would not affirm any of these "facts".[32] Also, there are even more items that many or even most scholars think can be verified about Jesus, though they are lacking in universal consensus.

Many items in the Gospels comport with existing knowledge pertaining to the historical settings in which the Gospels are situated. Bauckham (2017, pp. 39–92) has shown that when ancient documents and inscriptions are considered, the names mentioned in the Gospels and the book of Acts are not only the common names of Jews living in Israel of that period, and not those of Jews elsewhere, they also appear with roughly the same frequencies in the Gospels and Acts that we find in extrabiblical sources. At the very minimum, this suggests that all of the Gospel authors—or the sources from which they drew—were acquainted with Israel during the time of Jesus.

---

[32] Ehrman (2016, p. 221) is an exception when it comes to whether Jesus was known as a miracle worker during his ministry: "I want to consider whether it is absolutely certain that Jesus was already understood to be a miracle worker even in his own day, prior to his death. My view of that question is a minority position, but one that I want to explain. I think the answer is no. I am not saying that I know for certain that Jesus was not considered a miracle worker during his life. But I do think there are grounds for doubt". Ehrman may well be the only member subscribing to this "minority position".

We also know that places mentioned in the Gospels actually existed (e.g., Capernaum, Bethlehem, Bethsaida, Nazareth, Jerusalem, the Mount of Olives). We know that several of the people mentioned in the Gospels actually existed, and lived during the period in which they were situated (e.g., Augustus, Quirinius, Tiberius, the Herods, Pontius Pilate, Caiaphas, John the Baptist, Jesus).

It is germane that Mark was in a position to receive accurate reports about Jesus. This is especially true if Papias's report is correct that Mark wrote what he remembered Peter saying. Yet, even if it is not the case, the author still wrote within only a few decades of Jesus's life, and certainly while some of the eyewitnesses were alive.[33] Paul's undisputed letters and the book of Acts inform us that Jesus's disciples continued to teach about him publicly for more than two decades after his death (Gal. 1:17–18; 2:1–10; Acts 1:8; 4:16; 5:28; 6:7; 8:1, 14; 9:26; 11:27; 12:25; 13:13; 15:2, 4–6; 16:4; 21:17–18).[34] This brings us to the very doorstep of the time period of when Mark was written.[35] These sources also inform us that the Christian church was headquartered in Jerusalem for the first few decades of its existence, and that it served as the supreme doctrinal authority to which even Paul submitted (Acts 15:1–2; 21:17–26).[36] Whatever decisions were made by the Jerusalem leadership applied equally for churches outside the city (Acts 15:1–29, esp. vv. 19–33). Traditions were passed along to the churches, who were commanded to keep them. Thus, although there can be no doubt that stories of Jesus were corrupted as they circulated from person-to-person in an uncontrolled manner, there also can be no doubt that stories of Jesus were guarded by the early church leaders and Jesus's personal disciples, who continued to tell those stories for decades.

Not only was Mark in a good position to receive accurate reports of Jesus, Jesus's teachings would have been quite easily recalled by his disciples, even decades later. Unlike today's pastors, who have to create a new sermon every week for the same congregation, Jesus was an itinerant teacher, who may have had no more than a dozen or so sermons, some of which he taught countless times. He sent his disciples out to teach what they had heard him say. What they had heard Jesus teach, they now taught countless times. They went out in twos, providing the opportunity for one to correct the other when the integrity of Jesus's teaching had been compromised. They returned and heard Jesus teach even more. After his post-resurrection departure, they continued teaching for decades. This scenario is far more likely than the one advocated by scholars such as Ehrman (2016, pp. 3, 4, 62, 65, 101, 102, 289) who suggest that the authors of the Gospels included stories of Jesus in the form that those stories had taken after being circulated carelessly for decades. Those scholars do not take into consideration the continuing role of the eyewitnesses. As Taylor (1933, p. 41) wrote, "If the Form-Critics are right, the disciples must have been translated to heaven immediately after the Resurrection". It also assumes that the Gospel authors lacked the desire or the sense to sift through stories about Jesus, attempt to filter questionable ones, or prefer those stories that were thought to be rooted in the eyewitnesses, some of whom were still alive.

Like any effective teacher, Jesus would likely have desired to communicate his teachings in a memorable form. So, it is no surprise to observe in the Gospels that Jesus taught in parables and

---

[33] In his work *Memory, Jesus, and the Synoptic Gospels*, McIver (2011, pp. 189–209) considers population estimates of where Jesus frequently ministered, such as Capernaum and Jerusalem. He then estimates the number of eyewitnesses to Jesus who were ages fifteen and above at the time of Jesus's ministry, to be in the neighborhood of 62,000. Noting two major studies on lifespans in the time of Jesus, he shows that out of 100,000 live births, between 671 and 1644 survived to the age of eighty. After all is considered, McIver concludes that between 13,000 and 15,000 eyewitnesses would have been alive thirty-five years after Jesus's death (around the time many think Mark was written), and 600 to 1100 would still have been alive sixty years after His death (when many think John, the final Gospel, was written).

[34] The apostles were in Jerusalem during the days of Paul's persecution of the church. They were there three years after his conversion (Gal. 1:17–18). They were there fourteen years later (Gal. 2:1–10). Finally, they were still there when Paul met with James, and was subsequently arrested for an incident in the Jerusalem temple (Acts 21:17–33), which occurred c. 57–58 CE.

[35] See an earlier note in which I mention how Nick Peters and I gathered the opinions of seventy-five critical scholars on the matters of the authorship and dating of Mark's Gospel, written between 1965 and 2018.

[36] We may add that Paul states that spiritual teachings came from the church in Jerusalem (Rom. 15:25–27; cf. 1 Cor. 9:11). See Licona (2010, pp. 226–28).

employed rhetoric, such as hyperbolic language: "You cannot be my disciple unless you hate your family" (Luke 14:26; cf. Matt. 10:37), or "If your right eye causes you to sin, tear it out and throw it away" (Matt. 5:29; 18:9; Mark 9:47).

This all pertains to what Jesus said. What about what he did? We tend to recall events better when they either impact us in a profound manner, or elicit our strong emotions, such as grief, joy, and astonishment. Those of us who live in the United States and who are old enough to recall the terrorist attacks of September 11, 2001, can remember where we were, the moment that we learned that planes had flown into the two towers of the World Trade Center. Most of us can even remember what the weather was like on that day. Yet, most of us would be unable to remember what the weather was on September 11 last year.

Joe Galloway was a combat reporter during the Vietnam War, and he accompanied Lt. Col. Hal Moore and his team of American Special Forces during the three-day Battle of Ia Drang River Valley in November 1965.[37] Galloway was later interviewed in the television series titled *Vietnam in HD* (Jackson 2011). On one occasion during the interview, Galloway spoke of his experience during those days of battle, obviously still impacted by them, even after thirty-five years.

> I left that landing zone X-Ray battlefield knowing that young Americans had laid down their lives so that I might live. They had sacrificed themselves for me and their buddies. What I was learning was that there's some events that are so overwhelming that you can't simply be a witness. You can't be above it. You can't be neutral. You can't be untouched by it. Simple as that. You see it. You live it. You experience it. And it will be with you all of your days. (Jackson 2011)

If the events in the Gospels actually occurred, and let us say that you had been there, observing Jesus healing paralytics, the blind, lepers, and the demon-possessed, you saw him walk on water, raise the dead, be crucified, then shortly thereafter saw him alive and well, it is quite likely that you would be able to recall at least the general details of those events decades later.

Now this is not to assume the possibility of miracles, or that Jesus actually performed them. Instead, it is to contend that, if Jesus did perform miracles, his disciples and other eyewitnesses of those miracles would likely have been able to recall them, even decades later. I am also not suggesting that we should think that we are reading the very words of Jesus, rather than the gist of what he said. Moreover, there is no guarantee that the authors of the Gospels were committed to reporting only the events that had occurred, without adding non-historical elements for effect, or even inventing some stories. Nor is there any guarantee that all of his disciples' recollections of what he said and did were perfect, since memory is imperfect. However, with matters of great importance, we usually remember the gist of what occurred and what was said with a fair amount of accuracy, even decades later. So, the essence of Jesus's teachings and deeds could easily have been recalled fairly accurately, even at a much later date, especially since at least some of his disciples continued recalling them during that period in their own preaching and teaching. Thus, Mark was in a good position to receive these, regardless of whether Peter was his main source.

5. No More than a Very Small Percentage of Items Reported by the Author have a Reasonable Chance of Being Errors

Common errors are present throughout Suetonius's *Lives of the Divine Caesars*. Edwards (2000a, p. vii) writes, "Suetonius himself certainly offers little in the way of chronological narrative and it would be rash to rely on the factual accuracy of the stories he tells about the Caesars". She cautions, "As a

---

[37] Moore and Galloway later coauthored the award-winning book, *We Were Soldiers Once ... and Young: Ia Drang: The Battle That Changed the War in Vietnam* (Moore and Galloway 1992), and its sequel, *We Are Soldiers Still: A Journey Back to the Battlefields of Vietnam* (Moore and Galloway 2008). The 2001 motion picture *We Were Soldiers* (Wallace 2001) is based on the first book.

general rule, one should avoid relying on any of Suetonius' statements relating to numbers (e.g., dates, ages, prices)" (Edwards 2000b, p. xxxi). Even with his *Augustus*, the finest of Suetonius's *Lives of the Divine Caesars*, Wardle (Wardle 2014, p. 28; Hurley 2001, pp. 1–2) opines that "it is certain that Suet. does not offer 'the truth' about Aug".

There is another factor that must be considered, and for which every author is guilty to varying degrees: prejudicial selectivity. Let us suppose that a biography of Martin Luther King Jr. is written for the purpose of inspiring others to devote their lives to defending the oppressed. So, the biographer focuses on King's heroic work in the Civil Rights Movement of the 1960s while omitting any mention of his marital infidelities, since that information is irrelevant to the biographer's objective. Even if every detail reported in that biography were true, readers would be viewing a sanitized portrait of Martin Luther King Jr. through the author's somewhat distorting lens. How does this impact how we answer the question of reliability?

Along with most ancient biographers of his day, Suetonius was prejudicially selective in what he reported about Augustus, for whom he was especially fond. Although he does not omit negative stories about Augustus, he downplays them. For example, he must include the common knowledge that Augustus stole a pregnant Livia from her husband and married her, that he engaged in repeated adulteries throughout their marriage, and that he had an appetite for deflowering virgins. Nevertheless, Suetonius adds that Augustus loved Livia until the day he died, and that she was beside him until death, even kissing him on his deathbed (Wardle 2014, pp. 37–39). For Suetonius, Augustus's infidelities were small matters in his otherwise chaste life.

Suetonius provides a string of acts illustrating Augustus's tendency to be harsh and ruthless. But these are followed by reports that are apparently meant to soften the negative impact that these stories of his harsh acts may have on readers. For example, he writes,

> And the praetor Quintus Gallius, who was holding double tablets under his clothes while fulfilling his duty of paying respects, he suspected of concealing a sword but did not dare to search him on the spot in case something else were discovered; a little later he had him dragged from the tribunal and tortured like a slave by centurions and soldiers and, when he did not confess, ordered him to be killed, having first gouged out the man's eyes with his own hand. (Suet. *Aug.* 27.4 [Wardle])[38]

Suetonius follows this with the alternate account provided by Augustus, which has elements of truth: "However, [Augustus] himself writes that Gallius had requested an audience, made an attempt on his life, and was thrown into prison by him; then having been banned from the city, he was sent away and perished in a shipwreck or an ambush by brigands" (Suet. *Aug.* 27.4 [Wardle]).[39] Stories of Augustus's harsh behavior are then followed by Augustus's twice consideration of handing Rome back to the senate, his beautification of the city, other improvements that he made to it, and the creation of laws that protected the innocent (Suet. *Aug.* 28–34).

Wallace-Hadrill (1986, p. 245) concludes his review of Jacques Gascou's massive volume devoted to assessing Suetonius as a historian with the following:

> The Suetonius who emerges from this important study will not necessarily win the confidence and approval of present-day historians; but he will have to be read in a more sophisticated way, with greater awareness of the strengths and weaknesses of the ambivalent genre within which he writes, and of his standpoint and his ability to manipulate his material to suit his conceptions.

If most of what Suetonius reports about Augustus is true, while often stated in a manner that leads readers to a mental picture that is somewhat distorted, to what extent does that challenge the

---

[38] Translation by Wardle (Suetonius 2014, p. 50).
[39] See also Wardle's comments in his commentary on the text (Suetonius 2014, pp. 209–12).

historical reliability of the *Augustus*? How much selectivity may we allow an author when it affects the overall portrait? It seems we should assess both the facts and the mental picture. And what if the objective of the biography is didactic or to inspire readers to live virtuously? For example, as stated earlier, a modern biography of Martin Luther King Jr. may be written for the sole purpose of inspiring others to devote their lives to defending the oppressed. Accordingly, the biographer would focus on King's heroic work, while omitting any mention of his adulteries, since that information is irrelevant to the biographer's objectives. We might judge that biography as being historically reliable in what it reports, while being cognizant of the author's intent for writing, which consequently has resulted in a portrait that is incomplete and somewhat distorted. Yet, can a reasonable understanding of "historical reliability" tolerate such qualifications? This is a challenge that must be faced when examining and speaking about the historical reliability of ancient historical literature in a broad sense, and thus it requires more thought.

Turning to Mark, and bracketing its theological claims and miracle reports,[40] there are only a few items that have a reasonable chance of being incorrect: Mark's claim that Abiathar was high priest when David ate the consecrated bread (Mark 2:25–26; cf. 1 Sam. 21:1–6), three occasions where Mark may be geographically confused,[41] the day on which Jesus was anointed, and a few minor chronological items in his Passion narrative. Plausible solutions have been offered for all of these, which may or may not be true. Yet, even if every last one of the items just mentioned are truly errors, they make up an extremely small percentage of Mark's Gospel.

Are we viewing Jesus through Mark's distorting lens? It is difficult, if not impossible, to tell. However, it is worth mentioning that we can observe awkward content in Mark, which Matthew and Luke have either softened or omitted altogether. Whereas most of the miracles in Mark, and all of them in Matthew and Luke only require that Jesus say the word or either touch the person or be touched by the person, we find two occasions in Mark where Jesus's method differs is a strange way.[42] In Mark 7:31–35, a man who is deaf and has a speech impediment is brought to Jesus, who puts his fingers in the man's ears, spits and touches the man's tongue, and says, "Be opened", and the man is healed. Matthew 15:29–31 is aware of the event, but does not provide details, while Luke omits the story. In Mark 8:22–26, Jesus spits in the eyes of a blind man and lays hands on him, but the man is not healed completely. So, Jesus lays his hands on the man again, and the man can now see clearly. Matthew and Luke omit this story. Thus, although we cannot tell if Mark has softened stories that he heard about Jesus, we can observe the other evangelists softening Mark's portrayal of Jesus.

---

[40] As stated earlier, when it comes to theological matters in the Gospels, these cannot be confirmed by using the tools available to historians. Thus, we cannot say that those items are historically reliable or historically unreliable. Nevertheless, that does not prohibit historians from deciding on the non-theological elements in a narrative. For example, although historians are incapable of confirming that Jesus's death atones for sin, they are able to confirm that Jesus died by crucifixion.

[41] First, in Mark 5:1, 13, the distance of Gerasa from the Sea of Galilee, since Gerasa is about thirty miles from the Sea of Galilee. Second, in Mark 6:45, Jesus commands his disciples to get in a boat and cross over to Bethsaida, which is on the northeast side of the lake, but they instead land at Gennesaret (6:53). However, in Matthew 14:22, 34, he commands them to get in a boat and cross over to the other side, and they land in Gennesaret. Third, in John 6:16–21, his disciples get into a boat, begin to cross to Capernaum, and they land where they had intended. Gennesaret and Capernaum are on the northwest side of the lake. For more on this occasion of possible geographical confusion in Mark, see my online article (Licona 2016) at https://www.risenjesus.com/mark-confused-pertaining-location-feeding-5000. Third, in Mark 7:31, we read of an awkward journey from Tyre through Sidon to the Sea of Galilee in the midst of the region of the Decapolis.

[42] In his historical and theological study, *Jesus the Miracle Worker*, Twelftree (1999) provides lists of Jesus' miracles, and the summaries of his miracle activities (107–39; 144–64, 370n2; 386n1). The Gospel of Mark reports twenty-three miracle stories or summaries of his miracle activities in: Mark 1:21–28, 29–31, 32–34, 40–45; 2:1–12; 3:1–6, 7–12; 4:35–41; 5:1–20, 21–43 (two miracles); 6:30–44, 45–52, 53–56; 7:24–30, 31–37; 8:1–10, 22–26; 9:14–29, 32–34 (Q); 10:46–52; 11:12–14, 20–26. The Gospel of Matthew reports of twenty-eight of Jesus' miracles and summaries of his miracle activities in: Matt. 4:23–24; 8:1–4, 5–13 (Q), 14–15, 16–17, 23–27, 28–34; 9:1–8, 18–26 (two miracles), 27–31, 32–34, 35; 11:2–6 (absent in Mark); 12:9–14, 15–21, 22–30 (Q); 14:13–21, 22–33 (Matthew includes Peter walking on water, which is unique to Matthew; also found in John 6:16–21), 34–36; 15:21–28, 29–31; 17:14–20, 24–27 (unique to Matthew); 19:1–2 (Matthew mentions Jesus' healings here, while the parallel text in Mark 10:1 does not); 20:29–34; and 21:14–17 (unique to Matthew), 18–22. The Gospel of Luke reports twenty-two miracle stories. and summaries of his miracle activities in: Luke 4:31–37, 38–39, 40–41; 5:1–11 (unique to Luke), 12–16, 17–26; 6:6–11, 17–19; 7:1–10 (Q), 11–17 (unique to Luke); 8:22–25, 26–39, 40–56 (two miracle stories); 9:10–17, 37–43a; 11:14–23 (Q); 13:10–17 (unique to Luke); 14:1–6 (unique to Luke); 17:11–19 (unique to Luke); 18:35–43; and 22:50–51 (unique to Luke).

6. Conclusions

In this essay, a provisional definition of "historically reliable" has been provided which suggests that we must think of historical reliability in view of the literary conventions that were in play at the time of writing (Blomberg 2014, p. 213). To say that a particular historical work in antiquity is "historically reliable" does not require reports to have accuracy with the precision of a legal transcript, or that it be free of error or embellishment. "Historically reliable" means that, at the very minimum, that the account provides an accurate gist or an essentially faithful representation of what occurred. In the words of Pelling (2002, p. 160), it is "true enough". Based on the four provisional criteria for historical reliability in a broad sense, we have seen that we have some grounds for thinking that the Gospel of Mark in the Bible is historically reliable in this sense, perhaps even more so than Suetonius's *Life of Augustus*. That being said, serious challenges that require more thought remain.

Conflicts of Interest: The author declares no conflict of interest.

Abbreviations

Euseb.	Eusebius
Hist. eccl.	*Historia ecclesiastica* (*Ecclesiastical History*)
Pap.	Papias
Frag.	*Fragments*
Suet.	Suetonius
Aug.	*Divus Augustus* (*Life of the Divine Augustus*)
Jul. (or *Iul.*)	*Divus Julius* (*Life of the Divine Julius*)
Tit.	*Divus Titus* (*Life of the Divine Titus*)

References

Bauckham, Richard. 2017. *Jesus and the Eyewitnesses: The Gospels as Eyewitness Testimony*, 2nd ed. Grand Rapids: Eerdmans.

Blomberg, Craig L. 2007. *The Historical Reliability of the Gospels*, 2nd ed. Downers Grove: IVP Academic.

Blomberg, Craig L. 2014. *Can We Still Believe the Bible?: An Evangelical Engagement with Contemporary Questions*. Grand Rapids: Brazos Press.

Bradley, Keith R. 1998. Introduction. In *Lives of the Caesars*, Rev. ed. Loeb Classical Library 31. Translated by J. C. Rolfe. Cambridge: Harvard University Press, pp. 1–29.

Bradley, Keith R. 2012. Suetonius. In *The Oxford Classical Dictionary*, 4th ed. Edited by Simon Hornblower, Antony Spawforth and Esther Eidinow. Oxford: Oxford University Press, pp. 1409–10.

Downing, F. Gerald. 1980. Redaction Criticism: Josephus' *Antiquities* and the Synoptic Gospels (I). *Journal for the Study of the New Testament* 2: 46–65. [CrossRef]

Downing, F. Gerald. 2011. Writers' Use and Abuse of Written Sources. In *New Studies in the Synoptic Problem: Oxford Conference, April 2008; Essays in Honour of Christopher M. Tuckett*. Bibliotheca Ephemeridum Theologicarum Lovaniensium 239. Edited by P. Foster. Leuven: Peeters, pp. 523–48.

Drobner, Hubertus R. 2007. *The Fathers of the Church a Comprehensive Introduction*. Translated by Siegfried S. Schatzmann. Peabody: Hendrickson.

Edwards, Catharine. 2000a. Introduction. In *Lives of the Caesars*. Oxford World's Classics. Translated by Catharine Edwards. Oxford: Oxford University Press, pp. vii–xxx.

Edwards, Catharine. 2000b. Note on the Text and Translation. In *Lives of the Caesars*. Oxford World's Classics. Translated by Catharine Edwards. Oxford: Oxford University Press, p. xxxi.

Ehrman, Bart D. 2016. *Jesus before the Gospels: How the Earliest Christians Remembered, Changed, and Invented Their Stories of the Savior*. San Francisco: HarperOne.

Eve, Eric. 2014. *Behind the Gospels: Understanding the Oral Tradition*. Minneapolis: Fortress Press.

Eve, Eric. 2017. The Growth of the Nature Miracles. In *The Nature Miracles of Jesus: Problems, Perspectives, and Prospects*. Edited by Graham H. Twelftree. Eugene: Cascade Books, pp. 66–85.

Gascou, Jacques. 1984. *Suétone Historien*. Bibliothèque des Écoles françaises d'Athènes et de Rome, fasc. Rome: Ecole française de Rome, p. 255.

Gathercole, Simon. 2018. The Alleged Anonymity of the Canonical Gospels. *Journal of Theological Studies* 69: 447–76. [CrossRef]

Goh, Benson. 2016. Galba: A Comparison of Suetonius's and Plutarch's Biographies and Tacitus's *Histories* with Implications for the Historical Reliability of the Gospels. In *Biographies and Jesus: What Does It Mean for the Gospels to Be Biographies?* Edited by Craig S. Keener and Edward T. Wright. Lexington: Emeth Press, pp. 173–200.

Gundry, Robert H. 1994. *Matthew: A Commentary on His Handbook for a Mixed Church under Persecution*, 2nd ed. Grand Rapids: Eerdmans.

Hill, Charles E. 2007. The Fragments of Papias. In *The Writings of the Apostolic Fathers*. T&T Clark Library of Biblical Studies. Edited by Paul Foster. London: T&T Clark, pp. 42–51.

Holmes, Michael W., ed. 2007. *The Apostolic Fathers: Greek Texts and English Translations*, 3rd ed. Grand Rapids: Baker Academic.

Howard, Ron. 1995. *Apollo 13*. 2 videodiscs. Universal City: Universal Pictures, DVD.

Hurley, Donna W. 2001. Introduction. In *Divus Claudius*. Cambridge Greek and Latin Classics. Edited by Donna W. Hurley. Cambridge: Cambridge University Press, pp. 1–22.

Hurley, Donna W. 2014. Suetonius' Rubric Sandwich. In *Suetonius the Biographer: Studies in Roman Lives*. Edited by Tristan Power and Roy K. Gibson. Oxford: Oxford University Press, pp. 21–37.

Jackson, Sammy. 2011. *Vietnam in HD: Episode 1: The Beginning: 1965–1965*. New York: History Channel, DVD.

Jefford, Clayton N. 2006. *The Apostolic Fathers and the New Testament*. Peabody: Hendrickson.

Keener, Craig S. 2016. Otho: A Targeted Comparison of Suetonius's Biography and Tacitus's History, with Implications for the Gospels' Historical Reliability. In *Biographies and Jesus: What Does It Mean for the Gospels to Be Biographies?* Edited by Craig S. Keener and Edward T. Wright. Lexington: Emeth Press, pp. 143–72.

Keener, Craig S. forthcoming. *Christobiography: Memories, History, and the Reliability of the Gospels*. Grand Rapids: Eerdmans.

Koester, Helmut. 2000. *Introduction to the New Testament. Vol. 2. History and Literature of Early Christianity*, 2nd ed. New York: Walter de Gruyter.

Körtner, Ulrich H. J. 1983. *Papias von Hierapolis*. FRLANT 133. Göttingen: Vandenhoeck & Ruprecht.

Körtner, Ulrich H. J. 2010. The Papias Fragments. In *The Apostolic Fathers: An Introduction*. Edited by Wilhelm Pratscher. Translated by Elisabeth G. Wolfe. Waco: Baylor University Press, pp. 159–79.

Kranz, Gene. 2000. *Failure Is Not an Option: Mission Control from Mercury to Apollo 13 and Beyond*. New York: Simon & Schuster.

Licona, Michael R. 2010. *The Resurrection of Jesus: A New Historiographical Approach*. Downers Grove: IVP Academic.

Licona, Mike. 2016. Was Mark Confused Pertaining to the Location of the Feeding of the 5000? *Risen Jesus*. August 22. Available online: https://www.risenjesus.com/mark-confused-pertaining-location-feeding-5000 (accessed on 21 February 2019).

Licona, Michael R. 2017. *Why Are There Differences in the Gospels?: What We Can Learn from Ancient Biography*. New York: Oxford University Press.

Lovell, Jim, and Jeffrey Kluger. 1994. *Lost Moon: The Perilous Voyage of Apollo 13*. Boston: Houghton Mifflin.

McIver, Robert K. 2011. *Memory, Jesus, and the Synoptic Gospels*. Resources for Biblical Study 59. Atlanta: Society of Biblical Literature.

Mellor, Ronald. 1999. *The Roman Historians*. New York: Routledge.

Moore, Harold G., and Joseph L. Galloway. 1992. *We Were Soldiers Once . . . and Young: Ia Drang—The Battle That Changed the War in Vietnam*. New York: Random House.

Moore, Harold G., and Joseph L. Galloway. 2008. *We Are Soldiers Still: A Journey Back to the Battlefields of Vietnam*. New York: Harper.

Pelling, Christopher. 2002. *Plutarch and History: Eighteen Studies*. Swansea: Classical Press of Wales.

Power, Tristan. 2014. Introduction: The Originality of Suetonius. In *Suetonius the Biographer: Studies in Roman Lives*. Edited by Tristan Power and Roy K. Gibson. Oxford: Oxford University Press, pp. 1–18.

Qureshi, Nabeel. 2014. *Seeking Allah, Finding Jesus: A Devout Muslim Encounters Christianity*. Grand Rapids: Zondervan.

Russell, D. A. 1963. Plutarch's Life of Coriolanus. *Journal of Roman Studies* 53: 21–28. [CrossRef]

Schoedel, William R. 1967. Polycarp, Martyrdom of Polycarp, Fragments of Papias. In *The Apostolic Fathers*. Edited by Robert McQueen Grant. Camden: Thomas Nelson, vol. 5.

Schoedel, William R. 1992. Papias (Person). In *The Anchor Yale Bible Dictionary*. Edited by David Noel Freedman. New York: Doubleday, pp. 140–42.

Suetonius. 2014. *Life of Augustus [Vita Divi Augusti]*. Ancient History Series; Translated by D. Wardle Clarendon. Oxford: Oxford University Press.

Tatum, W. Jeffrey. 2014. Another Look at Suetonius' *Titus*. In *Suetonius the Biographer: Studies in Roman Lives*. Edited by Tristan Power and Roy K. Gibson. Oxford: Oxford University Press, pp. 159–77.

Taylor, Vincent. 1933. *The Formation of the Gospel Tradition: Eight Lectures*. London: Macmillan.

Twelftree, Graham H. 1999. *Jesus the Miracle Worker: A Historical and Theological Study*. Downers Grove: InterVarsity Press.

Van Voorst, Robert E. 2000. *Jesus Outside the New Testament: An Introduction to the Ancient Evidence*. Studying the Historical Jesus. Grand Rapids: Eerdmans.

Wallace, Randall. 2001. *We Were Soldiers*. Los Angeles: Paramount Pictures, DVD.

Wallace-Hadrill, Andrew. 1995. *Suetonius*, 2nd ed. Bristol Classical Paperbacks. London: Bristol Classical Press. First published 1983.

Wallace-Hadrill, Andrew. 1986. Suetonius as Historian—Jacques Gascou: *Suétone Historien*. (Bibliothèque des Écoles françaises d'Athènes et de Rome, 255.) pp. Xvi + 874. Rome: École française de Rome, 1984 (Obtainable from de Boccard, Paris). *Classical Review* 36: 243–45. [CrossRef]

Wardle, D. 2014. Introduction. In *Life of Augustus [Vita Divi Augusti]*. Ancient History Series. Translated by D. Wardle Clarendon. Oxford: Oxford University Press, pp. 1–40. First published 1983.

Woodfill, Jerry. 2019. Origin of Apollo 13 Quote: 'Failure Is Not an Option'. *Space Acts*. Available online: http://www.spaceacts.com/notanoption.htm (accessed on 31 January 2019).

Yarbrough, Robert W. 1983. The Date of Papias: A Reassessment. *Journal of the Evangelical Theological Society* 26: 181–91.

religions

MDPI

Article

A Deep-Language Mathematical Analysis of Gospels, Acts and Revelation

Emilio Matricciani [1,*] and **Liberato De Caro** [2]

[1] Dipartimento di Elettronica Informazione e Bioingegneria, Politecnico di Milano, 20133 Milan, Italy
[2] Istituto di Cristallografia, Consiglio Nazionale delle Ricerche (IC-CNR), 70126 Bari, Italy;
liberato.decaro@ic.cnr.it
* Correspondence: emilio.matricciani@polimi.it

Received: 14 March 2019; Accepted: 5 April 2019; Published: 9 April 2019

check for updates

Abstract: The paper aims at casting some light on the interrelations among the Gospels, Acts and Revelation. We do not consider words ranking and their frequency of occurrence, as largely done in the literature, but we analyze, statistically, some mathematical aspects of the texts, which the authors were not conscious of. We use mathematical methods developed for specifically studying deep-language parameters of literary texts, such as the number of words per sentence, the number of characters per word, the number of words per interpunctions, the number of interpunctions per sentence, all very likely peculiar to the writer's style, after having recalled the punctuation in classical languages. First, we consider the full texts of the canonical Gospels, Acts and Revelation, then the partial texts attributable to the Triple Tradition (Matthew, Mark and Luke), to the Double Tradition (Matthew and Luke), Own Tradition (Matthew and Luke) and Q source. The mathematical/statistical tool used confirms and reinforces some general results concerning the Gospels, Acts, Revelation and Q source, but also evidences some interesting differences concerning the number of words per sentence and words per interpunctions, likely casting some light on the capacity of the short-term memory of the readers/listeners of these texts. All these New Testament writings fit very well in the larger Greek literature of the time. The existence of a proto gospel seems more probable than other possible hypotheses.

Keywords: Acts; canonical Gospels; characters; Double Tradition; interpunctions; John; Luke; Mark; Matthew; own tradition; Q Source; Revelation; statistics; sentences; Triple Tradition; words; word interval

1. Introduction

The Gospels of Matthew (Mt), Mark (Mk) and Luke (Lk), called synoptic because they have much material in common, are very different from that of John (Jn). The concordance and difference among them have produced many studies on their likely interdependence, giving rise to the so-called Synoptic Problem (Foster 2011). Although some scholars have largely supported an oral solution, there is a strong consensus on a documentary interdependence among the synoptic gospels (Reicke 1986). The traditional hypothesis, dating back to Augustine of Hippo (IV–V century), assumes that the order of composition of the synoptic Gospels was Matthew, Mark, Luke (Augustinian hypothesis). At the end of the XVIII century, Griesbach (Griesbach 1790) proposed the order Matthew, Luke, Mark (Griesbach hypothesis), resumed in recent years by Farmer (Two-Gospel or neo-Griesbach hypothesis, (Farmer 1983)). At the end of the XVIII century, however, the priority of Mark has taken hold, which today turns out to be the dominant hypothesis (Foster 2011), for the following reasons.

Mark has 661 verses, far fewer than Matthew (1068 verses) and Luke (1149 verses). 80% of Mark's verses (meaning that they concern similar events) are found also in Matthew, and 65% in Luke.

Religions **2019**, *10*, 257; doi:10.3390/rel10040257

56

The Markan material found also in Matthew and Luke is referred to as the Triple Tradition (Tables 1–3). There are four main hypotheses that can account for the Triple Tradition:

1. Markan priority hypothesis: Mark was the first Gospel and copied by both Matthew and Luke;
2. Matthean priority hypothesis: Matthew was copied by Mark who, in turn, was copied by Luke (Augustinian hypothesis);
3. Lukan priority hypothesis: Luke was copied by Mark who, in turn, was copied by Matthew;
4. Griesbach hypothesis: Mark was third and he conflated Matthew and Luke (Griesbach 1790);

The material that Matthew and Luke share, about 220 verses—not present in Mark—is referred to as the Double Tradition (See Tables 1–3). There are three main hypotheses that can account for the Double Tradition:

1. Q hypothesis: Matthew and Luke copied the Double Tradition from a common written source, usually named Q;
2. Lukan posteriority hypothesis: Luke copied the Double Tradition from Matthew;
3. Matthean posteriority hypothesis: Matthew copied the Double Tradition from Luke.

Many scholars share the Markan priority hypothesis for the Triple Tradition and the Q hypothesis for the Double Tradition (Two-Source hypothesis). The Q hypothesis rests on the independence of Matthew and Luke, and is framed in terms of the failure to prove that Luke depends upon Matthew or vice versa. If Matthew and Luke are independent, the Double Tradition must be explained by an indirect relationship upon common material, called Q. Accordingly, Mark was written first. Matthew and Luke independently copied Mark for its narrative framework (the Triple Tradition) and independently added discourse material from the Q source, which should have been lost (Weisse 1838; Stein 1994; Tuckett 1983; Goodacre 2001).

The reconstruction of the most primitive text of the Q source, however, remains a major ongoing enterprise (Foster 2011; Mack 1993). Nevertheless, most scholars assume valid the Two-Source hypothesis, even if it has deficiencies concerning some "minor agreements" (Foster 2011; Neirynck et al. 1974; Streeter 1924), because there are verses in which Matthew and Luke agree but diverge from Mark. The presence of these verses does not seem to be immediately compatible with the Mark priority.

Besides the Two-Gospel or neo-Griesbach hypothesis (Farmer 1983), another solution to the "minor agreements" is to hypothesize that Matthew, Mark and Luke depend on a primitive Gospel, called the Proto-Matthew, which, accordingly, was combined by Luke and Matthew with another supplementary source (Goodacre 2001; Vaganay 1954; Boismard 1979). This hypothesis (Proto-Gospel hypothesis) has been further developed by other scholars (Rolland 1984; Burkett 2004).

In summary, in these developments, it is supposed that the common material among the three synoptic Gospels would derive from a proto gospel. This proto gospel would have undergone two independent revisions, A and B. Mark would have recombined these two revisions; A + B. Matthew would have-based his Gospel on A, Luke on B. Moreover, both Matthew and Luke would have also drawn from a common collection of Jesus' sayings, the Q source, as well as from other sources for their unique material, such as, for example, the Gospels of Infancy.

Other scholars, such as Butler (Butler 1951), have argued that Luke borrowed the material of the Double Tradition directly from Matthew, without referring to the hypothetical Q source. Even Mark would depend directly on Matthew. This hypothesis can be considered of Augustinian type because it proposes the Matthean priority hypothesis for the Triple Tradition and the Lukan posteriority hypothesis for the Double Tradition.

Another alternative approach to explain the problems of the Two-Source hypothesis, which received particular attention in the latest years, is Farrer's hypothesis. It assumes the Markan priority hypothesis for the Triple Tradition and the Lukan posteriority hypothesis for the Double Tradition. The Double Tradition is explained by Luke's further use of Matthew, thus dispensing with Q (Farrer 1955).

Going to the fourth gospel, there is more agreement that it does not depend on the Synoptics and vice versa, at least in their definitive versions, the canonical Gospels (Smith 1984). As a result, John can tell very little about the composition of the synoptic Gospels. Moreover, Acts are traditionally attributed to Luke, and Revelation is traditionally attributed to John. These attributions have been extensively discussed by scholars (Boring 1998). In principle, all these New Testament writings could be compared to search probable literary interrelations.

Given this general and not exhaustive overview of the complexity of the literary interdependence among some of the most important New Testament writings, the purpose of this paper is to help to cast some light on the interrelations among the Gospels (Mt, Mk, Lk, Jn), Acts (Ac) and Revelation (Re), by considering deep-language statistics not consciously controllable by the authors. For our analysis, we use some of the mathematical and statistical tools developed for specifically studying literary texts (Matricciani 2019), such as the number of words per sentence, P_F, the number of characters per word, C_p, the number of words per interpunctions, I_P, the number of interpunctions per sentence, M_F, all very likely peculiar to a writer's style. In other words, we do not consider words ranking and frequencies of occurrence, as largely done in the literature—items not directly linked to the four parameters just mentioned—but we analyze statistically some aspects of the texts, which the authors were not conscious of. Our innovative approach has allowed assessing mathematical similarities and differences in a large corpus of literary texts written by the Italian mystic Maria Valtorta (Matricciani and Caro 2018).

After this Introduction, in Section 2 we recall some mathematical parameters of text analysis; in Section 3 we summarize the main points on punctuation in classical Latin and Greek texts; in Section 4 we study the full texts of Matthew, Mark, Luke, Acts, and Revelation; in Section 5 we consider the texts of the so-called Triple Tradition (Matthew, Mark and Luke) and Q source; in Section 6 we consider the Double Tradition (Matthew and Luke) and Q; in Section 7 we consider the Own Tradition (Matthew and Luke) and Q; in Section 8 we show the relationship between the number of words per interpunctions and the number of words per sentence to evaluate the readability of the various texts; this section shows also a geometrical representation of the texts useful to evaluate at glance how identical or different the texts are; in Section 9, to place the New Testament writings in the larger Greek literature context of the time, we compare the mathematical/statistical results to those found in classical works of this literature; in Section 10, to obtain some indirect hints for discriminating the different hypotheses on Gospels' genesis, we review our results with a graphical synthesis; finally in Section 11 we discuss the overall results and indicate some future work.

Table 1. List of the verses considered in Luke, in the indicated texts. The list of names (genealogy) in Verses 3.23–3.38 has not been considered in the statistical analyses.

Luke Full Text	All Verses Except 3.23–3.38 (Genealogy)
Only in Luke ("Own")	1.1 et seq.; 2.1 et seq.; 7.11–17; 7.36–50; 8.1–3; 9.51–55; 10.1–12; 10.16–20; 10.29–42; 11.27–28; 12.13–20; 13.1–17; 14.1–14; 15.8–32; 16.1–15; 16.19–31; 17.11–19; 18.1–14; 19.1–10; 19.41–44; 24.13–53
Matthew, Mark and Luke ("Triple Tradition")	3.1 et seq.; 4.1–30; 4.38–44; 5.1 et seq.; 6.1–19; 8.4–56; 9.1–48; 10.25–28;11.14–24; 11.29–33; 11.37–54; 12.33–48; 13.18–20; 14.34–35;16.18; 17.1–10; 17.20–37; 18.15–43; 19.28–40; 19.45–48; 20.1 et seq.; 21.5–37; 22.1 et seq.; 23.1 et seq.; 24.1–12
Matthew and Luke ("Double tradition")	6.20–49; 7.1–10; 7.18–35; 9.57–62; 10.13–15; 10.21–24; 11.1–13; 11.34–35; 12.1–12; 12.22–32; 12.49–59; 13.22–35; 14.15–33; 15.1–7; 16.16–17; 19.11–27
Q (Theory of the two sources)	3.1–9; 3.15–17; 4.1–13; 6.20–23; 6.27–49; 7.1–10; 7.18–28; 7.31–35; 9.57–62; 10.1–16; 10.21–24; 11.1–4; 11.9–35; 11.39–52; 12.2–40; 11.42–46; 11.49–59; 13.18–21; 11.24–30; 11.34–35; 14.11–13; 14.16–35; 15.3–10; 16.13; 16.16–18; 17.1–4; 17.6; 17.23–37; 19.11–27; 22.28–30

Table 2. List of the verses considered in Mark, in the indicated texts.

Only in Mark ("Own")	4.26–28; 7.31–37; 8.22–26;16.9–11
Matthew, Mark and Luke ("Triple Tradition")	Full text except the verses indicated in "Own" and "Dual Tradition" and Verses 1.1–1.17 (Genealogy)
Matthew and Mark ("Double Tradition")	4.33–34; 6.45–56; 7.1–30; 8.1–19; 11.12–14; 11.20–25; 14.3–9; 15.16–20

Table 3. List of the verses considered in Matthew, in the indicated texts. The list of names (Genealogy) in Verses 1.1–1.17 17 has not been considered in the statistical analysis.

Matthew Full Text	Except 1.1–1.17
Only in Matthew ("Own")	1.1 et seq. (all chapter 1); 2.1 et seq.; 4.23–25 (from Verse 4.23 to Verse 4.25); 5.17–20; 5.27.37; 6.1–18; 9.35–38; 10.34–42; 12.15–21; 13.36–52; 17.24–27; 18.19–35; 20.1–16; 21.28–32; 25.31–46; 27.1–10;28.11–15
Matthew, Mark and Luke ("Triple Tradition")	3.1 et seq.; 4.1–17; 5.13–16; 8.1–4;8.14–17; 8.23–34; 9.1–23; 10.1–33;12.1–14; 12.22–50; 13.1–35; 13.53–58; 14.1–21; 16.1 et seq.; 17.1–23; 18.1–10; 19.13–30; 20.17–34; 21.1–17; 21.23–27; 21.33–46; 22.15–46; 23.1–36; 24.1 et seq.; 26.1–5; 26.14–75; 27.11–26; 27.32–66; 28.1–10
Matthew and Luke ("Double Tradition")	5.1–11; 5.21–26; 5.38–48; 6.19–34; 7.1 et seq.; 8.5–13; 8.18–22; 9.27–34; 11.1 et seq.; 18.12–18; 22.1–14; 23.37–38; 25.1–30

2. Some Mathematical Parameters of Text Analysis

Statistics of the Greek language used in the New Testament have been widely calculated by counting words and establishing their frequencies of occurrence (Van Voorst 2001; Poirier 2008; Brodie 2004; Abakuks 2015; Mealand 2016; Gareiou and Zervas 2018).

In this paper, we do not study word frequencies, but analyze the number of words per sentence, P_F, the number of characters per word, C_p, the number of words per interpunctions, I_P, the number of interpunctions per sentence, M_F, all parameters very likely peculiar to a writer's style or, in any case, to a particular text. Notice that M_F gives also the number of word intervals in a sentence, because $I_P = P_F/M_F$.

In particular, the number of words per interpunctions, referred to as the word interval I_P (Matricciani 2019), namely the number of words between two successive interpunctions, is an interesting parameter because it very likely linked, empirically, to the capacity of the short–term memory—described by Miller's "7 ∓ 2 law" (Miller 1955)—required of the readers, with appropriate cultural background, to read the text more easily. The word interval is, in fact, spread in the same range of Miller's law and, if converted into a time interval through an average reading speed, as shown for Italian (Matricciani 2019; Matricciani and Caro 2018), it is spread in the same range of time that the immediate memory needs to record the stimulus for memorizing it in the short-term memory.

We think that the study of these linguistic parameters and their statistics, not consciously controllable by the authors, can cast some light on the interdependence of the four canonical Gospels, of Acts and Revelation. However, before proceeding with the mathematical/statistical analysis of the complete original Greek versions, we summarize, in the next section, what is known about the punctuation of classical (Greek and Latin) texts, because P_F, I_P, and M_F do depend on punctuation.

3. Punctuation in Classical Texts

We summarize the main points on punctuation in classical Latin and Greek texts, following Parkes (Parkes 1992). Punctuation is typical of written language and its history follows that of the written medium. In the Greek and Roman times, the written word was regarded as a record of the spoken word and texts were mostly read aloud. Starting from the sixth century, writing came to be regarded as conveying information directly to the mind through sight, so that silent reading became the norm.

Before, as texts were mostly read aloud, a reader might murmur the sounds of the words to himself, but the ideal reader was one that declaimed the text with well-modulated pronunciation in which the text was carefully phrased by appropriate pauses. Silent reading was so rare that Augustine was astonished when in Milan, in the years 386–87, he saw the Bishop Ambrose reading without making a sound, as he recalls in his *Confessions*[1]. In any case, the ancient perception was that the written word was a record of the spoken word to be always heard in a reader's mind.

From Antiquity, no manuscript containing the author's own handwriting has survived. This lack of autograph material is attributed to the practice of dictating one's own literary works, letters, and even notes, to scribes. Because the work of scribes was mechanical, they reproduced as faithfully as possible what had been transmitted to them, without further interpretation, therefore they did not introduce punctuation. Consequently, the text was difficult to be read at first sight, even though they indicated major divisions, such as chapters and paragraphs, a practice, which seems to go back to the second century B.C.

In the first century, in Latin manuscripts, words were separated by interpunctions, but this practice ceased by the end of the first century, and thereafter Roman scribes imitated Greek ones by copying texts without separating words (the so-called *scriptio continua*), or indicating any pauses within a major section of the text. When a text was written in *scriptio continua*, it required careful preparation before it could be read aloud with appropriate pronunciation and expression. Rendering a text in *scriptio continua* required an interpreter to identify many elements, such as letters, syllables, words, before conveying to their own mind, or to listeners, the full meaning of the text. Reading at first sight was thus unusual and unexpected.

Pauses in a text, however, started to be annotated thanks to the initiative of the reader who would insert them according to the difficulty of the text and to a reader's comprehension. Many efforts were made to preserve, restore and explain texts, and to make texts more readable to a wider audience. Moreover, well-educated readers realized that the comprehension of literary language was declining and starting to affect the integrity of the texts, therefore they corrected and annotated their own copies for the benefit of friends and future readers.

For a religion of the book, as is the Christian Faith, grammatical culture was fundamental to the study of Scripture; therefore, at the higher levels, Christian scholars looked for the best manuscripts, corrected and annotated them, using the apparatus of textual criticism employed by classical scholars. In the third century, Origen (185–254) introduced the critical signs developed in the second century B.C. by Aristarchus in Alexandria.

Christianity attracted believers from all levels of society, and contrary to the elite audience of classical pagan literary texts, the Christian audience covered the whole spectrum of literacy. Some Christians read for themselves, but most of them could not read and listened to texts read aloud in churches, which, therefore, had to be paused for better delivering their correct meaning. In other words, the punctuation of the Bible became especially important when it was read in church, so that the reading and the Christian message could reach the whole community, both in the Latin and Greek speaking parts of the Roman Empire.

In a period dominated by oratory, the principal function of pauses, whether in speaking or reading, was not only to allow the reader to take a breath but also to phrase the delivery of a speech, or the reading of a text, to convey its meaning correctly. Pausing therefore belonged to reading, not to writing or copying, and during the first six centuries, wherever punctuation was employed, it was inserted by readers, or by scribes, as they read their own copies.

One of the weaknesses of the data about interpunctions is that it is not known how well the scribes interpreted the original intent of the authors. We can assume it was close. However, we must

---

[1] *The Confessions of Saint Augustine*, Book VI, chapter 3: "But when he was reading, his eye glided over the pages, and his heart searched out the sense, but his voice and tongue were at rest." English translation by Edward B. Pusey, Grand Rapids, MI: Christian Classics Ethereal Library.

also acknowledge that it was not perfect. In conclusion, the actual punctuation in the New Testament texts in Greek is likely reliable because many scholars read these texts very carefully, and inserted interpunctions for improving text intelligibility and conveying the Christian faith without errors. Moreover, we can figure out that all these texts were treated homogenously, therefore, if we consider correct the inserted interpunctions in the New Testament writings, then our mathematical analysis, partially based on interpunctions, is justified and should be reliable.

4. Full Texts

In this section, we consider the full texts of Matthew, Mark, Luke, John, Acts and Revelation[2]. Afterwards we will consider the partial texts, which, as recalled in the Introduction, have been recognized as common to two or more authors. In the Gospels of Matthew and Luke, we have deleted the verses that list the names of Jesus' ancestors (genealogy), to avoid some polarization of the statistics concerning, mainly, sentence length and word interval.

Our comparison considers the density and probability distribution functions (i.e., the probability that the indicated value is not exceeded) of the four parameters defined in Section 1, and the conclusions are based on the Kolmogorov–Smirnov test, mostly adopted for comparing probability distribution functions, as summarized in Appendix C of Matricciani and Caro (2018). For each of the four parameters, the mathematical model of the probability density function is a three-parameter log-normal function, as described in Appendix B of Matricciani and Caro (2018), each referred (scaled) to text block of 500 words (instead of 1000 because of the shorter literary texts here considered): see Appendix A of Matricciani and Caro (2018). The threshold of the log-normal model for all variables, i.e., their minimum value, is 1. In other words, the density is shifted 1 unit to the right. We report the fundamental statistical results of the various selections in Tables 4–7. From these data, the three-parameter log-normal probability density functions are derived as shown in Appendix B of (Matricciani and Caro 2018).

Table 4. Full Texts. Average number of characters per word C_P, words per sentence P_F, interpunctions per sentence (also, number of word intervals) M_F, words per interpunctions (word interval) I_P. The number between parentheses gives the standard deviation for text blocks of 500 words.

Text	Characters per Word C_P	Words per Sentence P_F	Interpunctions per Sentence M_F	Words per Interpunctions I_P
Matthew	4.906 (0.157)	20.27 (3.66)	2.825 (0.413)	7.182 (0.778)
Mark	4.955 (0.182)	19.14 (4.35)	2.683 (0.693)	7.165 (0.479)
Luke	4.910 (0.134)	20.47 (3.68)	2.892 (0.419)	7.105 (1.075)
John	4.542 (0.169)	18.56 (2.75)	2.743 (0.336)	6.785 (0.855)
Acts	5.099 (0.280)	25.47 (5.17)	2.905 (0.467)	8.766 (1.070)
Revelation	4.658 (0.125)	30.70 (5.78)	3.970 (0.805)	7.785 (0.721)

Finally, notice that if different versions of Greek texts were analyzed, the statistical results reported below would not change in any significant way because of the large number of words, sentences, interpunctions considered. As an example, in the version we have analyzed the episode narrated in John 8,1–11 (about a woman caught in adultery) is not present, because, as is known (Ehrman 2000), this episode is missing in some of the early manuscripts. If these 11 verses were present, only the totals of the four parameters mentioned above would be slightly affected, but not in a significant way. The impact would be even smaller if some words were changed, as it can be in other manuscripts. Recall that the meaning of a text has no importance in our mathematical analysis.

---

[2]   The Greek texts have been downloaded from the web site http://www.bibbiaedu.it of the Catholic Institution of the Conferenza Episcopale Italiana (CEI) *Fondazione di Religione Santi Francesco d'Assisi e Caterina da Siena*. Last access, 31 March 2019.

Table 5. Triple Tradition. Average number of characters per word C_P, words per sentence P_F, interpunctions per sentence (also, number of word intervals) M_F, words per interpunctions (word interval) I_P. The numbers between parentheses give the standard deviations for text blocks of 500 words.

Text	Characters per Word C_P	Words per Sentence P_F	Interpunctions per Sentence M_F	Words per Interpunctions I_P
Matthew	4.958 (0.160)	20.26 (3.08)	2.888 (0.428)	7.046 (0.573)
Mark	4.929 (0.152)	19.20 (2.50)	2.628 (0.291)	7.331 (0.640)
Luke	4.931 (0.126)	20.40 (2.84)	2.871 (0.330)	7.136 (0.687)

Table 6. Double Tradition. Average number of characters per word C_P, words per sentence P_F, interpunctions per sentence (also, number of word intervals) M_F, words per interpunctions (word interval) I_P. The numbers between parentheses give the standard deviations for text blocks of 500 words.

Text	Characters per Word C_P	Words per Sentence P_F	Interpunctions per Sentence M_F	Words per Interpunctions I_P
Matthew	5.009 (0.171)	19.83 (3.26)	3.085 (0.538)	6.489 (0.470)
Luke	4.906 (0.163)	20.10 (2.43)	3.095 (0.587)	6.727 (1.060)

Table 7. Own Tradition. Average number of characters per word C_P, words per sentence P_F, interpunctions per sentence (also, number of word intervals) M_F, words per interpunctions (word interval) I_P. The numbers between parentheses give the standard deviations for text blocks of 500 words.

Text	Characters per Word C_P	Words per Sentence P_F	Interpunctions per Sentence M_F	Words per Interpunctions I_P
Matthew	4.855 (0.137)	23.57 (4.20)	3.043 (0.529)	7.800 (0.777)
Luke	4.884 (0.136)	23.12 (4.44)	3.074 (0.468)	7.545 (0.888)

Figure 1 shows the density and probability distribution functions of the number of words per sentence, P_F, for each text. We can notice almost a total coincidence of the functions for Matthew and Luke (the two curves overlap), a significant difference with John and very large differences of the four Gospels with Acts and Revelation (the corresponding curves are very different).

If Luke is the author both of the Gospel and Acts, then it seems that when he writes the Gospel he is likely forced to follow a common literary or oral source, as recalled in the Introduction, but when he writes the Acts he is free to follow his own literary style and, therefore, modulates the length of sentences accordingly, also because of the different narrative occasions of the Acts.

If John is the author both of the Gospel and the Revelation, in Revelation he modulates the length of sentences very differently from his Gospel. Other explanations, of course, could hold: (i) the author is not same person; (ii) the original texts have been successively rearranged by other authors before the final editing.

The results of the Kolmogorov–Smirnov test for P_F are reported in Table 8 and confirm the conclusions drawn from a visual inspection of the functions shown in Figure 1. Each number in Table 8 gives the probability (or confidence level, %) that two texts are mathematically different. Therefore, 0% refers to identical texts, 100% to completely different texts. From these results, we can realize how different the texts examined are, by considering the confidence level we wish to adopt.

The test clearly shows that Matthew and Luke are indistinguishable (confidence level 1.25%, practically 0%); Mark is a little different from Matthew (45.49%) and Luke (52.70%), while John is different from Matthew (80.25%) and Luke (85.81%), but not so much from Mark (36.83%). Acts is very different from Luke (99.89%), and John is very different from Revelation (>99.99%, in practice 100%).

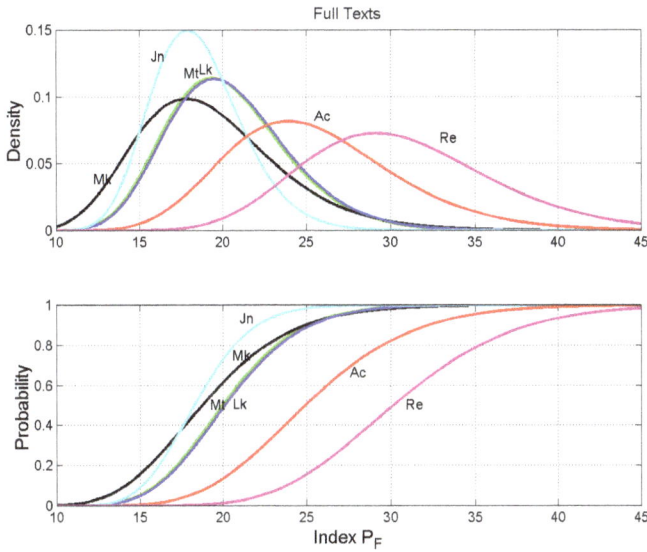

Figure 1. Probability density functions (upper panel) and probability distribution functions (lower panel) of the number of words per sentence P_F. *Matthew*: green line; *Mark*: black line; *Luke*: blue line; *John*: cyan line; *Acts*: red line; *Revelation*: magenta line.

A synthetic index can be the root mean square (RMS) value for each text, also reported in Table 8. It can give some quick and general overview of the likely interdependence of the texts. We can see that the four Gospels have very similar RMS values (~75%); John 83.85%. Both Acts and Revelation (~99.5%) are different from all other texts.

Table 8. Full Texts. Kolmogorov–Smirnov test results for P_F (below the diagonal of zeros) and C_P (above the diagonal). The values reported are the confidence level (%) that the indicated couple of probability distributions are not identical. For example, the confidence level that the number of words per sentence, P_F, in Mark and Luke are not identical is 1.25%, therefore the two probability distributions are, in effect, indistinguishable. The confidence level that the number of characters per word, C_P, in Mark and Luke are not identical is 29.25%, therefore the two probability distributions are not very different, thus indicating that the words contained in their dictionary are of about the same length. The root mean square (RMS) value is calculated as follows. Example, Luke's P_F :
$$\text{RMS} = \sqrt{\frac{1.25^2 + 52.70^2 + 85.81^2 + 99.89^2 + 100^2}{5}} = 77.61\%.$$

Text	Matthew	Mark	Luke	John	Acts	Revelation	RMS
Matthew	0	29.65	9.92	99.98	94.41	98.68	76.97
Mark	45.49	0	28.41	99.95	65.70	99.18	71.87
Luke	1.25	52.70	0	>99.99	95.61	99.63	77.42
John	80.25	36.83	85.81	0	>99.99	74.21	95.39
Acts	99.91	99.92	99.89	99.99	0	99.92	92.04
Revelation	>99.99	>99.99	>99.99	99.99	97.57	0	94.86
RMS	75.49	72.37	77.61	83.85	99.46	99.52	

Figure 2 shows the density and probability distribution functions of the number of characters per word, C_P, for each text. Again, we can notice the almost total coincidence of the functions for Matthew, Luke and Mark, and a large difference with John, Acts and Revelation. If Luke is the author both of the Gospel and Acts, then, as for P_F, it seems that when he writes the Gospel he is forced to follow a common dictionary (referring to the length of words), but when he writes the Acts he is free to use different word lengths, his own dictionary, also because he is narrating events quite different from those reported in the Gospel. If John is the author both of the Gospel and the Revelation, he seems to modulate the length of words very differently in the two texts.

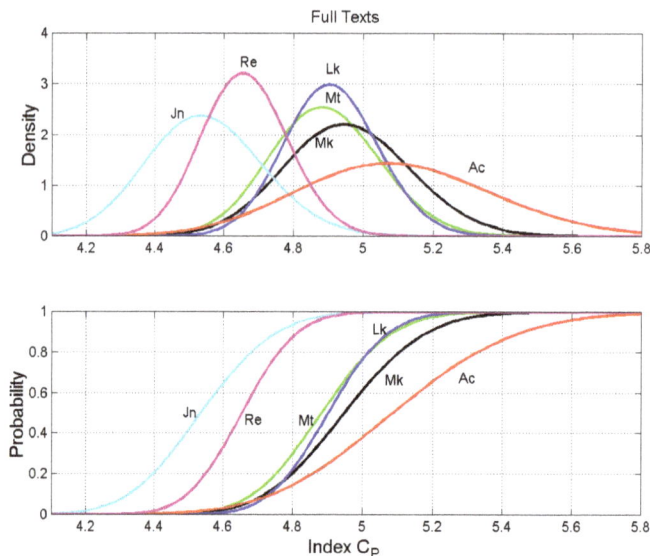

Figure 2. Probability density functions (upper panel) and probability distribution functions (lower panel) of the number of words per sentence C_P. *Matthew*: green line; *Mark*: black line; *Luke*: blue line; *John*: cyan line; *Acts*: red line; *Revelation*: magenta line.

The results of the Kolmogorov–Smirnov test for C_P are reported in Table 8. The test clearly shows that Matthew and Luke are indistinguishable (confidence level 9.92%). John is very different from Matthew, Luke and Mark (confidence level >99.95%). Acts is very different from Luke (95.61%) and John is different from Revelation (74.21%).

Figure 3 shows the density and probability distribution functions of the number of interpunctions per sentence, M_F, for each text and Table 9 reports the results of the Kolmogorov–Smirnov test. In addition, in this case, there is a total coincidence of the functions of Matthew and Luke, but now also John agrees with them. Mark and especially Revelation are at the extremes. Revelation does not agree with John, but now Acts does agree with Luke. It seems that Luke, both in the Gospel and in the Acts, "uses" the same style as far as interpunctions are concerned, even though the number of words per sentence, P_F, does not follow this trend, as Figure 1 shows. Of course, interpunctions were inserted later, as discussed in Section 3, consequently, Acts and Luke must differ in the word interval statistics, as we show next.

The results of the Kolmogorov–Smirnov test for M_F, reported in Table 9, confirm our visual observations and conclusions. Matthew, Luke and John are practically indistinguishable (9.63% and 24.32%), Mark is different from them (confidence level 82.94%). Acts and Luke are also indistinguishable (6.13%). John and Revelation are very different (>99.99%). Revelation is different from all other texts.

The number of words per interpunctions, referred to as the word interval I_P, namely the number of words between two successive interpunctions, is an important parameter because it seems to be linked to the capacity of the short-term memory required of the readers to read the text more easily (Matricciani 2019; Matricciani and Caro 2018).

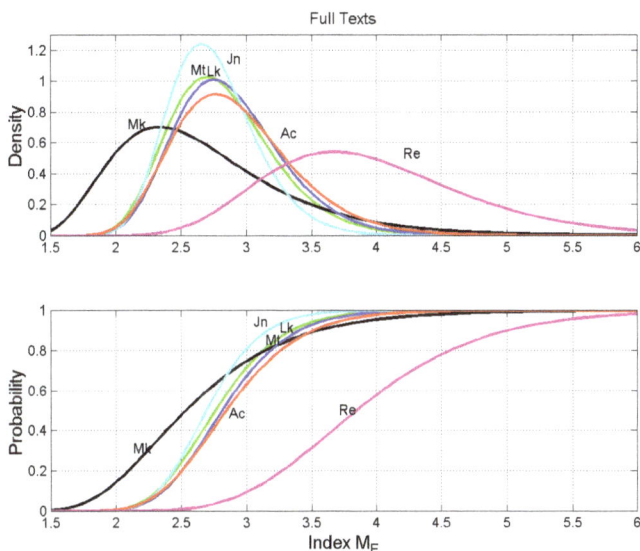

Figure 3. Probability density functions (upper panel) and probability distribution functions (lower panel) of the number of interpunctions per sentence M_F. *Matthew*: green line; *Mark*: black line; *Luke*: blue line; *John*: cyan line; *Acts*: red line; *Revelation*: magenta line.

Table 9. Full Texts. Kolmogorov–Smirnov test results for I_P (below the diagonal of zeros) and M_F (above the diagonal). The values reported are the confidence level (%) that the indicated couple of probability distributions are not identical.

Text	Matthew	Mark	Luke	John	Acts	Revelation	RMS
Matthew	0	82.94	9.63	24.32	22.74	>99.99	60.13
Mark	30.51	0	89.89	81.70	89.72	99.99	89.09
Luke	39.61	77.86	0	48.89	6.13	>99.99	64.19
John	78.00	94.17	45.87	0	65.71	>99.99	69.25
Acts	>99.99	>99.99	>99.99	>99.99	0	>99.99	67.71
Revelation	92.22	96.74	96.61	99.74	99.07	0	>99.99
RMS	73.60	83.93	76.25	86.03	99.81	96.91	

Figure 4 shows the density and probability distribution functions of I_P, for each text. We can notice that the probability distributions of Matthew and Luke are quite similar, with Mark and John significantly different, as the Kolmogorov–Smirnov test results, reported in Table 9, show. As we have anticipated, Acts and Luke differ very much in the word interval statistics (confidence level >99.99%). In addition, John and Revelation are very different (99.74%). In conclusion, Acts and Revelation are different from all other texts, as shown by the RMS values (99.81% and 96.01%).

Notice that the RMS values of M_F are lower than those of I_P (except for Revelation) therefore indicating some more homogeneity in the probability distribution of interpunctions.

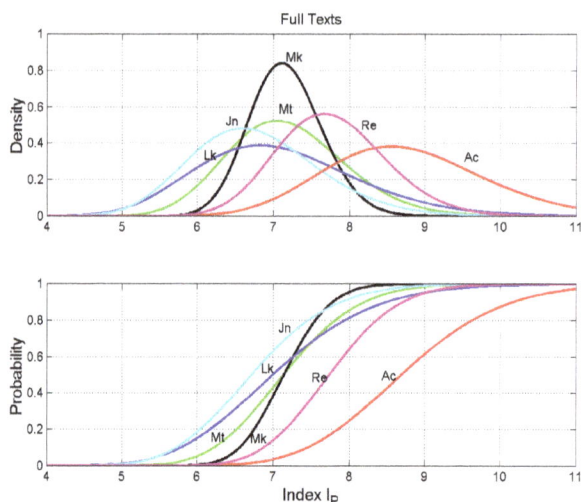

Figure 4. Probability density functions (upper panel) and probability distribution functions (lower panel) of the number of words per sentence I_P. *Matthew*: green line; *Mark*: black line; *Luke*: blue line; *John*: cyan line; *Acts*: red line; *Revelation*: magenta line.

5. Triple Tradition

In this section, we analyze the statistics of the four parameters in the texts of Matthew, Mark and Luke referred to as the Triple Tradition (Tables 1–3), and compared them to the Q source (Table 1).

Figure 5 shows the density and probability distribution functions of P_F, for each text, and Table 10 reports the results of the Kolmogorov–Smirnov test. We can notice that the functions of Matthew and Luke are practically identical (confidence level 3.03%) and slightly closer to Q (Matthew–Q 34.83%; Luke–Q 26.27%) than to Mark (Matthew–Mark 46.21%; Luke–Mark 50.66%). Mark and Q are significantly different (78.80%). The RMS values are similar for Matthew and Luke and larger for both Mark (60.31%) and Q (52.00%).

Table 10. Triple Tradition and Q. Kolmogorov–Smirnov test results for P_F (below the diagonal of zeros) and C_P (above the diagonal). The values reported are the confidence level (%) that the indicated couple of probability distributions are not identical.

Text	Matthew	Mark	Luke	Q	RMS
Matthew	0	15.03	22.10	63.87	39.97
Mark	46.21	0	6.61	40.26	25.10
Luke	3.03	50.66	0	58.28	36.19
Q	34.83	78.80	26.27	0	55.07
RMS	33.45	60.31	32.99	52.00	

In conclusion, these results indicate that Matthew, Luke and Q are very likely interdependent. Mark is likely linked to Matthew and Luke, or vice versa (confidence level about 50%), and less to Q. These findings substantially agree with the results found in the Full Texts analysis of Section 4.

Figure 6 shows the density and probability distribution functions of C_P, for each text and Table 10 reports the results of the Kolmogorov–Smirnov test. We can notice that the functions of Matthew, Luke and Mark are practically identical and loosely linked to Q. The RMS values indicate that all texts share the same set of word lengths, with Q the most different. These results indicate that Matthew, Mark and Luke are using words of very similar length, a common dictionary as far as the number of characters per word is concerned, and agree with the results of the Full Texts analysis of Section 4.

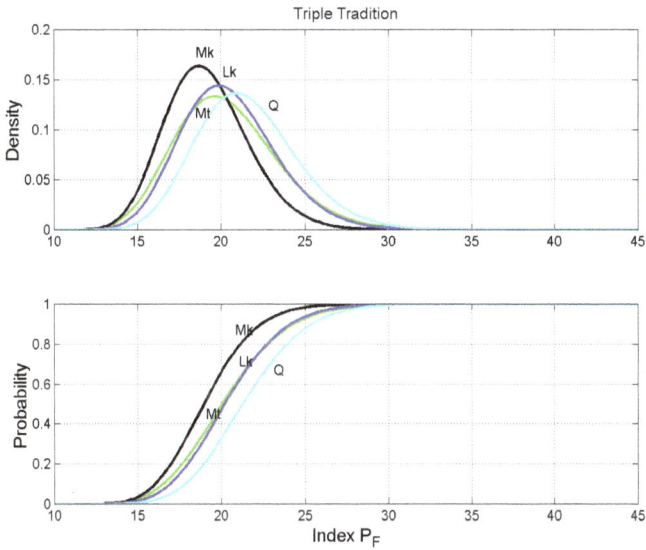

Figure 5. Triple Tradition. Probability density functions (upper panel) and probability distribution functions (lower panel) of the number of words per sentence P_F. *Matthew*: green line; *Mark*: black line; *Luke*: blue line; Q: cyan line.

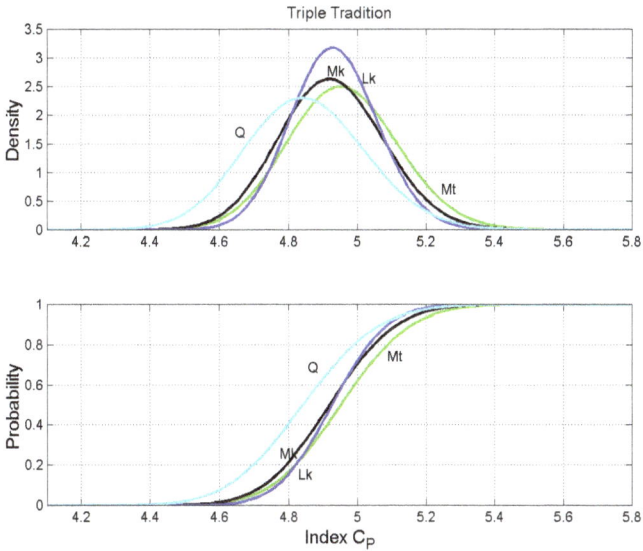

Figure 6. Triple Tradition and Q. Probability density functions (upper panel) and probability distribution functions (lower panel) of the number of words per sentence C_P. *Matthew*: green line; *Mark*: black line; *Luke*: blue line; Q: cyan line.

Figure 7 shows the density and probability distribution functions of M_F, for each text. We can notice that the functions of Matthew and Luke are practically identical (7.70%), with Mark and Q significantly different from them, as the Kolmogorov–Smirnov test results, reported in Table 11, show.

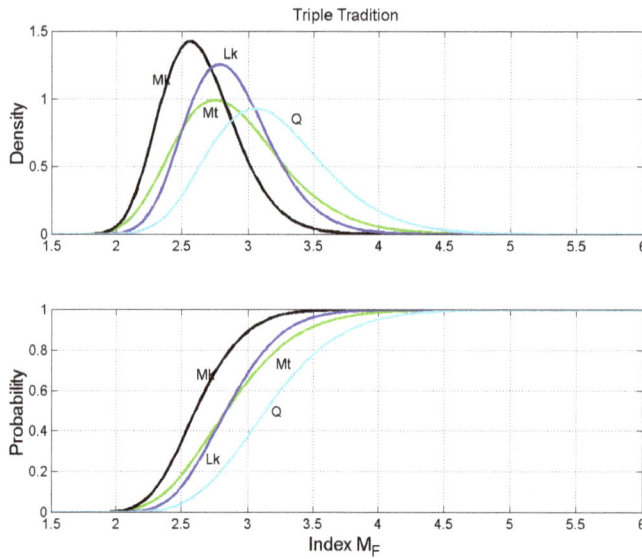

Figure 7. Triple Tradition. Probability density functions (upper panel) and probability distribution functions (lower panel) of the number of words per sentence M_F. *Matthew*: green line; *Mark: black line; Luke*: blue line; *Q*: cyan line.

Figure 8 shows the density and probability distribution functions of I_P, for each text. The functions of Matthew and Luke are very similar, with Mark different from Matthew (54.01%) and Q (72.01%) but not from Luke (23.57%), as reported in Table 11.

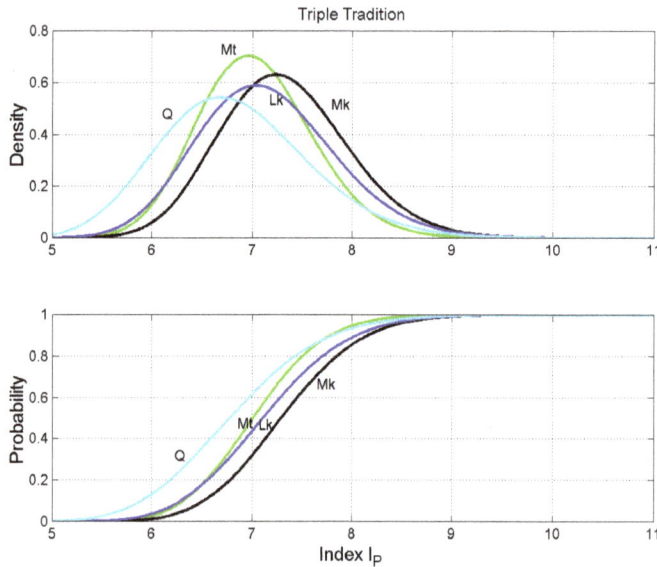

Figure 8. Triple Tradition and Q. Probability density functions (upper panel) and probability distribution functions (lower panel) of the number of words per interpunctions (word interval) I_P. *Matthew*: green line; *Mark*: black line; *Luke*: blue line; *Q*: cyan line.

Table 11. Triple Tradition and Q. Kolmogorov–Smirnov test results for I_P (below the diagonal of zeros) and M_F (above the diagonal). The values reported are the confidence level (%) that the indicated couple of probability distributions are not identical.

Text	Matthew	Mark	Luke	Q	RMS
Matthew	0	81.58	7.70	67.98	61.47
Mark	54.01	0	81.40	74.24	79.15
Luke	14.65	23.57	0	11.31	47.66
Q	37.56	72.01	39.76	0	58.50
RMS	38.91	53.72	27.99	52.21	

6. Double Tradition

In this section, we analyze the statistics of the four parameters in the texts of Matthew and Luke, referred to as the Double Tradition (Tables 1–3), compared to the Q source.

Figure 9 shows the density and probability distribution functions of P_F, for each text. We can notice that Matthew, Luke and Q are practically identical. They have about the same RMS values (Table 12).

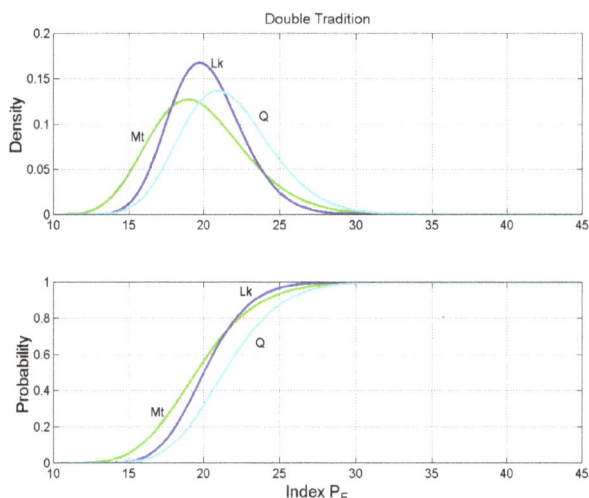

Figure 9. Double Tradition and Q. Probability density functions (upper panel) and probability distribution functions (lower panel) of the number of words per sentence P_F. *Matthew*: green line; *Luke*: blue line; *Q*: cyan line.

Table 12. Double Tradition. Kolmogorov–Smirnov test results for P_F (below the diagonal of zeros) and C_P (above the diagonal). The values reported are the confidence level (%) that the indicated couple of probability distributions are not identical.

Text	Matthew	Luke	Q	RMS
Matthew	0	27.74	60.03	46.76
Luke	9.43	0	15.05	22.32
Q	36.82	28.66	0	43.76
RMS	26.88	21.33	32.99	

Figure 10 shows the density and probability distribution functions of C_P, for each text. As for P_F, Matthew and Luke are very similar (27.74%), but now Q is enough different from Matthew (60.03%).

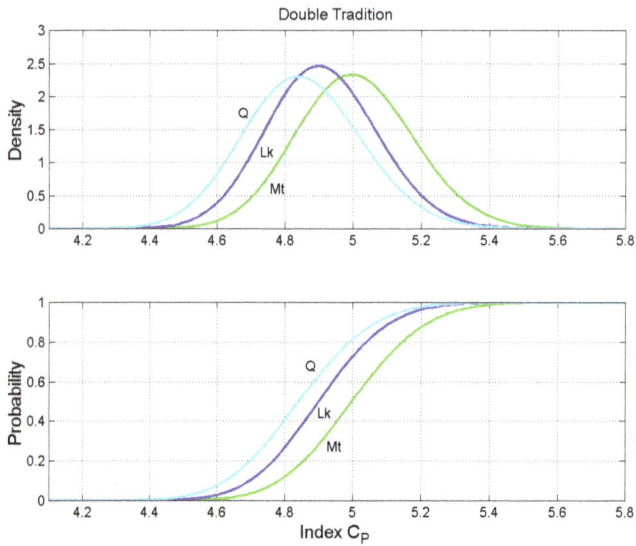

Figure 10. Double Tradition. Probability density functions (upper panel) and probability distribution functions (lower panel) of the number of characters per word C_P. *Matthew*: green line; *Luke*: blue line; *Q*: cyan line.

Figure 11 shows the density and probability distribution functions of M_F, for each text and Table 13 reports the Kolmogorov–Smirnov test results. Matthew and Luke are practically identical, Q is very close to them. In other words, the scribes/readers who inserted the interpunctions treated these verses in the same way.

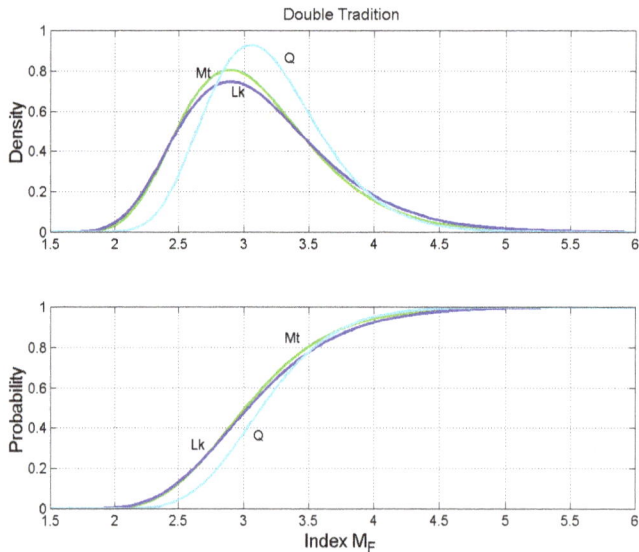

Figure 11. Double Tradition. Probability density functions (upper panel) and probability distribution functions (lower panel) of the number of interpunctions per sentence M_F. *Matthew*: green line; *Luke*: blue line; *Proto–Luke*: blue dashed line; *Q*: cyan line.

Table 13. Double Tradition and Q. Kolmogorov–Smirnov test results for I_P (below the diagonal of zeros) and M_F (above the diagonal). The values reported are the confidence level (%) that the indicated couple of probability distributions are not identical.

Text	Matthew	Luke	Q	RMS
Matthew	0	0.50	11.73	8.30
Luke	29.70	0	11.71	8.29
Q	37.38	11.31	0	11.72
RMS	33.76	22.47	27.62	

Figure 12 shows the density and probability distribution functions of I_P, for each text and Table 9 reports the Kolmogorov–Smirnov test results. Matthew, Luke and Q are similar (29.70%, 37.38% and 11.31%).

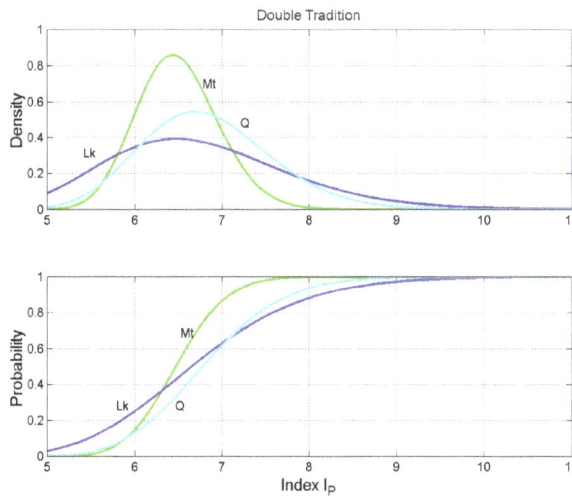

Figure 12. Double Tradition. Probability density functions (upper panel) and probability distribution functions (lower panel) of the number of words per interpunctions (word interval) I_P. *Matthew*: green line; *Luke*: blue line; *Q*: cyan line.

7. Own Tradition

In this section, we analyze the statistics of the four parameters derived in the texts of Matthew and Luke referred to as the Own Tradition (Tables 1–3), compared to the Q source (Table 1).

Figure 13 shows the density and probability distribution functions of P_F, for each text and Table 14 reports the Kolmogorov–Smirnov test results. It is clear that, surprisingly, Matthew and Luke are identical. In other words, the unique ("Own") verses of Matthew and Luke are statistically identical to those of the Double Tradition.

Table 14. Own Tradition and Q. Kolmogorov–Smirnov test results for P_F (below the diagonal of zeros) and C_P (above the diagonal). The values reported are the confidence level (%) that the indicated couple of probability distributions are not identical.

	Matthew	Luke	Q	RMS
Matthew	0	3.77	4.87	4.35
Luke	3.34	0	16.77	12.15
Q	37.50	34.26	0	12.35
RMS	26.62	24.34	35.92	

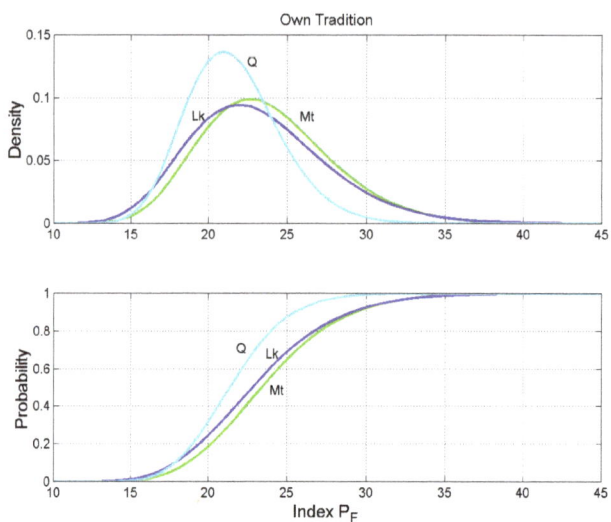

Figure 13. Own Tradition. Probability density functions (upper panel) and probability distribution functions (lower panel) of the number of words per sentence P_F. *Matthew*: green line; *Luke*: blue line; Q: cyan line.

Figure 14 shows the density and probability distribution functions of C_P, for each text and Table 14 reports the Kolmogorov–Smirnov test results. Again, as for P_F, Matthew, Luke and Q are identical.

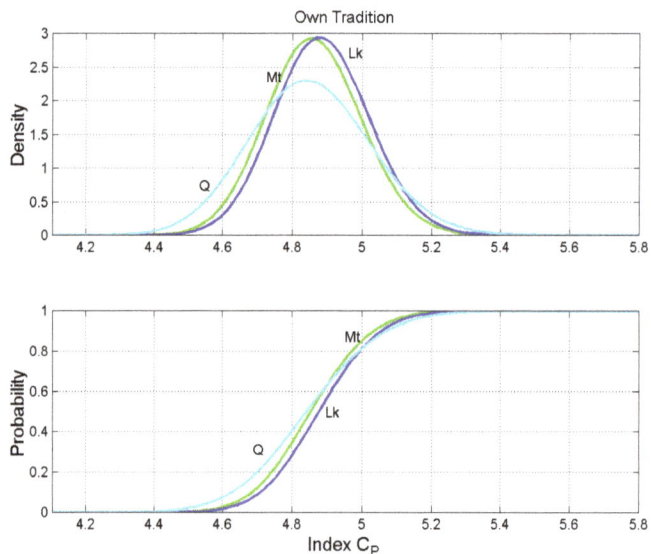

Figure 14. Own Tradition. Probability density functions (upper panel) and probability distribution functions (lower panel) of the number of characters per word C_P. *Matthew*: green line; *Luke*: blue line; Q: cyan line.

Figure 15 shows the density and probability distribution functions of M_F, for each text and Table 15 reports the Kolmogorov–Smirnov test results. It is clear that all curves are practically identical, and in more agreement with the Double Tradition (Figure 11) than with the Full Texts (Figure 3) or Triple Tradition (Figure 7). In other words, the Own Tradition is very similar to the Double Tradition.

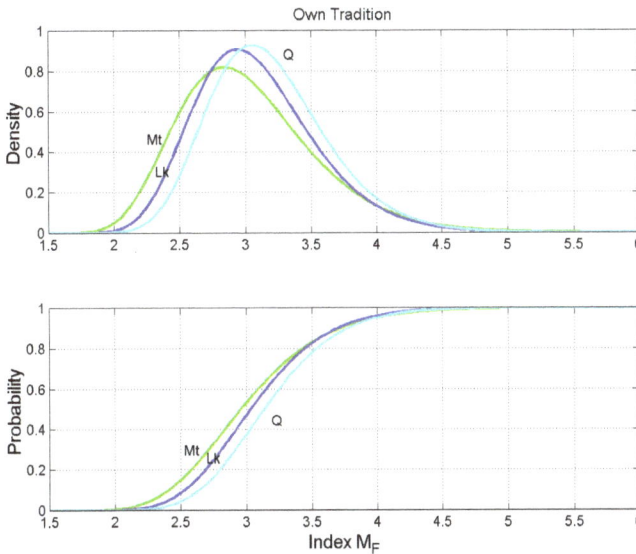

Figure 15. Own Tradition. Probability density functions (upper panel) and probability distribution functions (lower panel) of the number of interpunctions per sentence M_F. *Matthew*: green line; *Luke*: blue line; *Q*: cyan line.

Table 15. Own Tradition and Q. Kolmogorov–Smirnov test results for I_P (below the diagonal of zeros) and M_F (above the diagonal). The values reported are the confidence level (%) that the indicated couple of probability distributions are not identical.

Text	Matthew	Luke	Q	RMS
Matthew	0	5.47	20.89	15.27
Luke	14.73	0	10.30	8.25
Q	83.91	73.90	0	16.47
RMS	60.24	53.28	79.06	

Figure 16 shows the density and probability distribution functions of I_P, for each text. Here differences are very marked. Matthew and Luke are practically coincident (14.73%), while Q is clearly different (83.91%). This is mainly due to the differences in the number of words per sentence, P_F. These findings seem to indicate that the capacity of the short-term memory required of the reader is significantly different for each text in the Double and Own Traditions, except for Q.

Finally, Table 16 reports, for an overview, the global RMS values of the confidence levels (from the previous tables), for the couple Matthew and Luke, in the Triple, Double and Own Traditions. We can notice that in any case the two texts are practically indistinguishable, with the Own Tradition giving values lower than those of the Double Tradition. From Tables 10–13 and 16 we can calculate the overall RMS values: 13.89% for the Triple Tradition, 20.86% for the Double and 15.23% for the Own Tradition, therefore confirming the unexpected result that the Own Tradition is made of texts which are not really different from those of the Double Tradition or Triple Tradition.

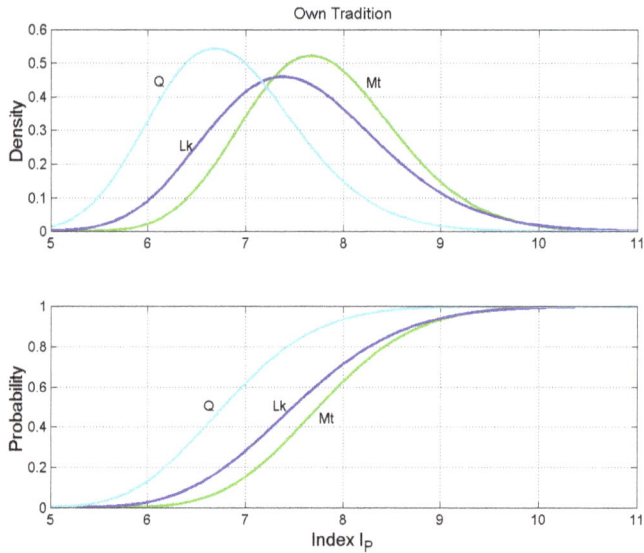

Figure 16. Own Tradition. Probability density functions (upper panel) and probability distribution functions (lower panel) of the number of words per interpunctions (word interval) I_P. *Matthew*: green line; *Luke*: blue line; *Q*: cyan line.

Table 16. Confidence levels (%) for the indicated Traditions (only Matthew and Luke).

Tradition	P_F	C_P	M_F	I_P	RMS
Triple Tradition	3.03	22.10	7.70	14.65	13.89
Double Tradition	9.43	27.74	0.50	29.70	20.86
Own Tradition	3.34	3.77	5.47	14.73	8.25
RMS	6.03	20.59	5.46	20.93	

8. Relationship between I_P and P_F, Readability and Geometrical Representation of Literary Texts

The number of words per interpunctions, I_P, and the number of words per sentence, P_F, are linked by a direct proportionality (Matricciani 2019; Matricciani and Caro 2018). Moreover, the readability of a text depends mostly on P_F, as shown for Italian (Matricciani 2019; Matricciani and Caro 2018), with a readability index that decreases (the text is less readable) as P_F and I_P increase. Therefore, we can estimate, to a first approximation, the relationship between I_P and the readability of the texts here considered, by using the averages values of I_P and P_F reported in Tables 4–7. Figure 17 shows the average value of I_P versus the average value of P_F.

In Figure 17, we have also inserted some important literary works of the Greek literature to assess where the New Testament writings are placed in this broader scenario. The comparison of the New Testament writings with these literary works will be discussed in the next section. Now, we examine only the New Testament writings.

From Figure 17 several interesting observations emerge. The most readable text is John, as it has the smallest value of P_F. The less readable is Revelation. Matthew and Luke are practically superposed, they have the same readability. Q is distinct from the synoptic Gospels. Mark is clearly distinct from Matthew and Luke, and even more from John.

The Triple Tradition gives results very close to the Full Texts results. Therefore, they have similar values of readability. On the contrary, the Double Tradition and the Own Tradition are far from each other and from the Full Texts. It is evident that the Own Tradition gives results very different from the other texts, and its texts are the less readable of the Gospels. Acts is very different from Luke and Revelation is very different from John.

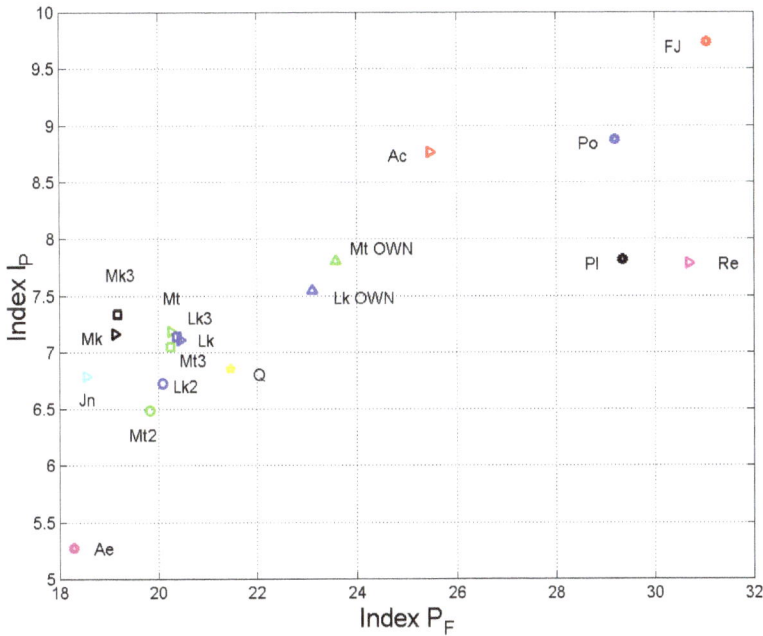

Figure 17. Average number of words per interpunctions, I_P, versus the average number of words per sentence, P_F. Triangles with vertex to the right refer to Full Texts. Squares refer to the Triple Tradition (e.g., Mt3). Circles refer to the Double Tradition (e.g., Mt2). Triangles with vertex up refer to the Own Tradition. *Matthew*: green; *Mark*: black; *Luke*: blue; *John*: cyan; *Acts*: red; *Revelation*: magenta; *Q*: yellow. *Aesop* (Ae): magenta star; *Polybius* (Po): blue star; *Plutarch* (Pl): black star; *Flavius Josephus* (FJ): red star.

A useful graphical and mathematical tool for comparing different literary texts is the vector representation, discussed by Matricciani (2019), obtained by considering the following six vectors of components[3] x and y : $\vec{R}_1 = (C_P, P_F)$, $\vec{R}_2 = (M_F, P_F)$, $\vec{R}_3 = (I_P, P_F)$, $\vec{R}_4 = (C_P, M_F)$, $\vec{R}_5 = (I_P, M_F)$, $\vec{R}_6 = (I_P, C_P)$ and their resulting vector of coordinates, x_R and y_R, given by:

$$\vec{R} = \sum_{k=1}^{6} \vec{R}_k \qquad (1)$$

Using the average values of Tables 4–7, with the vector representation (1) a literary text ends up at a point of coordinates x_R and y_R in the first Cartesian quadrant, as shown in Figure 18. The closer the mark is to the origin of the Cartesian axes (0,0), not shown, the more readable the text. In Figure 18, differences and similarities already observed in Figure 17 are again clearly evidenced, therefore confirming the general picture that emerges from our results.

---

3   The choice of which parameter represents the component x or y is not important. Once the choice is made, the numerical results will depend on it, but not the relative comparisons and general conclusions

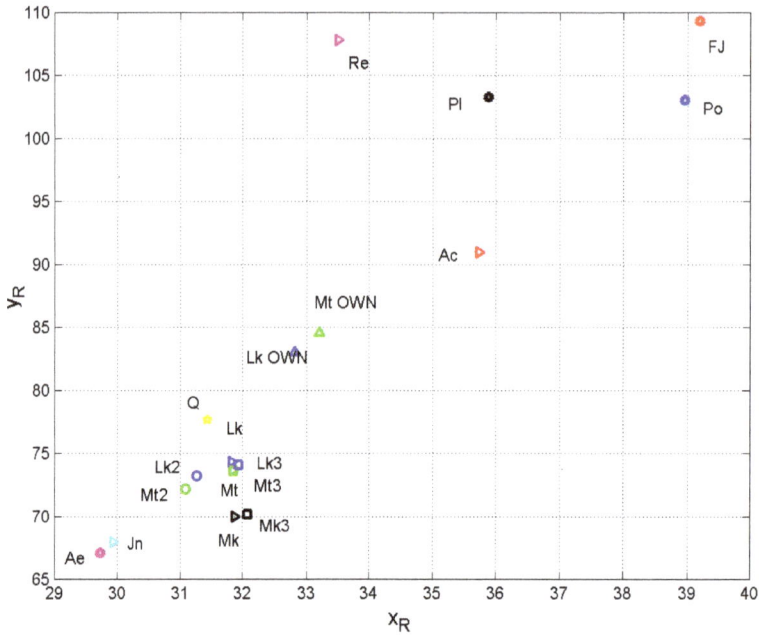

Figure 18. Coordinates x_R and y_R of the resulting vector (1) of the texts considered. Triangles with vertices to the right refer to Full Texts. Squares refer to the Triple Tradition (e.g., Mt3). Circles refer to the Double Tradition (e.g., Mt2). Triangles with vertices pointing up refer to the Own Tradition. *Matthew*: green; *Mark*: black; *Luke*: blue; *John*: cyan; *Acts*: red; *Revelation*: magenta; *Q*: yellow. *Aesop* (Ae): magenta star; *Polybius* (Po): blue star; *Plutarch* (Pl): black star; *Flavius Josephus* (FJ): red star.

9. Comparison with the Classical Greek Literature

The New Testament writings were written in Greek by authors who were very likely conscious of the classical Greek literary works. This is more than a guess for Luke, who was of Greek origin and very literate, e.g., see Ehrman (2000). These classical literary works can guide us to place the New Testament writings, here studied, in a more general context. To this purpose we have done the same mathematical/statistical analysis on three historical works that can be considered quasi contemporaneous of the New Testament writings, or were largely known, namely[4] the *Histories* by Polybius (II century B.C.), the *Parallel Lives* by Plutarch (I century A.C.), the *Jewish War* by Flavius Josephus (I century A.C), and the classical *Fables* by Aesop (V century B.C.). Table 17 lists the main statistics of these literary works.

Figures 17 and 18 show where these works are located. From Table 17 and Figures 17 and 18, we can notice some interesting facts:

(i) The Gospels are very close to Aesop's Fables, as we should expect because in both cases the audience addressed is a popular one. Compared to Polybius, Plutarch and Flavius Josephus, the words used in the Gospels are in fact shorter, below about 5 characters per word against 5.2 to 6; the number of words per sentence is smaller, about 20 words per sentence against about 30 (recall that this number should determine the readability); the word interval is smaller (a parameter very likely linked to the short-term memory capacity), 7 against 8~9.

---

4   These Greek literary works have been downloaded from the web site http://www.perseus.tufts.edu. Last access: 31 March 2019.

(ii) Revelation and Acts are closer to the historical works of Polybius, Plutarch and Flavius Josephus. On the models that might have inspired the author of Acts, see (Ehrman 2000). The four parameters of Acts and Revelation are closer to those of these historical works than to those of the Gospels.

Table 17. Examples of classical Greek literature. Totals of characters, words, sentences; average number of characters per word C_P, words per sentence P_F, interpunctions per sentence (also, number of word intervals) M_F, words per interpunctions (word interval) I_P. The number between parentheses gives the standard deviation for text blocks of 500 words.

Author	Characters	Words	Sentences	C_P	P_F	M_F	I_P
Polybius	1,530,968	256,495	8830	5.969 (0.438)	29.19 (7.45)	3.302 (1.200)	8.877 (1.975)
Plutarch	2,750,711	499,683	17,905	5.505 (0.362)	29.35 (22.81)	3.730 (2.288)	7.815 (2.428)
Flavius Josephus	670,313	121,717	4004	5.507 (0.218)	31.05 (7.61)	3.199 (0.657)	9.737 (1.523)
Aesop	204,913	39,122	2172	5.238 (0.167)	18.29 (3.34)	3.463 (0.511)	5.275 (0.382)

10. A Synthetic Overview of the Statistical Results

In Figure 19, we have connected the three marks reported in Figure 18 for the Double, Triple and Own Traditions, for Matthew and Luke. The resulting triangles give, for each author, a pictorial estimate of the area involved in their literary statistics. The green triangle refers to Matthew, the blue triangle, smaller and practically overlapped to the green triangle, refers to Luke. The red triangle extends Luke's literary area (blue + red) to the Acts.

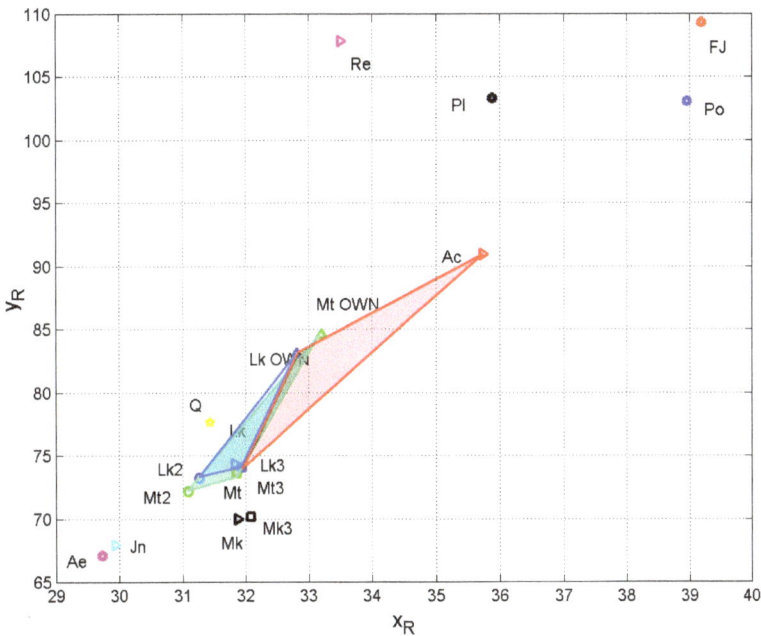

Figure 19. Coordinates x_R and y_R of the resulting vector (1) of the texts considered. Same symbols as Figure 18. The green triangle refers to Matthew; the blue triangle refers to Luke. The red triangle extends Luke's literary area (blue + red) to the Acts.

From this synthetic overview, we can notice that Luke spans a total area given by the sum of the blue and red triangles. Conversely, Matthew is much more limited and contains the blue triangle, which is the expression of the literary style of Luke when he wrote his Gospel. In other words, these results say that Luke had the ability to use different styles, one for the Gospel, another one for the Acts. However, when he writes the Gospel the blue triangle spans an area smaller that Matthew's area. Therefore, under the hypothesis of the existence of a proto gospel, these findings may suggest that when Luke wrote his Gospel he was practically compelled to rely on material from a previous written tradition (from which also Matthew drew his material), as he explicitly states in the prologue, a material characterized, however, by statistics quite different of those of the Acts, a book he apparently wrote without turning to an earlier tradition. In other words, all these data seem to support the hypothesis of a proto Gospel, maybe due to Matthew, an interesting conjecture that could bring future mathematical/statistical work to be done on proto Gospels.

11. Discussion and Conclusions

From the statistical results reported and discussed in the previous sections we can conclude that, for any of the four parameters considered, Revelation is significantly different from any other text.

Let us now examine the other texts, by considering first the number of interpunctions per sentence M_F. From the functions shown in Figures 3, 7, 11 and 15 we can notice that, for any text considered, the probability density and the probability distribution functions of M_F can be considered practically identical. In other words, the punctuation of Acts, of the Full Texts, of the Triple Tradition, Double Tradition and Own Tradition texts, is very similar. Moreover, Q is very similar to these texts. This result strengthens the historical reconstruction done by Parkes (Parkes 1992), and summarized in Section 3, on how the interpunctions were inserted in the New Testament. The statistical homogeneity of M_F seems to confirm that interpunctions were not inserted by the original authors, but by well-educated scribes and readers, as outlined in Section 3. However, the doubt remains whether the scribes and readers interpreted correctly the original intent of the authors.

Let us consider the number of characters per word, C_p. Its average value is typical of a particular language but authors are a little free to select words with number of characters statistically different, as it is shown, for example, in the Italian literature (Matricciani 2019). Our analysis has shown that only Matthew's, Mark's and Luke's Gospels share the same probability distributions (see Figures 2, 6, 10 and 14). This finding reinforces the hypothesis that very likely a common written/oral tradition on Jesus's sayings and events was available to these authors. On the contrary, John's Gospel and Revelation draw words from a different set, and different form that of Matthew and Luke. Acts shows a very different selection of word length compared to Luke, allegedly written by the same author. As also underlined by the analysis of the other parameters, the alleged Luke when he writes the Acts is largely free from the common tradition from which he extracted the sayings and events narrated in Gospel. Q is quite similar to Luke and Matthew.

Let us now discuss the results concerning the two parameters most linked to author's style (see Matricciani 2019), namely the number of words per sentence, P_F, and the number of words per interpunctions, I_P. Before doing so, let us state that, although the interpunctions inserted do determine these parameters, it must be said that the scribes, who inserted them, did it for rendering a correct understanding of the text. In other words, they should have not changed in any significant way the length of a sentence (hence, P_F), or the length of clauses and its natural pauses within a sentence (hence, I_P), although there is always the doubt about the correct interpretation of the original intent of the authors.

As for P_F, Acts and Revelation are definitely different from the Gospels. Because the readability of a text mostly depends on this parameter (Matricciani 2019; Matricciani and Caro 2018), we can say that Acts and Revelation are more difficult to read, as evidenced in Figures 17 and 18. On the contrary, the Gospels appear very similar if we consider the Full Texts, the Triple Tradition and the Double Tradition (Figures 1, 5 and 9). Very surprisingly, the unique texts of Matthew and Luke (the Own Tradition, Figure 13) are very alike and similar to the texts of Matthew and Luke in the Double or Triple Traditions, as if they were describing facts and events with a style taken from a common literary source or present in the same oral tradition. Q is very similar to Matthew and Luke. Therefore, the results obtained seem to support particularly the proto-Gospel hypothesis, among all the different conjectures on Gospels genesis, summarized in the Introduction. From this common tradition, it seems that each author extracted facts and sayings, and chose a particular order presentation of them, according to the audience they were writing for, besides the theological aspects. This finding could be further studied by analyzing, with the same mathematical/statistical approach, the texts proposed by scholars as proto-Luke, proto-Matthew, and so on, to assess which hypothesis is more reliable.

As for I_P, Acts and Revelation are definitely different from the Gospels, and confirm what has already been observed for P_F on their readability. The Full Texts and the Triple Tradition are very similar, as if the authors had drawn their texts from a common literary or oral tradition, in which texts were addressed to people with alleged similar capacity of short-term memory. On the contrary, the subsets of Double and Own Traditions are at the extremes of the general picture depicted in the Full Texts: the Double Tradition considers shorter values of I_P, and identically for both Matthew and Luke, while the Own Tradition shows longer values of I_P, again identically for both Matthew and Luke. The relationship between I_P and P_F (Figure 17) and the geometrical representation of the texts (Figure 18) confirm the above observations.

All these New Testament writings fit very well in the larger Greek literature of the time. As shown in Figures 17 and 18, the Gospels are much closer to Aesop's Fables, while Acts and Revelation are closer to the historical works of Polybius, Plutarch and Flavius Josephus.

In conclusion, the mathematical/statistical tool used in this paper confirms and reinforces some general results found in the vast literature on the New Testament concerning the Gospels, Acts, Revelation and Q source, but also evidences some interesting differences concerning especially the number of words per sentence and words per interpunctions, maybe casting some light on the capacity of the short-term memory of the readers/listeners of these texts. Moreover, the findings concerning the surprising coincidence of the Own Tradition in Matthew and Luke may reinforce the hypothesis of the existence of a proto Gospel, maybe due to Matthew.

Author Contributions: E.M. conceived, designed and performed the calculations; both authors discussed and wrote the paper.

Funding: This research received no funding.

Conflicts of Interest: The authors declare no conflict of interest.

References

Abakuks, Andris. 2015. *The Synoptic Problem and Statistics*. Boca Raton: CRC Press.

Boismard, Marie-Émile. 1979. The Two–Source Theory at an Impasse. *New Testament Studies* 26: 1–17. [CrossRef]

Boring, M. Eugene. 1998. *The History and Theology of the New Testament Writings*. Minneapolis: Fortress.

Brodie, Thomas L. 2004. *The Birthing of the New Testament. The Intertextual Development of the New Testament Writings*. Sheffield: Sheffiled Phoenix Press.

Burkett, Delbert. 2004. *Rethinking the Gospel Sources: From Proto–Mark to Mark*. London: A&C Black.

Butler, Basil Christopher. 1951. *The Originality of St. Matthew*. Cambridge: Cambridge University Press.

Ehrman, Bart D. 2000. *The New Testament. A Historical Introduction to the Early Christian Writings*. Oxford: Oxford University Press.

Farmer, William R. 1983. *New Synoptic Studies. The Cambridge Gospel Conference and Beyond*. Macon: Mercer University Press.

Farrer, Austin M. 1955. *Studies in the Gospels. Essays in Memory of R. H. Lightfoot*. Edited by D. E. Nineham. Oxford: Basil Blackwell, pp. 55–88.

Foster, Paul, ed. 2011. *New Studies in the Synoptic Problem: Oxford Conference, April 2008. Essays in Honor of Christopher M. Tuckett*. Leuven: Peeters, April 20.

Gareiou, Zoe, and Efthimios Zervas. 2018. Analysis of Environmental References in the Texts of the Four Gospels Using Descriptive Statistics. *Religions* 9: 266. [CrossRef]

Goodacre, Mark. 2001. *The Case against Q: Studies in Markan Priority and Synoptic Problem*. Norcross: Trinity Press.

Griesbach, Johann Jakob. 1790. *Commentatio qua Marci evangelium totum e Matthaei et Lucae commentariis decerptum esse monstratur*. Jena: Officina Stranckmannio-Fickelscherria, vols. I–II.

Mack, Burton L. 1993. *The Lost Gospel. The Book of Q & Christian Origins*. San Francisco: Harper One.

Matricciani, Emilio. 2019. Leggibilità della lingua italiana: rivisitazione della formula GULPEASE e legami con la "legge del 7 ∓ 2". *Nuova Secondaria*, Ed. La Scuola, Part 1: February 2019, 6, 79–87; Part 2: March 2019, 7, 80–86.

Matricciani, Emilio, and Liberato De Caro. 2018. A Mathematical Analysis of Maria Valtorta's Mystical Writings. *Religions* 9: 373. [CrossRef]

Mealand, David L. 2016. The Seams and Summaries of Luke and of Acts. *Journal for the Study of the New Testament* 38: 482–502. [CrossRef]

Miller, George A. 1955. The Magical Number Seven, Plus or Minus Two. Some Limits on Our Capacity for Processing Information. *Psychological Review* 63: 343–52.

Neirynck, Frans, Theo Hansen, and Frans van Segbroeck. 1974. *The Minor Agreements of Matthew and Luke against Mark with a Cumulative List*. Bibliotheca Ephemeridum Theologicarum Lovaniensium. Leuven: Peeters Publishers, vol. 37.

Parkes, Malcolm B. 1992. *Pause and Effect. An Introduction to the History of Punctuation in the West.*. Abingdon: Routledge.

Poirier, John C. 2008. Statistical Studies of the Verbal Agreements and their Impact on the Synoptic Problem. *Currents in Biblical Research* 7: 83–123. [CrossRef]

Reicke, Bo Ivar. 1986. *The Roots of the Synoptic Gospels*. Minneapolis: Fortress Press.

Rolland, Philippe. 1984. *Les premiers Evangiles. Un noveau regard sur le probléme synoptique*. Les Paris: Editions du Cerf.

Smith, Dwight Moody. 1984. *Johannine Christianity*. Columbia: University of South Carolina Press.

Stein, Robert H. 1994. *The Synoptic Problem: An Introduction*. Grand Rapids: Baker Book House.

Streeter, Burnett Hillman. 1924. *The Four Gospels*. London: Macmillan.

Tuckett, Christopher M. 1983. *The revival of the Griesbach Hypothesis*. Cambridge: Cambridge University Press.

Vaganay, Leon. 1954. *Le problem synoptique*. Paris: Descleé & Co.

Van Voorst, Robert E. 2001. *Building Your New Testament Greek Vocabulary*, 3rd ed. Atlanta: Society of Biblical Literature.

Weisse, H. 1838. *Die evangelische Geschichte kritisch und philosopisch bearbeitet. Leipzig: Breitkopf und Hartel*. Leipzig: Breitkopf und Hartel.

religions   MDPI

Article

Biblical Performance Criticism: Survey and Prospects

Peter S. Perry

School of Theology, Fuller Theological Seminary, Phoenix, AZ 85014, USA; peterperry@fuller.edu

Received: 22 January 2019; Accepted: 7 February 2019; Published: 18 February 2019

check for updates

Abstract: Biblical Performance Criticism (BPC) analyzes communication events of biblical traditions for audiences. Every communication event of a tradition has four aspects: a communicator, traditions re-expressed, an audience, and a social situation. This essay surveys the history of BPC and its current prospects and points to the future work of developing a fine-grained theoretical foundation for its work. In the analytical mode, a scholar gathers and examines data from a past performance event to describe it, and its effects, in detail. In the heuristic mode, a performer presents a tradition to an audience in order to better understand its dynamics. In the practical mode, a person reflects on the performance of biblical traditions in daily life. In these ways, BPC reunites biblical scholarship fragmented by critical reduction, and bridges the academic and popular use of biblical traditions.

Keywords: performance criticism; biblical interpretation; oral tradition; communication; relevance theory; memory; translation; rhetoric

1. Introduction

Biblical traditions have been presented and re-presented in various ways throughout history.[1] The Bible itself indicates ways that its early audiences may have experienced it. Moses is portrayed in Deuteronomy as retelling the story of the exodus from Egypt while the Israelites stand on the bank of the Jordan River ready to enter Canaan (Deut 9:1). The book of Proverbs imagines parents repeating its wisdom to their children (e.g., 1:8). Singers and musicians practice psalms to sing in the courts of the Jerusalem Temple (1 Chr 25). Ezra the scribe reads the scroll of the Law of Moses to the people gathered in the restored walls of Jerusalem, and Levites help further teach and explain it to the audience (Neh 8). Luke depicts Jesus standing to read from an Isaiah scroll before sitting to teach (Luke 4). Matthew and Luke describe Jesus teaching similar words in two locations, a Sermon on the Mount and a Sermon on the Plain (Matt 5–7; Luke 6: 17–49). Acts portrays Paul and other apostles summarizing the history of Israel, climaxing with Jesus, to people gathered in synagogues (e.g., Acts 13:16–41). Paul asks that his letters be read to all believers in Thessalonika (1 Thess 5:27). John expects the book of Revelation to be read aloud, likely to many audiences (Rev 1:3). These examples suggest the ways in which almost all the biblical material functioned in communication events.

Biblical Performance Criticism (BPC) is both a way to understand communication events of biblical traditions and a method for exploring meaning-making in those events.[2] By "performance," we mean a communication event re-expressing traditions for an audience (Perry 2016, p. 28; see Schechner 2013, p. 29). In every biblical communication event there is a performer, a tradition called "biblical," an audience, and a situation. Meaning-making is not restricted to any one of these four elements but occurs in the ephemeral communication event and its processing by participants during and after the event. As both epistemology and method, BPC is used analytically, heuristically, or practically.

---

[1] Thanks to Carolyn Alsen, Lee Johnson, Jeanette Mathews, James Maxey, Bernhard Oestreich, and Phil Ruge-Jones for their insightful comments on a draft of this article.

[2] See https://www.biblicalperformancecriticism.org/ for more resources and bibliography.

2. A Brief History of BPC

Biblical Performance Criticism incorporates the insights of many disciplines and reframes those disciplines to analyze communication events rather than simply texts and contexts. Beginning with form criticism, many modern critical disciplines read biblical texts in terms of the interaction of: (1) someone speaking; (2) someone hearing; (3) a tradition; and (4) a social situation.

BPC emerges from, and depends on, the insights from many critical disciplines. As the early 20th century began, form critics (e.g., Gunkel, Noth, von Rad, Dibelius, and Bultmann) analyzed biblical traditions as anonymous oral traditions that circulated as genre fragments, applied in various social situations and eventually collected and written. In the 1930s, oral-tradition scholars Milman Parry and Lord (1960) discovered that Bosnian storytellers used repeated type scenes and formulas in a way that helped to understand Homer's Greek epics. These insights were further refined by Ong (1998), Havelock (1982), Finnegan (1988), and Foley (1988), and first applied to New Testament traditions by Kelber (1983) and to the Hebrew Bible by Niditch (1996). Rhetorical criticism, as developed by Kennedy (1984) and Betz (1989), analyzed the way biblical authors tried to persuade audiences with reasoning, emotion, and their character. Narrative critics helped biblical scholars analyze texts as stories with characters, setting, time, plot, and point of view (Rhoads et al. 2012). Memory studies examined how memory is socially constructed, i.e. by a group of people who tell and retell memories that organize relationships, space, and time for that group (Kirk and Thatcher 2005). Media studies analyzed and compared the way the medium (e.g., face-to-face, written, live radio, recorded video) affects communication (Boomershine 1987; Rodríguez 2014). Text critics such as Parker (1997) demonstrated that some variations between manuscripts may be the result of different performances and memories of the material. Performance criticism, emerging out of cultural anthropology and theater studies (Bauman 1977, Carlson 2004, Schnechner 2013, Conquergood 2002), further illuminated embodied actions that are rehearsed and performed (Doan and Giles 2005; Mathews 2012). Each of these scholar's work and methods elucidate some aspect of communication events between someone who speaks or writes, an audience, a biblical tradition, and a social situation.

2.1. Biblical Performance Criticism 1.0

Scholars influenced by each of these disciplines came together in what I am calling BPC 1.0. This version of BPC was characterized by three movements: distinguishing oral from written communication, elucidating the ancient world as a primarily oral culture, and performing memorized biblical texts face-to-face for audiences. By drawing a sharp contrast between oral and written cultures, these modern scholars and performers created a theoretical space for reconceiving how biblical texts were composed, used, and received.

Inspired by oral tradition studies outside the guild of biblical scholarship (Milman and Parry, Ong, Finnegan), Kelber, Niditch, J. Dewey and others identified textual characteristics, formulas, patterns, rhythms, and lexemes as residue of their oral composition and performance. Ong compared oral and written communication in binary oppositions: i.e., communication in primarily oral cultures was additive rather than subordinative, aggregative rather than analytic, redundant rather than economical, conservative rather than innovative, concrete rather than abstract, agonistic rather than neutral, participatory rather than objective, and so on (Ong 1998, pp. 36–57). Within these binary constructions, Dewey (1995), Wire (2011), and others, re-evaluated texts contemporary with the Bible for evidence of oral communication. Shiner (2003), Dewey (2009), Botha (2012), and others analyzed rhetorical figures such as parataxis, prosopopoeia, ring composition, and hyberbaton as signs that a text was composed for oral performance and aural reception. For example, Mark's gospel has an abundance of *kai* parataxis, which in synoptic passages Matthew and Luke seem to have removed. This suggested that Mark was composed in oral performance rather than the more written "sounding" compositions by Matthew and Luke (Wire 2011, pp. 80–84). This "morphological" approach to oral traditions (so named by Rodríguez) searches for the textual residue of oral composition and performance (Rodríguez 2014, p. 56; cf. Lord 1995; Vatri 2017 calls this a philological approach).

The second movement of BPC 1.0 elucidated the dynamics of ancient oral culture. Distinct from any morphological or philological evidence discovered in ancient texts, these scholars described media cultures, that is, the way a group's behavior, attitudes, and values were shaped around particular communication media. Evidence of oral communication is abundant, for example, Apuleius' *Golden Ass* is evidence for informal storytellers; Dio Chrysostom describes walking through a horse track in Asia Minor and seeing someone "reading a poem aloud, another singing, and another telling some story or myth" (*Or.* 20.10 LCL; see Hearon 2009). Mark's gospel contains an aside, "let the [public] reader understand" (13:14); Paul and John expect their letters to be read aloud (1 Thess 5:27; Col. 4:16; Rev 1:3). Scholars such as Kelber (1995), Horsley and Draper (1999), Loubser (2013), and Rhoads (2009) distinguished between cultures that communicate orally and print cultures inaugurated by the printing press and modern mass production of texts. They point out that even Matthew, Luke and John, who use less *kai* parataxis than Mark, wrote and were received in a culture where few (estimated by Harris 1989, and Herzer 2001, to be between 3% and 10% of the population) could pick up a scroll and fluently verbalize the text for an audience. If only a few could read aloud fluently, then the primary way people experienced these texts was through the performance of a lector, someone who studied the text ahead of time to speak aloud for a group. In 1983, Boomershine founded the Society of Biblical Literature (SBL) section "the Bible in Ancient and Modern Media" (BAMM) to develop a methodology for interpreting the Bible in both media cultures. Boomershine (1995), Ward (1995), Shiner (2003), Shiell (2004), and others mined ancient texts to describe how they may have been used in oral performance. They argued text itself was subordinate to the face-to-face performance of the text. Works were composed with attention to sound, including pacing, tone, and volume. Memory played an essential role for both performer and audience. Performer and audience interacted, and audience members interacted with each other in ways that influenced meaning. Emotions were considered in composition, performance, and reception. The bodies of performer and audience were integral to the event: standing, sitting, gesturing, moving, facial expressions, eye contact, applause or foot stomping could influence how a tradition was received (Shiner 2003). The performance space affected how the event was experienced. Person (2010) and Rodríguez (2014) extended the work of Foley to describe the simultaneous variability and stability of oral traditions. Rodríguez calls this a "contextual" approach to oral traditions because it describes a group's values, attitudes, and behaviors that constitute a media culture (Lord 1995 "philosophical"; Vatri 2017).

In the third movement of BPC 1.0, scholars performed texts. Rhoads, Shiner, Boomershine (1988, 2015), and Ruge-Jones memorized biblical texts (including whole books such as Mark and Galatians) to perform from memory with dramatic gestures and use of voice. In a two-part article that announced BPC as "an emerging criticism," Rhoads argued that the written text was like a musical score or a play by Shakespeare (Rhoads 2006a, 2006b). No one would argue that you could understand Mozart by simply looking at the notes on a page, or the *Merchant of Venice* by simply reading it silently. Biblical texts were intended to be vocalized and embodied. Boomershine (1988), Swanson (2004), and Ward and Trobisch (2013) developed techniques and advice for modern readers to perform biblical traditions for modern audiences. Maxey (2009) incorporated face-to-face performances of texts into translation theory and practice. These performers discovered new insights through their performances, and their audiences were moved in ways they had not experienced through silent readings or monotone presentations.

Many contributions were made by scholars of this first stage of BPC, more than can be listed here. In general, we can summarize these as follows: (1) they exposed how the Bible was misunderstood if it was reduced down to one element (the written text) rather than the interaction of all four elements (performer, audience, tradition, and situation); (2) as a result, they opened up a new space in scholarship for re-conceiving the composition, performance, and reception of biblical traditions; (3) they restored the embodiment of these traditions as an analytical category; (4) they highlighted overlooked or minimized evidence for the role of memory, delivery, emotion, sound, physical space, and audience interaction; and (5), they proved the value of modern face-to-face performances of texts for both performers and audiences to better understand their dynamics and impact.

Early criticism came from within the circle of those working in disciplines related to BPC. For example, Kelber's ground breaking *The Oral and Written Gospel* (1983) was criticized for promoting a false "Great Divide" that bifurcated orality from literacy. Kelber recalibrated his position to emphasize that the two media are interconnected and interdependent (Kelber 2013, pp. 174–86). Wendland criticized the lack of theoretical foundations (Wendland 2008). Spencer Miller (2013) and Esala (2015) exposed the western cultural assumptions that lurk behind BPC. Rodríguez problematized the category of "orality studies" as aspirational when referring to the first century since the evidence is primarily textual (2014). Parataxis, prosopopoeia, ring composition, and other rhetorical figures cannot be considered marks of solely oral composition since they are also used in written compositions. He advocated "media criticism" as the preferred name for this discipline rather than the ambiguous and often misunderstood "performance criticism."

Looking back, we can see that much of BPC 1.0 was necessarily radical in its rhetoric. Strong and clear distinctions were needed to break through the unstated communication assumptions that dominated scholarship. Exaggerated binaries allowed performance realities to be heard over the standard set of analytical categories. Although these "divides" proved persuasive to some, they failed when subjected to close scrutiny. Echoing Foley, if BPC 1.0 was "in retrospect too coarse-grained, we should remember that it was their initial approximations that created a new field of inquiry and made later, more fine-grained investigations possible" (Foley 2015, p. 106).

Broader criticism of BPC and its subsequent refinement has launched what I am calling BPC 2.0. Hurtado (2014) brought public criticism from outside the circles of BPC scholars. He questioned the default assumption held by some that texts were memorized by early Christians word-for-word and performed with little or no reference to a physical text. He challenged the premise that silent reading of texts was rare in the first century CE. He criticized the word "performance" as either so broad as to refer to everything as performance, or so narrow as to refer to what actors do in a theater. He implied that a modern performance (i.e., memorizing and performing aloud with gestures and movement) could not shed any light on an ancient performance. The best we can do, Hurtado suggests, is carefully study the manuscript evidence.

Hurtado's critiques do not apply to many BPC scholars today (Iverson 2016). As noted, BPC had already been changing as a result of internal critiques. The rhetorical value of "great divides"—speech vs. writing, oral vs. print cultures, memory vs. text, public vs. individual reading, aloud vs. silent—had exhausted its usefulness.

2.2. Biblical Performance Criticism 2.0

Biblical Performance Criticism is now many groups and movements, each with their own focus and interests. Analysis of texts as evidence of performances has spread far beyond "the Bible in Ancient and Modern Media" and "Performance Criticism of the Bible and other Ancient Texts" (begun in 2007). For example, the Society for Comparative Research on Iconic and Performative Texts (SCRIPT) was founded in 2010.[3] In 2018, forty-seven sections of the annual SBL meeting included papers addressing some aspect of performance, including: a paper on ritual texts and ritual performances in a section on papyrology; another on women's roles in Roman funerals in a section on Greco-Roman religions; and another on embodiment and emotion in the Lukan infancy narrative.

In general, we can summarize that BPC 2.0 is moving in at least six directions yielding finer-grained analysis of communication of biblical traditions. These directions include:

1. Describing ancient communication events in as much detail as possible based on the evidence, with attention to all four aspects of a performance, Johnson (2017), Oestreich (2016), and others

---

[3] http://script-site.net/index.html.

have written careful historical reconstructions of ancient performance scenarios. Wright (2017) has exposed a wealth of data about ancient communal reading events.

2. Clarifying ancient media cultures. Person (2010, 2011), Rodríguez (2014), Keith (2014), and others describe the interaction of spoken and written traditions within specific media cultures indicated by evidence in the Hebrew Bible and New Testament.

3. Exploring the dynamics of social memory. Kirk (2018), Thatcher, and Rodríguez have applied models of social memory to New Testament traditions.

4. Analyzing the sound of ancient texts and their probable impact on audiences. Based on detailed discourse analysis and study of ancient pronunciation, Lee and Scott (2009), Brickle (2012, 2018), Nässelqvist (2015, 2018) and others have developed and are refining methods for mapping the sounds of Greek New Testament texts, the ways sound delimit passages and indicate aural intensity, intonation/pitch, volume, speed, and voice quality (Lee 2018). Vatri's application of cognitive linguistics to processing of classical Attic prose offers a promising avenue for biblical scholars (2017).

5. Applying the insights of BPC to translation theory. Maxey (2009, 2016), Esala (2015), Wendland (2012) and others are using performance to translate biblical traditions more effectively.

6. Using performance to teach biblical languages and biblical studies. Buth,[4] West (2016), and Halcomb (2014) are examples of teachers using performance to teach Greek and Hebrew. Because performance is fully embodied, learning is visual, auditory, and kinesthetic.

Further work needs to be done, especially in three areas:

1. Re-engaging rhetorical criticism, especially in terms of memory and delivery, two of the five tasks of the orator described by ancient theorists. The works of Shiner (2003) and Shiell (2004) are the last major works in this area, and the deposit of biographies, speeches, and letters remains to be explored for evidence of how memory and delivery influenced their composition, performance, and reception.

2. Incorporating analysis of power relationships in the composition, performance, and reception of traditions (West 2007; Spencer Miller 2015), including those that maintain a binary division between scholars and performers (Conquergood 2002).

3. Developing a robust and fine-grained theoretical foundation for how modern performances may illuminate ancient performances (see an initial proposal below).

As BPC becomes more diverse, it will be important that scholars listen and learn from each other outside their areas of specialization, especially to develop a clear theoretical framework. What follows is an initial movement towards that goal.

3. What Is Biblical Performance Criticism?

3.1. Defining "Performance"

We are defining "performance" as a communication event re-expressing traditions before an audience. Performance refers to more than dramatic presentations on a stage; it also refers to lectors reading, choirs singing, teachers teaching, writers writing, and so on—any time a tradition is re-presented. Reading a text aloud is a species of performance. "Performance" is inherently a contested term, which is appropriate because the communication of traditions is usually contested in meaning and significance (Carlson 2004, pp. 4–5; Perry 2016, pp. 27–31). When someone dismisses a communication event as "mere performance," it is an attempt to minimize the effects of that communication. Not all communication events are performances. What makes a communication event

---

[4]   https://www.biblicallanguagecenter.com/; See also https://www.glossahouse.com

a performance is its re-expression of a tradition, its "not for the first time" quality before an audience (Schechner 2013, p. 29).

As a *communication* event, a performance needs to be understood within a framework of how human beings communicate. Everyone operates with some kind of explicit or implicit model of communication, and every biblical studies discipline is strengthened when grounded theoretically in a robust communication theory (Sheppers 2018, p. 174).

An implicit communication theory for many biblical scholars is the code theory that assumes a speaker or writer encodes an idea into language or signals in some media (speech, writing, audio, video) and the audience decodes the signal into the intended meaning. This assumes that the idea is completely contained in the utterance, that all media are equally encodable, and that encoding/decoding abilities are the only requirements for participants in communication. Much of the language we use about communication of biblical traditions assumes a code model. "Transmission" implies that a text is like a radio signal and all we need is to be tuned to the right station. "Reception" perhaps suggests more participation by an audience, but still suggests a relatively passive role. When scholars imply that a text "means" something without discussion of the social situation or audience, they assume a code model of communication. Diagrams such as the following visualize the code model:

Author –> Text –> Reader
Speaker –> Speech –> Hearer

The code model of communication is inadequate. Consider a standard example in linguistic textbooks: a person shouts, "fire." No other words are used. The meaning of this utterance depends on the situation: a firing squad, a theater, or a job evaluation. The utterance itself is insufficient to determine meaning. The situation, the medium, the relationship of the speaker to audience, the ability for the audience to hear and understand the command—each are essential to communication. Take the medium of a command to a firing squad: the voice is optimized for a large group to simultaneously respond but a written note is not. The captain of a firing squad who passes a note that commands, "fire," would likely not receive a simultaneous volley. By using one word, a speaker assumes her audience[5] can draw on both perception and memory to quickly understand. Whatever communication theory is used for the analysis of biblical traditions, it should acknowledge that: (1) all utterances are underdetermined, which makes inadequate any analysis of a text independent of author, a particular audience, and their situation; (2) different media offer both resources and restrictions for communication; (3) both speakers/authors and hearers/readers will use perception and memory *in addition* to the utterance to infer meaning; and (4) all communication is in some way embodied.

There are many current models used to describe communication. My preference is Relevance Theory (RT) because it is simple and yet powerful in its explanations of communication dynamics (Sperber and Wilson 1996).[6] RT is based on fieldwork in cognitive linguistics and has proven applicable across cultures. It describes well how metaphor, irony, and humor work. A good introductory article on RT for biblical studies is Pattemore (2011), and for applying RT to written communication, Wilson (2018).

Briefly put, RT asserts that all human beings naturally and unconsciously communicate by maximizing effects with adequate effort. Three ideas are important: effect, processing effort, and context. Language is one kind of signal (e.g., verbal, written, non-verbal) used as evidence by the hearer along with perception, memories, ideas, and opinions to infer meaning. The *inferential* nature of communication overturns simplistic, deterministic models that suggest an utterance will be understood by all audiences in the same way. A speaker is limited by her language, media, preferences and knowledge of the hearers, and chooses signals she believes will produce the desired effects with reasonable effort. Some of these effects will only be implied. In RT, the word "context" is used to

---

5 Following Relevance Theory's traditional usage, I will refer to speakers as female and hearers as male.
6 Other communication theories offer different resources, e.g., Peircian semiotics; as an introduction, see Hodgson (2007)

describe the perceptions, ideas, thoughts, memories and opinions that can be mentally represented. A speaker who is confident that she shares context with her audience may use minimal signals to imply a great deal of meaning. When Paul asks Philemon to prepare a room for him, he assumes that Philemon understands the details of what that means (Phlm 22). Hearers may draw implications beyond what the speaker implied. For example, Philemon may think he needs to buy more food before Paul comes.

When shared context is not available, the processing effort may be too difficult for an audience. For example, for many modern readers of the Bible, the effect of reading the genealogy of Noah (Gen 5) may not seem worth the effort. In the technical sense, the "relevance" of a communication event refers to the effects experienced by the audience for some processing effort, for example, strengthening or weakening assumptions, emotions, attitudes, beliefs, or actions. Some readers may stop processing before optimal relevance is reached; others may sense that there will be further effects that are worth their time and energy to process (e.g., thought, research, discussion with others.) Others will over-process an utterance and go beyond what is intended.

RT helps to understand media dynamics in communication. If human beings, by virtue of our cognitive makeup, naturally balance effects and efforts (as limited by the speaker's abilities and preferences), then an author will optimize the communication for the chosen media. Vatri (2017) warns against assuming that optimization for spoken communication precludes written communication. RT predicts that, based on previous memories and experiences with various media, an author will unconsciously and consciously optimize communication for the ways the author imagines the audience will use the media. A letter can be optimized both for silent as well as spoken reading. Face-to-face communication offers the additional signals of facial expressions, intonation, pace and pauses, gestures, and interaction with the audience that are not available in writing. Written texts, on the other hand, offer paratextual evidence (e.g., handwriting style, paper and ink quality and color, marginal marks or comments). Physical texts are available for repeated examination and more processing time, while face-to-face communication is linear and requires more rapid processing.

RT emphasizes the bodily nature of all communication. In face-to-face communication, the entire body is being observed by the audience and consciously or unconsciously used with other signals to draw inferences about the speaker's meaning. In BPC 2.0, we are moving away from the terms "oral" and "orality." It is not "oral" communication, as if the voice could be separated from the body ("face-to-face" communication is a preferable term). Writing and reading are also embodied activities. Describing a communication event must involve some kind of description of bodies. Was the writer seated and writing on papyrus on a knee or perched at a keyboard looking at a screen? Both are embodied communication events utilizing different media technologies so that an audience may experience particular effects.

Performance Criticism seeks to describe and analyze communication *events*. The meaning making is not located in one aspect of communication, but the event which brings together the speaker/author, utterance, audience, and situation. This event is, by nature, ephemeral, dynamic, and processed over time. A communication event is never precisely repeatable and so is ephemeral. Even if the same words are spoken by the same person to the same audience, inevitably something has changed in at least one of the people involved and their perception of the situation. As a result, the inferences drawn are different.

As an event, the four aspects are in a dynamic and not a static relationship. The audience may cheer or boo or interrupt a speaker, which in turn may change the words, affect, pace, and so on of the speaker. A reader studying a text may be interrupted by the situation and draw new inferences based on the interruption. A lector reading a text before a congregation may stumble over a word and the congregation misunderstand the idea. The dynamics of each communication event are unique, and any analysis of an event must include as much detail as possible.

Communication events are not necessarily fully processed in that moment. The nature of traditions (discussed below) is that they have been adapted to changes in culture over time and have endured.

Such adaptability and persistence suggest that the inferences drawn from tradition are not exhausted by a single communication event but continue to provide fodder for processing that produces new or richer effects. The Bible represents a collection of traditions that have been presented weekly, even daily, for some audiences. Take, for example, a reading from the Torah in synagogue. A hearer may process it for a moment and draw some conclusions. Then a rabbi stands to speak on the passage. The hearer processes both this new communication event, which involves a second processing of the Torah portion. He may leave the synagogue in conversation with another participant that leads to further effects. Situations may emerge later that day or week that trigger further processing. As we describe communication events, we also must acknowledge that the hearer's processing may continue beyond the time period of the event itself.

3.2. Defining "Biblical Performance"

Foley defines tradition as "a dynamic, multivalent body of meaning, ... a living and vital entity with synchronic and diachronic aspects that over time and space will experience (and partially constitute) a unified variety of receptions" (Foley 1995, p. xii). This definition is richer than we can unpack in this essay, but three points suffice. First, "tradition" may include written texts but is always more. A group that uses a text refers to it as a locus of meaning within a network of other memories, values, attitudes, behaviors, and objects—including other texts. Taken out of a network of traditional referents, a text has few communicative effects. In this way, "tradition" constitutes a body of meaning in which groups compose, receive, and perform. Second, tradition is living; something new happens in each performance. Composition within a tradition creates something new even as it relates to the larger body of meaning. While there are a variety of performances and receptions, the variety is not unlimited but bounded by that which allows audiences to perceive and describe it as within a discrete, unified tradition. The third point is a critique: this particular instance of Foley's definition is disembodied, describing tradition as an entity independent of the human bodies that receive, experience, and perform traditions.

Traditions, as dynamic bodies of meaning, are embedded and integral to human cultures. Socially patterned behavior, such as reciting commandments, singing psalms, or reading aloud sacred texts, embody the beliefs, attitudes, values, and behaviors of a group. The gestures, intonation, language, and other signals only have meaning within a cultural framework that assigns them value and significance. The performance of traditions takes place within the matrix of power relationships within and outside the group and establishes both individual and group identity (Perry 2016, pp. 29–31).

Oral tradition is embodied, collective memory not comparable to a computer accessing RAM.[7] Foley writes, "[T]he oral singers tell us at least five things. First, memory in oral tradition is emphatically not a static retrieval mechanism for data. Second, it is very often a kinetic, emergent, creative activity. Third, in many cases it is linked to performance, without which it has no meaning. Fourth, memory typically entails an oral/aural communication requiring an auditor or audience. Fifth, and as a consequence of the first four qualities, memory in oral tradition is phenomenologically distinct from 'our memory.'" (Foley 2006, p. 84; quoted in Person 2011, p. 537). Lord gives the examples of saying "please" or "thank you" (Person 2011, p. 537). We do not consciously memorize these responses to social situations. We observe them, internalize them, and in certain situations we perform them as a learned reflex.

Rather than speaking of memorization of traditions, which suggests rote, word-for-word recall, we speak of *internalization*. Internalization happens when a person or group has repeated experiences of a tradition to the point that they embody the tradition in their speech, thought patterns, and even bodily responses. A single word may trigger the entire tradition in a way that a person who has

---

[7] We distinguish here between cultural, or collective, memory and memory as a cognitive category, such as used in RT. The two are related; see the essays in (Kirk 2018).

internalized a song can imagine the whole song simply by hearing a few notes. This is what Foley calls the "referential function" of a traditional unit (Foley 1991, p. 6). For example, for those who have internalized Psalm 23, all it takes is for someone to say, "The Lord is my shepherd," and the entire psalm will be brought to mind, along with the situations in which the psalm was performed. It will bring to mind not only words, but emotions, relationships, and experiences. Some will not be able to recite the psalm word for word as an individual but could with others reciting the psalm aloud.

Biblical traditions are those traditions that include and refer to the texts that a group calls "the Bible." (We note that *which* texts are included in this designation has been a point of dispute even into the 21st century, with, for example, Roman Catholics including the Apocrypha.) The films "The Prince of Egypt" and "Jesus of Montreal" are, by this definition, performances of biblical traditions. Even though they clearly do not follow a biblical text word for word, and one is animated and the other is a complete recontextualization of the story of Jesus, both include and refer to the texts included in the Bible. In this sense, biblical tradition is always plural. (Foley 2015 writes, "'Oraltradition' is a very plural noun.")

When we do speak of "a tradition" we mean it in relationship to other biblical traditions, as a node in a larger network of meaning. Analyzing one text requires unavoidably linking to other texts, with each text representing multiple performances of a tradition in relationship to other performances. From this point of view, rather than speaking of stemma of textual criticism, it is more accurate to speak of each individual manuscript as evidence of a tradition of performing that text. The search for an "original text" does not match the reality of a community that uses a particular manuscript, which may vary from those used by other communities.

4. Method and Epistemology

BPC understands meaning to be produced in a communication event that involves a performer, audience, traditions re-expressed, and a situation. The meaning is always pluriform: the performer and each audience member may experience effects in unique ways and in varying degrees. For example, Mark's gospel portrays the centurion at Jesus' cross saying, "This is truly God's Son!" Scholars have argued whether this is meant to be a statement of faith, irony, or mockery (Iverson 2011; see discussion in Collins 2007). A performer may decide to perform this phrase sarcastically to observe audience responses, which may include:

- Rejecting this interpretation as contrary to experience;
- Taking offense;
- Ignoring the sarcasm and irony and identifying with a confession of faith;
- Hearing it as simply confusing; or,
- Affirming the irony with delight.

Each person will construct meaning based upon the performance event, the specific situation (both locally and culturally), their individual memories triggered (including prior memories of the traditional material, the performer, and the others gathered), as well as their particular cognitive processing of all the above together.

Cultural memory and culturally-shaped processing are essential to understand meaning-making in the performance event. West (2007), Powell (2001), and Spencer Miller (2013, 2015) are helpful in describing the ways audiences process Bible texts differently based on their cultural framework. When we speak of "epistemology" as the study of the production of knowledge, we are referring to a cognitive process within a cultural communication schema. There is no abstract communication; all communication takes place using a culturally determined symbol system by a performer and audience drawing on memories shaped by a culture's grid that prioritizes and signifies certain values, attitudes, and behaviors over others.

What holds all this meaning-making together is the performance event itself of traditional material. The particular performance event—no matter how diverse the meaning-making—is unitary.

The traditional material—no matter how transformed in the performance event—is still in some degree of continuity with other performances if the audience can recognize it as relating to the tradition. Finally, a third element of commonality is available in the basic biology of the performer and audience. All human beings have basically the same cognitive processing capabilities and bodily resources for communication, such as two hands, five fingers, eyes, mouth, and so on (Perry 2016). We subconsciously depend on our similar bodies and cognitive apparatus to communicate and these make communication across cultures even possible.

Reframed by these realities about human communication, the task of biblical studies, then, is the comparison of performance events, traditions, and/or cognitive processing of traditions. These are the three elements in common that allow for "apples-to-apples" comparisons. We can compare two performances of any material (say, Mark's passion narrative and Shakespeare's Macbeth), based on performance alone, to think about similarities and differences and the impact on audience and performers. The interface between performance of biblical traditions and other kinds of performance has largely been practiced outside the guild of biblical studies. (Artists, writers, theater critics, philosophers, and linguists have been doing it for years.) We can compare two performances of a particular tradition (say, Mark's passion narrative) to investigate the convergent and divergent effects. Reception Criticism and Reader-Response Criticism have historically operated in this field. We can also specifically investigate how a particular person (or type of person) processed a specific tradition to make meaning in a particular cultural framework. Unwittingly, biblical studies has been operating largely in this third region because of its singular and deterministic outcomes. When historical critics, narrative critics, and others have said, "The text means *this*," they have unconsciously been saying, "I have processed the text based on my memories, cultural predispositions, and situation and it means this to me."

This suggests that there are three modes of BPC: "analytical," "heuristic," and "practical." The analytical mode of BPC examines the remains of performance events as an archeologist examines an ancient site, looking for clues of the performer, audience, traditional material, and situation, trying to reconstruct the performance event. This mode is similar to what historical critics have done for over a century, using information from the text under analysis in addition to related texts and discoveries from archeology, social sciences, and other critical methods to estimate what a text likely meant to a particular ancient audience.

The heuristic mode of BPC creates contemporary performance events in order to discover what meanings may be produced. This mode may be compared to the physicist who creates quantum events in order to study the interaction of particles in real time. A performer of Mark's passion narrative may speak the centurion's words three different ways for an audience, with reverence, shock, and mockery, in order to observe and explore audience reactions to each. We have often called the person who practices the analytic mode the "scholar" and the heuristic mode the "performer."

The practical mode of BPC is the daily performance of biblical materials that happens every Sabbath and Sunday, every Bible study, every YouTube video and coffee shop conversation when someone performs a biblical tradition, with or without the awareness that they are performing. Ancient lectors and scribes might not have identified themselves as performing, but their activities fit our definition. To the degree that the performers and audiences are aware of the performative nature of the event and reflect on the aspects of performer, audience, tradition, and situation, they are practicing the practical mode of BPC. For example, when John Chrysostom comments on the task of preaching a text, it is a kind of BPC. When someone reflects on producing a Bible YouTube video (voice, pacing, word choice, eye contact, gestures, visuals, etc.), it is a kind of BPC. This kind of practical BPC should be distinguished from the analytical mode; one could analyze a preaching event in the analytical mode of BPC, but this would be different than the preacher's reflections.

Each of these modes has their own particular production of knowledge, or epistemology. In the analytic mode, knowledge is produced by an analyst creating coherence between data and cultural frameworks of communication. The analyst is the scholar who tries to discover as much as possible about a performance event: a performer and audience that only may have left traces behind, a biblical tradition encoded often only in texts, and a situation that often is described only in generalizations. Because of the nature of the human brain, the analyst seeks coherence among this data, tries to assemble them like fragments of parchment in the right positions that will allow her to imagine the whole. The framework for assembling these pieces is culturally determined; the performance event will have its own cultural framework of knowledge, independent of the analyst. The analyst also will have a cultural framework. The analyst will inevitably impose her own cultural framework on the performance event, and more so to the extent she is unaware of her own cultural prioritization of values, attitudes, and behaviors. For example, some (myself included) have taken the stories in all four gospels about the women discovering the empty tomb to suggest performance events when Mary Magdalene and the women told the story over and over again (Hearon 2004). Further data are assembled to describe the kinds of locations and audiences where these witnesses may have told the story, how the sounds were spoken, etc. The data for this hypothesis are the data of female-only first witnesses, with the likelihood of male rejection of their witness (verified by Luke's account), and the larger cultural framework of devaluing women's witness (evidenced by Jewish, Greek, Roman, and later Christian sources). My own cultural framework includes a desire to retrieve women's voices in early Christian stories, which may bias my own reading. The coherence (and thus meaning-making) takes place in the analyst's mind as the data and cultural frameworks are processed. The epistemology may take on the appearance of objectivity, which is seductive for those who want certainty, but the analytical mode is individual and subjective. This is not to dismiss the utility of the analytical mode, but only to emphasize that the analyst should be transparent about their cultural frameworks and predispositions and hesitant about making deterministic or objective claims.

In the heuristic mode, the BPC practitioner creates real-time events to study the pluriformity of meaning-making. The performer may have done some analytical work to hypothesize about the effects on early audiences of a tradition in order to create similar effects on a contemporary audience. Or the performer may want to experiment with different kinds of performance variables to see how they affect the meaning-making in a particular audience. Swanson (2004) suggests that in a reading circle each person takes a different emotion in which to perform a passage. By holding other variables constant, the audience can be engaged to see how the text meant differently by changing the emotion of a performance. In this mode, the epistemology is centered on the relationship between the performer and the audience, fully embracing that the performer's intention may or may not be received by the audience. Meaning-making is indeterminate until after the performance, and even until further processing of the event by interactions between the performance and the audience. Post-performance discussion often becomes the site for conscious meaning-making; in the midst of performance, an audience is often overwhelmed with information and emotion, and often it is the emotion that sticks in a person's mind (Perry 2016). For example, in my own experimentation with performances of the book of Revelation, audiences have largely not been able to tell me what Revelation was "about," but they would tell me they felt "hopeful," "fearful," "confused," or other similar emotions. With more questions, and conversation among the audience, they are then able to make more declarative statements about the "meaning" of Revelation for them (Perry 2016). In this way, the heuristic mode of BPC shifts the focus onto the audience's processing of performances.

The practical mode of BPC also has an operative epistemology. Unlike the other two modes, there is no degree of detachment or separation between the practitioner and performer. The performer may not even think of herself as a "performer" of biblical traditions; she just does it and reflects on what she is doing in order to improve the communication effects for her audience in a given situation. The meaning-making for both performer and audience is more focused on the situation. The performer is often moved to deliver the biblical traditions in response to the given situation; the audience expects relevance in the performance. The performer will evaluate the performance event based on how her intentions were realized, or not, for the audience and the extent to which the audience responded as desired. The audience will evaluate the performance event based on expectations and meaning will be often less about declarative statements than emotion and validation or challenge of values, attitudes, and behaviors. For example, someone who produces a YouTube video of the Gospel of Mark assumes that the performance in the video is useful in some way to viewers, relevant for their time, and that it will make some kind of impact.[8] A person who finds such a video is looking for some kind of impact, which may or may not be satisfied by watching the video. Likely, the creator of the video will give some signal of his intentions and some viewers will leave comments in the thread of discussion that may indicate what impact it had.

5. Conclusions

In its analytical, heuristic, and practical modes, Biblical Performance Criticism 2.0 offers a new paradigm for biblical studies that brings together scholars of various critical disciplines and those who perform biblical traditions. It is not necessary to be a specialist in every critical method; each one offers insight into the communication event. BPC provides a way to reintegrate the insights of scholarship into a whole. At the same time, it bridges both theoretically and practically, the gap that has emerged from the academic study of the Bible and its use by communities that perform and receive its traditions.

Funding: This research received no external funding.

Conflicts of Interest: The author declares no conflict of interest.

References

Bauman, Richard. 1977. *Verbal Art as Performance*. Long Grove: Waveland Press.
Betz, Hans Dieter. 1989. *Galatians: A Commentary on Paul's Letter to the Churches in Galatia*. Hermeneia. Minneapolis: Fortress Press.
Boomershine, Thomas E. 1987. Biblical Megatrends: Towards a Paradigm for the Interpretation of the Bible in Electronic Media. In *SBL Seminar Papers*. Atlanta: Scholars Press, pp. 144–57.
Boomershine, Thomas E. 1988. *Story Journey: An Invitation to the Gospel as Storytelling*. Nashville: Abingdon.
Boomershine, Thomas E. 1995. Jesus of Nazareth and the Watershed of Ancient Orality and Literacy. *Semeia* 65: 7–36.
Boomershine, Thomas E. 2015. *The Messiah of Peace: A Performance-Criticism Commentary on Mark's Passion-Resurrection Narrative*. BPC 12. Eugene: Cascade.
Botha, Pieter J. J. 2012. *Orality and Literacy in Early Christianity*. BPC 5. Eugene: Cascade.
Brickle, Jeffrey E. 2012. *Aural Design and Coherence in the Prologue of First John*. London: T & T Clark.
Brickle, Jeffrey E. 2018. Caves, Cattle, and *Koinonia*: Acoustic Shadows. In *Sound Matters: New Testament Studies in Sound Mapping*. BPC 16. Edited by Margaret E. Lee. Eugene: Cascade, pp. 69–83.
Carlson, Marvin. 2004. *Performance: A Critical Introduction*, 2nd ed. London: Routledge.
Collins, Adela Yarbro. 2007. *Mark: A Commentary*. Hermeneia. Minneapolis: Fortress.
Conquergood, Dwight. 2002. Performance Studies: Interventions and Radical Research. *The Drama Review* 46: 145–56. [CrossRef]
Dewey, Joanna. 1995. Textuality in an Oral Culture: A Survey of the Pauline Traditions. *Semeia* 65: 37–65.
Dewey, Arthur J. 2009. Competing Gospels: Imperial Echoes, A Dissident Voice. In *The Bible in Ancient and Modern Media: Story and Performance*. BPC 1. Edited by Holly E. Hearon and Philip Ruge-Jones. Eugene: Cascade, pp. 64–79.
Doan, William, and Terry Giles. 2005. *Prophets, Performance, and Power*. London: Continuum.
Esala, Nathan. 2015. Ideology and Bible Translation: Can Biblical Performance Criticism Help? *The Bible Translator* 66: 216–29. [CrossRef]
Finnegan, Ruth. 1988. *Literacy and Orality: Studies in the Technology of Communication*. Oxford: Blackwell.

---

[8] For example, see Phil Ruge-Jones: https://www.youtube.com/watch?v=3OS_hpt_xeU.

Foley, John Miles. 1988. *The Theory of Oral Composition: History and Methodology*. Bloomington: Indiana University Press.

Foley, John Miles. 1991. *Immanent Art: From Structure to Meaning in Traditional Oral Epic*. Indianapolis: Indiana University Press.

Foley, John Miles. 1995. *The Implications of Oral Tradition. Oral Tradition in the Middle Ages*. Illinois, USA: University of Illinois Press, pp. 31–57.

Foley, John Miles. 2006. The Riddle of Q: Oral Ancestor, Textual Precedent, or Ideological Creation? In *Oral Performance, Popular Tradition, and Hidden Transcript in Q*. Edited by Rachard A. Horsley. Atlanta: SBL, pp. 123–40.

Foley, John Miles. 2015. Plenitude and Diversity: Interaction between Orality and Writing. In *The Interface of Orality and Writing: Speaking, Seeing, Writing in the Shaping of New Genres*. BPC 11. Edited by Annette Weiseenrieder and Robert B. Coote. Eugene: Cascade.

Halcomb, T. Michael W. 2014. *The First Steps to Learning Koine Greek*. Wilmore: GlossaHouse.

Harris, William V. 1989. *Ancient Literacy*. Cambridge: Harvard University Press.

Havelock, Eric A. 1982. *The Literate Revolution in Greece and Its Cultural Consequences*. Princeton: Princeton University Press.

Hearon, Holly E. 2004. *The Mary Magdalene Tradition: Witness and Counter-Witness in Early Christian Communities*. Collegeville: Michael Glazier.

Hearon, Holly E. 2009. The Storytelling World of the First Century and the Gospels. In *The Bible in Ancient and Modern Media: Story and Performance*. BPC 1. Edited by Holly E. Hearon and Philip Ruge-Jones. Eugene: Cascade, pp. 21–35.

Herzer, Catherine. 2001. *Jewish Literacy in Roman Palestine*. Texts and Studies in Ancient Judaism 81. Tübingen: Mohr Siebeck.

Hodgson, Robert. 2007. Semiotics and Bible Translation. *Semiotica* 163: 163–85. [CrossRef]

Horsley, Richard A., and Jonathan A. Draper. 1999. *Whoever Hears You Hears Me: Prophets, Performance, and Tradition in Q*. Salem: Trinity Press International.

Hurtado, Larry W. 2014. Oral Fixation and New Testament Studies?: 'Orality', 'Performance' and Reading Texts in Early Christianity. *New Testament Studies* 60: 321–40. [CrossRef]

Iverson, Kelly R. 2011. A Centurion's 'Confession': A Performance-Critical Analysis of Mark 15:39. *Journal of Biblical Literature* 130: 329–50. [CrossRef]

Iverson, Kelly R. 2016. Oral Fixation or Oral Corrective? A Response to Larry Hurtado. *NTS* 60: 183–200. [CrossRef]

Johnson, Lee A. 2017. Ancient Curses in Bath: Oral Oaths, Lead Etchings, and the Impact on Biblical Interpretation. *Oral History Journal of South Africa* 5: 1–16. [CrossRef]

Keith, Chris. 2014. *Jesus against the Scribal Elite: The Origins of the Conflict*. Grand Rapids: Baker Academic.

Kelber, Werner. 1983. *The Oral and Written Gospel: The Hermeneutics of Speaking and Writing in the Synoptic Tradition, Mark, Paul, and Q*. Philadelphia: Fortress Press.

Kelber, Werner H. 1995. Modalities of Communication, Cognition, and Physiology of Perception: Orality, Rhetoric, and Scribality. *Semeia* 65: 193–216.

Kelber, Werner H. 2013. *Imprints, Voiceprints, & Footprints of Memory: Collected Essays of Werner H. Kelber*. Atlanta: SBL.

Kennedy, George. 1984. *New Testament Interpretation through Rhetorical Criticism*. Chapel Hill: University of North Carolina Press.

Kirk, Alan. 2018. *Memory and the Jesus Tradition*. London: T & T Clark.

Kirk, Alan, and Tom Thatcher. 2005. *Memory, Tradition, and Text: Uses of the Past in Early Christianity*. Atlanta: SBL Press.

Lee, Margaret E. 2018. Sound Mapping Reassessed. In *Sound Matters: New Testament Studies in Sound Mapping*. BPC 16. Edited by Margaret E. Lee. Eugene: Cascade, pp. 8–26.

Lee, Margaret E., and Bernard Brandon Scott. 2009. *Sound Mapping the New Testament*. Salem: Polebridge.

Lord, Albert Bates. 1960. *The Singer of Tales*. Cambridge: Harvard University Press.

Lord, Albert Bates. 1995. *The Singer Resumes the Tale*. Edited by Mary Louise Lord. Ithaca: Cornell University Press.

Loubser, J. A. (Bobby). 2013. *Oral and Manuscript Culture in the Bible: Studies on the Media Texture of the New Testament—Explorative Hermeneutics*. BPC 7. Eugene: Cascade.

Mathews, Jeanette. 2012. *Performing Habakkuk: Faithful Re-Enactment in the Midst of Crisis*. Eugene: Wipf & Stock.

Maxey, James A. 2009. *From Orality to Orality: A New Paradigm for Contextual Translation of the Bible*. BPC 2. Eugene: Cascade.

Maxey, James A. 2016. Alternative Evaluative Concepts to the Trinity of Bible Translation. In *Translating Values: Evaluative Concepts in Translation*. Edited by Piotr Blumczynski and John Gillespie. London: Palgrave Macmillan, pp. 57–80.

Nässelqvist, Dan. 2015. *Public Reading in Early Christianity: Lectors, Manuscripts, and Sound in the Oral Delivery of John 1–4*. Leiden: Brill.

Nässelqvist, Dan. 2018. Underexplored Benefits of Sound Mapping in New Testament Exegesis. In *Sound Matters: New Testament Studies in Sound Mapping*. BPC 16. Edited by Margaret E. Lee. Eugene: Cascade, pp. 120–32.

Niditch, Susan. 1996. *Oral World and Written Word*. Louisville: Westminster John Knox.

Oestreich, Bernhard. 2016. *Performance Criticism of the Pauline Letters*. BPC 14. Eugene: Cascade.

Ong, Walter J. 1998. *Orality and Literacy: The Technologizing of the Word*. London: Routledge.

Parker, David C. 1997. *The Living Text of the Gospels*. Cambridge: Cambridge University Press.

Pattemore, Stephen. 2011. Relevance Theory, Intertextuality, and the Book of Revelation. In *Current Trends in Scripture Translation*. Edited by Philip A. Noss. Reading: UBS, pp. 43–60.

Perry, Peter S. 2016. *Insights from Performance Criticism*. Minneapolis: Fortress.

Person, Raymond F. 2010. *The Deuteronomic History and the Book of Chronicles: Scribal Works in an Oral World*. Atlanta: SBL Press.

Person, Raymond F. 2011. The Role of Memory in the Tradition Represented by the Deuteronomic History and the Book of Chronicles. *Oral Tradition* 26: 537–50. [CrossRef]

Powell, Mark Allan. 2001. *Chasing the Eastern Star: Adventures in Biblical Reader-Response Criticism*. Louisville: Westminster John Knox Press.

Rhoads, David. 2006a. Performance Criticism: An Emerging Methodology in Second Testament Studies—Part I. *Biblical Theology Bulletin* 36: 118–33. [CrossRef]

Rhoads, David. 2006b. Performance Criticism: An Emerging Methodology in Second Testament Studies—Part II. *Biblical Theology Bulletin* 36: 164–84. [CrossRef]

Rhoads, David. 2009. What is Performance Criticism? In *The Bible in Ancient and Modern Media: Story and Performance*. BPC 1. Edited by Holly E. Hearon and Philip Ruge-Jones. Eugene: Cascade, pp. 83–100.

Rhoads, David, Joanna Dewey, and Donald Mitchie. 2012. *Mark as Story: An Introduction to the Narrative of a Gospel*, 3rd ed. Minneapolis: Fortress Press.

Rodríguez, Rafael. 2014. *Oral Tradition and the New Testament: A Guide for the Perplexed*. London: Bloomsbury/T&T Clark.

Schechner, Richard. 2013. *Performance Studies: An Introduction*, 3rd ed. London: Routledge.

Sheppers, Frank. 2018. Discourse Segmentation, Discourse Structure, and Sound Mapping (Including an Analysis of Mark 15). In *Sound Matters: New Testament Studies in Sound Mapping*. BPC 16. Edited by Margaret E. Lee. Eugene: Cascade, pp. 133–178.

Shiell, William David. 2004. *Reading Acts: The Lector and the Early Christian Audience*. Leiden: Brill.

Shiner, Whitney. 2003. *Proclaiming the Gospel: First-Century Performance of Mark*. Harrisburg: Trinity Press International.

Spencer Miller, Althea. 2013. Rethinking Orality for Biblical Studies. In *Postcolonialism and the Hebrew Bible*. Edited by Roland Boer. Atlanta: SBL, pp. 35–68.

Spencer Miller, Althea. 2015. Creolizing Hermeneutics: A Caribbean Invitation. In *Islands, Islanders, and the Bible: Ruminations*. Edited by Jione Havea, Margaret Aymer and Steed Vernyl Davidson. Atlanta: SBL Press.

Sperber, Dan, and Deirdre Wilson. 1996. *Relevance: Communication and Cognition*, 2nd ed. Blackwell: Malden.

Swanson, Richard. 2004. *Provoking the Gospel: Methods to Embody Biblical Storytelling through Drama*. Cleveland: Pilgrim.

Vatri, Alessandro. 2017. *Orality and Performance in Classical Attic Prose: A Linguistic Approach*, 1st ed. Oxford: Oxford University Press.

Ward, Richard F. 1995. Pauline Voice and Presence as Strategic Communication. *Semeia* 65: 95–107.

Ward, Richard, and David Trobisch. 2013. *Bringing the Word to Life: Engaging the New Testament through Performing It*. Grand Rapids: Eerdmans.

Wendland, Ernst. 2008. Performance Criticism: Assumptions, Applications, and Assessment. *TIC Talk* 65: 1–11.

Wendland, Ernst. 2012. Comparative Rhetorical Poetics, Orality, and Bible Translation: The Case of Jude. In *Translating Scripture for Sound and Performance*. BPC 5. Edited by James A. Maxey and Ernst Wendland. Eugene: Cascade, pp. 139–78.

West, Gerald O. 2007. *Reading Other-wise: Socially Engaged Biblical Scholars Reading with Their Local Communities*. Atlanta: SBL.

West, Travis. 2016. *Biblical Hebrew: An Interactive Approach*. Wilmore: GlossaHouse.

Wilson, Deirdre. 2018. Relevance Theory and Literary Interpretation. In *Reading Beyond the Code: Literature & Relevance Theory*. Edited by Terence Cave and Deirdre Wilson. Oxford: Oxford University Press, pp. 185–204.

Wire, Antoinette Clark. 2011. *The Case for Mark Composed in Performance*. Eugene: Cascade.

Wright, Brian J. 2017. *Communal Reading in the Time of Jesus: A Window into Early Christian Reading Practices*. Minneapolis: Fortress.

religions   MDPI

Article

A Glossary of New Testament Narrative Criticism with Illustrations

James L. Resseguie

Winebrenner Theological Seminary, Findlay, OH 45840, USA; resseguiej@findlay.edu

Received: 10 February 2019; Accepted: 15 March 2019; Published: 21 March 2019

check for
updates

Abstract: This is the first stand-alone glossary of New Testament narrative-critical terms in the English language. It is an alphabetical listing of prominent terms, concepts, and techniques of narrative criticism with illustrations and cross-references. Commonly used terms are defined and illustrated, these include character, characterization, double entendre, misunderstanding, implied author, implied reader, irony, narrator, point of view, plot, rhetoric, and other constitutive elements of a narrative. Lesser-known terms and concepts are also defined, such as carnivalesque, composite character, defamiliarization, fabula, syuzhet, hybrid character, MacGuffin, masterplot, primacy/recency effect, and type-scene. Major disciplines—for example, narratology, New Criticism, and reader-response criticism—are explained with glances at prominent literary critics/theorists, such as Aristotle, Mikhail Bakhtin, Wayne Booth, Seymour Chatman, Stanley Fish, E. M. Forster, Gérard Genette, Wolfgang Iser, and Susan Sniader Lanser.

Keywords: narrative criticism; narratology; literary terms; literary criticism; reader-response criticism; New Criticism; close reading

1. Introduction

Narrative criticism focuses on how the New Testament works as literature. The "what" of a narrative (content) and the "how" (rhetoric and structure) are analyzed as a complete tapestry, an organic whole. Narrative critics are concerned primarily with the literariness of New Testament narratives or the qualities that make them literature. It is a shift away from traditional historical-critical methods to how the text communicates meaning as a self-contained unit, an undivided whole. Of the three main components of a literary work—author, text, reader—narrative criticism focuses primarily on the text. It attends to the constitutive features of narratives, such as characterization, setting, plot, literary devices, point of view, narrator, implied author, and implied reader.

The precursors of narrative criticism are Russian formalism, French structuralism, and New Criticism. In 1982, David Rhoads coined the term "narrative criticism" to describe this new literary approach to the Gospel of Mark (Rhoads 1982). Also in 1982, David Rhoads and Donald Michie analyzed Mark from a narrative-critical perspective, focusing specifically on the narrator, point of view, literary technique, setting, plot, and character (Rhoads and Michie 1982). In 1983, R. Alan Culpepper published a groundbreaking narrative-critical study on the Fourth Gospel. Culpepper was influenced by the literary critic Seymour Chatman who explored the narrative dynamics of a text in terms of its story (the content) and its discourse (the how). The influence of Chatman can be seen in Culpepper's opening statement to *Anatomy of the Fourth Gospel*: "Our aim is to contribute to the understanding of the gospel as a narrative text, what it is and how it works (Culpepper 1983, p. 5). This twofold emphasis on story ("what it is") and discourse ("how it works") became the focus of narrative criticism in its early years. Short articles on narrative criticism introduced readers to the basic concepts and techniques of the new discipline (Malbon 2008; Tull 2013; Resseguie 2013b; Resseguie forthcoming (a)

"Narrative Criticism/Narratology"). Full length introductions served as readers' guides to narrative criticism (Powell 1990; Marguerat and Bourquin 1999; Tolmie 1999; Resseguie 2005).

Initially, New Testament narrative criticism focused on the four canonical gospels and Acts, but later turned its attention to the narrative features of the book of Revelation (Barr 1998, 2016; Resseguie 1998, 2005, 2009, forthcoming (b) "Narrative Features"). Recently, a plethora of studies on characters and characterization in the gospels and Acts have relied on the insights of narrative criticism and narratology—for example, Rhoads and Syreeni (1999); Malbon (2000, 2009); Elliot (2011); Hunt et al. (2013); Skinner (2013); Skinner and Hauge (2014); and Dicken and Snyder (2016). Initially, narrative criticism relied on formalism and close readings of narrative texts. Today, it has moved beyond formalism and appropriated other approaches to the New Testament. It has examined the politics of the first century world (Horsley 2001; Carter 2004) and the social world of the New Testament (Rhoads 2004), applied feminist criticism to narrative criticism (Anderson 1983; Malbon 1983), incorporated the insights of reader-response criticism to narrative criticism (Powell 2001; Powell 2011; Resseguie 2016), and applied cognitive narratology to New Testament narrative criticism (Hongisto 2010; Green 2016; see Herman 2013).

This is the first stand-alone glossary of New Testament narrative-critical terms in the English language. It is an alphabetical listing of prominent terms, concepts, and techniques of narrative criticism with illustrations and cross-references. Inevitably some terms are missing from the glossary, and some readers may wonder why other terms are included. However, as a short compendium of narrative criticism, it contains many of the major terms, concepts, and techniques of New Testament narrative criticism. (Although this is the first stand-alone glossary of New Testament narrative criticism, Daniel Marguerat and Yvan Bourquin have an abbreviated glossary at the end of their introduction to narrative criticism (Marguerat and Bourquin 1999, pp. 173–78). Janice Capel Anderson and Stephen D. Moore also provide a glossary at the end of their introduction, *Mark and Method* (Anderson and Moore 2008, pp. 233–43).)

2. A Glossary of New Testament Narrative Criticism[1]

affective fallacy → **New Criticism**.

alazon → **character**.

ambiguity → **double entendre** and **misunderstanding**.

anagnorisis ("recognition") → **plot** and **type-scene**.

anaphora: "Anaphora" is the repetition of the same expression at the beginning of two or more successive clauses or sentences to add force to an argument. For example, the writer of the book of Hebrews reiterates the word "by faith" at the beginning of sentences to foreground a theological perspective:

> *By faith* we understand ...
>
> *by faith* Abel ...
>
> *by faith* Noah ...
>
> *by faith* Abraham ...
>
> *by faith* Isaac ...
>
> *by faith* Jacob ...
>
> *by faith* Joseph ...
>
> *by faith* Moses ...

---

[1] All the terms in this glossary are in alphabetical order and in **boldface**. Any term that is not itself the subject of an entry is also in **boldface** with a cross-reference to an entry where it is discussed.

> *by faith* the people passed through the Red Sea . . .
>
> *by faith* the walls of Jericho fell . . .
>
> *by faith* Rahab . . . (Hebrews 11).[2]

In Matthew 13, the gospel writer introduces a series of parables with the anaphoric phrase "the kingdom of heaven is like":

> *The kingdom of heaven is like* a mustard seed . . .
>
> *The kingdom of heaven is like* yeast . . .
>
> *The kingdom of heaven is like* treasure hidden in a field . . .
>
> *The kingdom of heaven is like* a merchant . . .
>
> *The kingdom of heaven is like* a net . . . (Matt. 13: 31, 33, 44, 45, 47).

antagonist → **character**.

antithesis → **parallelism**.

aside → **characterization**.

carnivalesque: "Carnivalesque" is a term coined by Mikhail Bakhtin to describe the upside-down world of carnival. As a literary device, carnivalesque flouts conventions of authority and inverts social hierarchies of the existing culture. It expresses "life drawn out of its *usual* rut" and "the reverse side of the world (*'monde à l'envers'*)" in which normally suppressed voices of the culture mock everyday social hierarchies and the voices of the status quo (Bakhtin 1984, p. 122). Bakhtin identifies four basic categories that characterize carnivalesque.

(1) The laws, prohibitions, restrictions, and hierarchical structures that are associated with everyday life are suspended in carnival. As a result, "a special carnival category goes into effect: *free and familiar contact among people*" (Bakhtin 1984, p. 123, emphasis Bakhtin).

(2) The latent sides of human nature reveal and express themselves in carnival. "The behavior, gesture, and discourse of a person are freed from the authority of all hierarchical positions (social estate, rank, age, property)" (Bakhtin 1984, p. 123). The everyday is overturned in favor of an inside-out world.

(3) Carnival combines "the sacred with the profane, the lofty with the low, the great with the insignificant, the wise with the stupid" (Bakhtin 1984, p. 123).

(4) The last of Bakhtin's carnivalistic categories is profanation. Blasphemy, mocking, and deriding are common acts of debasing during carnival.

The primary act of carnival is the mock crowning and subsequent de-crowning of a carnival king. It is a "dualistic ambivalent ritual" that typifies the inside-out world of carnival and the "*joyful relativity* of all structure and order" (Bakhtin 1984, p. 124, emphasis Bakhtin). In carnival, the one who is crowned is the opposite of a real king (a slave or jester), and the symbols of crown, scepter, and robe that symbolize structures of authority in the ordinary world take on new meaning in carnival's mock ritual. They become "almost stage props" that undermine the "heavy" and "serious" structures of the everyday world (Bakhtin 1984, p. 124). But coronation is incomplete without de-coronation: regal vestments are stripped off, the crown and scepter are removed, and the mock king is beaten. Although de-coronation appears to be "naked, absolute negation and destruction," it is actually a positive image of "constructive death" (Bakhtin 1984, p. 125).

---

[2] All scriptural references, unless otherwise noted, are from the New Revised Standard Version (NRSV).

The passion narrative of the First Gospel is imbued with the carnivalesque (Matt. 27:27–31). The soldier's investiture of the mock king emphasizes the "joyful relativity" of all structures and order. They place a scepter (reed) in Jesus's right hand and kneel before him in scornful honor (Matt. 27:29). Their gallows humor is a form of carnivalistic laughter that heightens both the dualistic and ambivalent symbols of this mock ritual. The gentile soldiers deride Jesus as "King of the Jews" (Matt. 27:29), but their carnivalistic laughter turns out to be true: Jesus is indeed "King of the Jews". De-crowning completes the act of mock coronation. Jesus's royal cloak and scepter are taken away and his own clothes are put on. The crowning and de-crowning appears to be absolute negation: jeering, abuse, spitting, and mockery of an imposter. But the celebration of negativity has a positive side. Jesus inaugurates a new kind of order, a different type of rule in which the old ways of structuring this world are shattered and are replaced with a new kind of kingship.

catastrophe → plot.

character: "Characters" are the **dramatis personae**—the persons in the story—who may be major or minor characters that play a role in the plot. The **protagonist** or hero is the chief character in the plot around whom the action centers. An **antagonist** is a rival or opponent of the protagonist. In the gospels, Jesus is the protagonist while the religious authorities are often pitted against him as the antagonists. **Flat** and **round characters** are terms used by E. M. Forster in *Aspects of the Novel* (Forster [1927] 2005) to describe character types. A flat character is a two-dimensional character constructed around a single idea or quality that is summed up in a single phrase or sentence. A round character is three-dimensional and possesses several complex traits. "The test of a round character is whether it is capable of surprising in a convincing way. If it never surprises, it is flat. If it does not convince, it is flat pretending to be round" (Forster [1927] 2005, p. 81). For example, Jesus and the disciples are round characters with complex and—in the case of the disciples—conflicting traits. The Pharisees, on the other hand, are flat characters that lack complexity and exhibit a single trait of duplicity or obstructiveness. As individuals, however, the Pharisees are complex and surprising (e.g., Nicodemus in John 3; Saul/Paul in Acts). Identifying a character as flat or round is not as important as identifying the singular traits that make a character complex and surprising, or unconvincing and predictable.

Flat and round characters can either be **dynamic** (developing) or **stati** (un-developing).c Dynamic characters undergo change throughout the course of a narrative, displaying new behaviors and changed outlooks and can step outside the bounds of the narrative. "The change may be a large or a small one; it may be positive or negative; but it is something significant and basic, not some minor change of habit or opinion" (Arp and Johnson 2017, p. 107). A dynamic character—or what Thomas Docherty calls **kinetic** character—is capable of being absent from the text. "This character's motivation extends beyond that which is merely necessary for the accomplishment of the design of the plot, and he or she 'moves' in other spheres than the one we are engaged in reading" (Docherty 1983, p. 224). On the other hand, static characters are cardboard figures that do not develop or change and cannot step outside the bounds of the narrative. They are simply a function of the plot (Docherty 1983, p. 224). Generally, round characters are dynamic and flat characters are static. But as Shlomith Rimmon-Kenan notes in *Narrative Fiction*, round characters can be complex yet un-developing and flat characters can be simple yet developing (Rimmon-Kenan 2002, pp. 40–41). The importance of plotting the development of a dynamic character cannot be underestimated. According to Laurence Perrine, the "change [in a character] is usually at the heart of the story and defining and explaining the change will be the best way to arrive at its meaning" (Arp and Johnson 2017, p. 107).

Other character types include **stock**, **composite character**, **foil**, **walk-on**, and **hybrid character**. A **stock character** is a type that appears repeatedly in narratives and is recognized as part of the conventions of a literary genre. In fairy tales, the cruel stepmother and the charming prince are stock characters (Harmon 2012, p. 456). In film noirs, the femme fatale, an attractive yet dangerous woman, is a stock character of this genre. In ancient Greek comedy, the **eiron** is a stock character along with its opposite type, the **alazon**. The eiron pretends to know less than he knows and speaks in understatement, while the alazon is the braggart who claims to know more than he knows. In John 9, the exchange between the man born blind and the religious leaders is a classic example of an eiron dissembling the boastful claims of an alazon. Although the religious authorities revile the man born blind and call him a man "born entirely in sins" (John 9:34), the healed man gains the upper hand by feigning ignorance: "Do you also want to become his disciples?" (John 9:27c). Then he lectures the learned authorities on basic theology:

> We know that God does not listen to sinners, but he does listen to one who worships him and obeys his will. Never since the world began has it been heard that anyone opened the eyes of a person born blind (John 9:31–32).

On the eiron-character type, see Whitenton (2016).

A **composite character** is similar to a stock character. But the term designates two or more historical figures that are construed as a single character. For example, Luke's development of the three Herods in the gospel and Acts—Herod the Great, Herod Antipas, and Herod Agrippa I—are historical rulers whose traits have merged to form a single composite character. Frank Dicken has shown that this "Herod" is an amalgamation of rulers who function in the narrative as "an actualization of Satan's desire to impede the spread of the good news though his ["Herod's"] rejection of the gospel message and through political persecution", for example the execution of John (Luke 9:7–9), Jesus (Acts 4:24–28), James (Acts 12:1–2), and the attempted execution of Peter (Acts 12:3–5) (Dicken 2014, p. 7). Pharaoh is also a composite/stock character who functions as an opponent and persecutor of the people of God. He appears at the exodus of the Israelites out of Egypt (cf. Exodus 14–15), re-appears in Matthew's Gospel as Herod (the Great) who seeks to destroy Israel's new Moses (cf. Matt. 2:1–18), and appears once more in Revelation as the "great dragon" or "ancient serpent" who pursues and persecutes the people of God on their journey to the new promised land, the new Jerusalem (cf. Rev. 12: 13–17).

A **foil** is literally a contrasting background such as a sheet of shiny metal that is placed under jewels to enhance their brilliance. In literature, a foil is a character that enhances the distinctive characteristics of another character through contrast (Harmon 2012, p. 202). For example, the wealthy who contribute out of their abundance are foils for the poor widow who puts into the treasury far less but gives far more (Mark 12:41–44; Luke 21:1–4). Narrative settings can contrast with each other and thus serve as foils. For example, Babylon, a city of oppression and exploitation, contrasts with the new Jerusalem, a city of abundance and perfection (Rev. 18 and 21–22). The throne on which Jesus is crucified and exalted—the cross—contrasts with the opulent throne of earthly rulers.

Walk-on is a term used by Seymour Chatman for characters that are not fully delineated and individualized but are "mere elements of the setting" (Chatman 1978, p. 139). They do not qualify as characters—even as stock characters—but are part of the background. Yet they can play an important role as human barricades or grumblers that voice conventional societal norms. For example, the crowd in Luke 19:1–10 is an immoveable barrier to Zacchaeus's quest to see Jesus, underscoring not only the difficulty of the tax collector's quest but also his resolve (19:3). Also, the crowd functions like an ancient Greek chorus that provides commentary and perspective on characters and the meaning of their actions. They voice the conventional religious and social attitudes of the first century. "He [Jesus] has gone to be the guest of one who is a sinner" (Luke 19:7). Roman soldiers are also walk-ons—faceless and nameless characters of the crucifixion that are necessary for the story but are seldom delineated. (An exception is the centurion of Luke 23:47 who is individualized—that is, given a voice—and is a foil to the authorities that condemned Jesus to death.)

A **hybrid character** blends characteristic of humans with the inhuman or the monstrous with human traits. Examples of mythological hybrids include the centaur with the face, arms, and trunk of a human and the body of a horse; the Greek sphinx with the face of a woman and the body of a lion with wings; and the manticore with the head of a man and three rows of teeth, the body of a lion, and a scorpion-like or dragon tail. Hybrid characters represent the divided and conflicted nature of humanity. For example, the centaur depicts the unbridled and uncontrollable side of humanity. The Greek sphinx represents the cunning, trickster nature of humans. In Sophocles' Oedipus narratives the sphinx devoured all who could not answer its puzzling riddle: "What is the creature that walks on four legs in the morning, two legs at noon, and three legs in the evening." Oedipus correctly answers the riddle (it is a human) and the sphinx throws herself to death. The manticore with its monstrous appearance and shark-like teeth represents the bestial or vicious trait of human beings.

Hybrid characters are also found in biblical literature, most notably the bizarre characters of the book of Revelation. The evil hybrids of Revelation are the locusts from the abyss (Rev. 9:3–11), the beast from the sea (Rev. 11:7; 13:1–10, 18; 17:8), and the beast from the land (Rev. 13:11–17; 16:13; 19:20; 20:10). For example, the locusts from the abyss combine human traits with monstrous characteristics: faces like human faces, hair like woman's hair, teeth like lions' teeth, and tails like scorpion tails. The merger of the human with the inhuman represents the collusion of the world below with this world in Revelation's three-part universe (the world above, this world, and the world below). They signify a world turned upside down and inside out and exemplify what the world would be like if God gave free and unrestrained reign to evil. The beast from the sea combines animal traits (leopard, bear, lion) with human characteristics (a human number, 666, in Rev. 13:18), and the beast from the land has two horns like a lamb yet is clearly human (Rev. 13:11).

Other hybrids of Revelation are of a different sort. The four living creatures in Rev. 4:6b-8 combine traits of the world above (six wings; eyes in front and behind and around and inside) with animal and human traits from this world (lion, ox, eagle, and human). Whereas the locusts represent this world torn asunder, the four living creatures depict a world in complete harmony with its Creator (Resseguie forthcoming (b) "Narrative Features").

characterization: Two commonly recognized methods for the presentation of characters are **showing** (also called **dramatic method** or **indirect presentation**) and **telling** (also called **direct presentation**). In showing, the author or narrator presents the characters talking and acting from which the reader infers character traits and motives. According to Seymour Chatman, a character trait is the minimal persistent quality of a character that enables the reader to distinguish one character from another (Chatman 1978, pp. 121–26). In showing, character traits are revealed through speech, actions, clothing, physical description, posture, affect, gender, and socio-economic status (Dinkler 2017, pp. 691–92). What characters say, what they wear, what they do, how they relate to others, and how they appear, reveal defining traits (Resseguie 2005, p. 121; Resseguie 2009, pp. 38–39). What others say about them and how they respond enhance characterization. In addition, literary foils amplify character traits while symbolic settings magnify characters' speech and actions. Michal Beth Dinkler has shown how silence—what is unsaid in the telling of a tale, including gaps and ambiguities—provides a window into a character's traits (Dinkler 2013). In Luke 7:36–50, the uninvited, unnamed woman is silent, yet her symbolic action speaks: "she honors Jesus as she anoints him" (Dinkler 2013, p. 122). Jesus also embraces silence in this scene when he accepts her actions and behavior without comment, setting the stage for conflict with the host, Simon the Pharisee.

Interior monologue (also called an **unspoken soliloquy**) is a conspicuous method of showing a character's traits. It is a "species of stream of consciousness which undertakes to present to the reader the course and rhythm of consciousness precisely as it occurs in a character's mind" (Abrams and Harpham 2015, p. 379). Robert Scholes and Robert Kellogg define interior monologue as "a direct, immediate presentation of the unspoken thoughts of a character without any intervening narrator" (Scholes et al. 2006, p. 177). Interior monologues in the gospels provide a glimpse into a character's motivations, thinking, and *Weltanschauung* (worldview). Philip Sellew and Michal Beth Dinkler offer several examples of interior monologues in Luke's parables (Sellew 1992; Dinkler 2015). For example, the rich farmer's self-talk in Luke 12:16–20 reveals a tragic flaw of hubris:

> "What should I do, for I have no place to store my crops?" Then he said, "I will do this: I will pull down my barns and build larger ones, and there I will store my grain and my goods. And I will say to my soul, "Soul, you have ample goods laid up for many years; relax, eat, drink, be merry" (Luke 12:17b–19).

An unspoken soliloquy in Luke 7:39 reveals not only Simon the Pharisee's point of view; it educates the reader on the cultural and religious perspectives of the first century. "If this man [Jesus] were a prophet, he would have known who and what kind of woman this is who is touching him—that she is a sinner." (Interior monologues are also found at Luke 12:42–46; 15:11–32; 16:1–8; 18:2–5; 20:9–16.)

An author/narrator also uses **names** and **epithets** to amplify character traits. Proper names are "saturated with meaning" and are prominent ways of highlighting characteristics (Hochman 1985, p. 37). For example, the character named Abaddon in Revelation means "destruction" (9:11), Apollyon means "Destroyer" (9:11), and the beast's name in 13:18 is a number saturated with meaning. In Mark 5:1–20, the foreign possessing power of the demoniac is called "Legion." Names—whether an expanded name or a shortened, personal name—mark seminal moments in a narrative and accent a character's development. The story of Mary Magdalene in John 20:1–18 is an example of the use of a personal name at a crucial point to heighten the importance of a discovery. The narrator uses Mary's full name—Mary Magdalene—as bookends of the narrative (John 20:1, 18). Then he shortens her name to "Mary" (John 20:11); meanwhile, the angels and Jesus address her as "woman" in their encounter with Mary (John 20:13, 15). But when the veil of incomprehension is lifted, and she recognizes the risen Jesus, both her formal name and the generic—"woman"—are cast aside, and she is called by her personal name "Mary" (John 20:16).

In the Fourth Gospel, Peter's priority as the first disciple who enters the empty tomb is marked by an expansion of his name. In John 20:2–10, Peter is introduced into the narrative with his full name, "Simon Peter" (John 20:2), which is the normal way the disciple is mentioned at the outset (Elliott 1972). Then the narrator shortens his name to "Peter" twice (in 20:3 and 20:4), which is the usual way of referring to him after the formal introduction. But at the crucial moment of discovery—when he enters the tomb and sees the linen wrappings and the soudarion rolled up by itself—the narrator discards the shortened name. He does not say, "*Peter . . .* went into the tomb," as might be expected. Rather, the narrator lengthens his name to call attention to the discovery and Peter's priority: "*Simon Peter . . .* went into the tomb" (John 20:6–7; Resseguie 2001, p. 150 n. 135). On names see Docherty (1983, chp. 2); Dawsey (1986, pp. 143–47).

An **epithet** is an adjective or adjectival phrase that describes a character's distinctive quality. In Revelation, John uses no less than five sobriquets or epithets to define Satan's character: "The *great dragon . . .* that *ancient serpent*, who is called the *Devil* and *Satan*, the *deceiver* of the whole world . . . was thrown down to earth" (Rev. 12:9). In the Fourth Gospel, an unnamed character is given a descriptive phrase not only to underline his unique relationship to Jesus (cf. John 13:25); it underscores his singular trait of privilege that enables him to "see" what other disciples cannot "see" (e.g., John 20:8; 21:7). This disciple—"the one whom Jesus loved" (John 13:23–26; 19:26–27; 20:2–10; 21:7, 20–23)—represents the ideal point of view of the gospel, the ideological perspective that John wants the reader to embrace (Resseguie 2013a, 2016).

An expanded description can alert the reader to a striking development in a narrative. A case in point are the descriptions given to the beloved disciple in John 20:2–9. The anonymous disciple is introduced with his traditional, identifying marker: "the other disciple, the one whom Jesus loved" (John 20:2). Afterwards, "the one whom Jesus loved" is dropped and the beloved disciple is referred to as "the other disciple" (John 20:3, 4). But the abbreviated designation, "the other disciple," is expanded at a key moment in the narrative: "Then the other disciple, *who reached the tomb first*, also went in, and he saw and believed" (John 20:8). Although Peter is the first to enter and see the discarded garments in the tomb, the beloved disciple is the first to reach the tomb and to interpret the significance of the abandoned grave clothes.

In telling, the narrator intervenes and adds authoritative comments on characters and their disposition. An omniscient/intrusive narrator—one who sees all and comments on what he or she sees—can peer into a character's mind and reveal his or her thinking, feelings, and motives (also called **inside view**). A narrator may also provide commentary on characters or events that gives the reader/hearer information that may or may not be available to the characters in the story. This commentary is called an **aside** (Rhoads et al. 2012, pp. 42–43; Sheeley 1992). For example, the narrator of Acts provides important information to the reader on the beliefs of the Sadducees and Pharisees through an aside: "The Sadducees say there is no resurrection, or angel, or spirit; but the Pharisees acknowledge all three" (Acts 23:8). (The NRSV puts this verse in parenthesis to show that it is an intrusive comment.) Whenever the narrator relies on telling, the reader does not need to infer the attributes of a character from what the character says or does. Rather the narrator provides information about a character's traits and motivations.

Other aspects of telling go beyond basic information and delve into a character's motivations and thinking. The narrator may also provide an evaluation or judgment concerning the character. For example, the disciples "did not understand about the loaves, *but their hearts were hardened*" (Mark 6:52). The phrase "their hearts were hardened" is the narrator's evaluation of the disciples' blindness. In the Fourth Gospel, the narrator tells the reader what to anticipate and how to evaluate an antagonist and his words. For example, when Judas is first introduced, the narrator adds this comment: Judas "was going to betray [Jesus]" (John 6:71). Later, when Judas complains about an expensive perfume that was used to anoint Jesus—an extravagance that he claims should have been used to help the poor—the narrator intervenes. He explains not only Judas's motive for the complaint; he also reveals a disqualifying trait that was previously unknown to the reader. "He said this not because he cared about the poor, but because he was a thief; he kept the common purse and used to steal what was put into it" (John 12:6). Because inside views are taken as authoritative comments by a **reliable narrator**—one that shares the perspective of the implied author—they influence how the reader reads the narrative, evaluates characters, and understands the ideological norms and beliefs of the narrative. (The opposite of a reliable narrator is an **unreliable** or **fallible narrator**, who does not share the perception, interpretation, and evaluation of the implied author. Although an unreliable narrator occurs in modern literature, he or she is unknown in New Testament literature.) On reliable and unreliable narrators see Booth (1983, pp. 158–59), and on the concept of unreliability see Shen (2013).

chiasmus (chiasm): "Chiasmus" or "chiasm" is derived from the Greek letter chi (written X). An X symbolizes the crossover pattern of words, phrases, clauses, or ideas that are repeated in reversed order. The simplest type of chiasmus is an A B B' A' pattern as seen in Mark 2:27:

> The *sabbath* was made (A)
>
> for *humankind* (B),
>
> and not *humankind* (B')
>
> for the *sabbath* (A').

In Luke 22:42, a chiasm illustrates the conflict Jesus has within himself concerning his mission and his desire to follow the Father's will:

> Father, if you are willing (A),
>
> remove this cup from me (B);
>
> yet, not my will (B')
>
> yours be done (A').

The first person singular (me, my) is placed within the second singular (you, yours), which underscores Jesus' resolve: his will is completely enclosed in the Father's will.

The writer of Ephesians uses a chiasmus of grace and peace to bracket the entire book:

> Grace to you (A)
>
> and peace . . . (B) (Ephesians 1:2).

Peace (B′) . . .

Grace (A′) . . . (Ephesians 6:23, 24).

And Paul uses an interlocking chiasmus to highlight the mystery of the Christian faith in 1 Timothy 3:16. Two worlds—the world above (spirit, angels, glory) and this world (flesh, Gentiles, world), which were separated or at odds with one another at the beginning, are joined together by the life, mission, and death of Jesus (Resseguie 2000, p. 817; Resseguie 2005, p. 60).

[Jesus] was revealed in flesh (A),

vindicated in spirit (B),

seen by angels (B′),

proclaimed among Gentiles (A′),

believed in throughout the world (A),

taken up in glory (B).

The first chiasm (A, B, B′, A′) interlocks with the second (B′, A′, A, B), as the following diagram illustrates:

flesh (A)

spirit (B)

angels (B′)

Gentiles (A′).

. . . .

angels (B′)

Gentiles (A′)

world (A)

glory (B).

close reading → **New Criticism.**
composite character → **character.**

defamiliarization: The Russian formalist Victor Shklovsky coined and popularized the concept of **defamiliarization** (**ostranenie**, which literally means "making strange") in his article "Art as Technique" (Shklovsky [1917] 2012). (The concept precedes Shklovsky and is found at least as early as the Romantic critic Coleridge [1817] 1983). Defamiliarization—also called **estrangement**—is the creative distortion of the world of ordinary perception to renew the reader's diminished capacity for fresh awareness. Everyday language leads to over-automatization or automatic perception that results in a stale view of the world. Defamiliarization jars the reader out of the lethargy of the habitual and forces the reader to see the world anew. The reader's renewed mode of perception is achieved through literary devices or techniques that disrupt automatic perception—slowing down the reading process so that the familiar no longer seems familiar. Shklovsky provides several examples of defamiliarization techniques: a novel point of view, the substitution of the unexpected for the expected, a subtle twisting of a commonplace phrase, and the deformation of a familiar context (Shklovsky [1917] 2012; Resseguie 1988, 1990, 1991). The process of "making strange" forces the reader to view worn-out rhetoric, familiar contexts, stereotyped phrases, and jaded conventions in unfamiliar ways.

Defamiliarization occurs wherever language and conventions are deformed. In Mark, a jarring phrase—"with persecutions"—gives the hearers (disciples) and readers pause:

Jesus said, "Truly I tell you, there is no one who has left house or brothers or sisters or mother or father or children or fields, for my sake and for the sake of the good news, who will not receive a hundredfold now in this age—houses, brothers and sisters, mothers and children, and fields *with persecutions*—and in the age to come eternal life" (Mark 10:29–30).

Initially the saying confirms the disciples' decision to follow Jesus—for loss is gain and what is left behind will be multiplied many times over. The expectation is established by first listing the family members and possessions that have been left behind: "house *or* brothers *or* sisters *or* mother *or* father *or* children *or* fields." It is then reinforced by listing what is gained in the plural: "houses *and* brothers *and* sisters *and* mothers *and* children *and* fields" (author's translation). The repetition of what is left behind along with what is gained creates in the reader what E. H. Gombrich calls the "etc. principle"—that is, "the assumption we tend to make ... that to see a few members of a series is to see them all" (Gombrich 1961, p. 220). With the reader's expectations firmly established, Mark shatters them with the unexpected phrase "with persecutions". Not only is the phrase surprising; it appears out of place in a saying intended to encourage the disciples in their decision to follow Jesus. Matthew and Luke, who are likely dependent on Mark, removed the offending words from their accounts (cf. Matt. 19:29; Luke 18:29–30).

The Russian formalists also recognized that a plot defamiliarizes a story. They used the terms **fabula** and **syuzhet** to differentiate between story and plot. The fabula is the basic story stuff of a narrative while the syuzhet is the representation of that story stuff as a concrete plot. A story can be made unfamiliar by its reformulation into a plot with jarring twists, omissions, digressions, and postponement of important information. In other words, the syuzhet is the fabula defamiliarized. Shklovsky uses Lawrence Sterne's *Tristram Shandy* as an example of a story that is deformed when it is reformulated into a concrete plot. The normal temporal-causal sequence of narrated events (the familiar way) is disrupted when reshaped into a plot that distorts the story (the unfamiliar way). Temporal displacements, digressions, and causal disruptions (e.g., placing the *effects* before their *causes*) impede the reader's ability to reassemble the story, and thus what may appear as a familiar story is upended by unfamiliar plotting. The defamiliarized plot causes the reader to pay attention and to see the story in a new, unjaded way. Similarly, a story within a gospel can be made more forceful by the temporal displacement of relevant information. The plot (syuzhet) of Luke 7:36–50 omits important information at the beginning and places it later, after the reader's expectations and judgments are firmly established (Resseguie 1991, pp. 145–46; Resseguie 2016, pp. 18–19). The chronological storyline (fabula) of Luke 7:36–50 is as follows:

(1) Simon invites Jesus to a dinner party.
(2) *But the Pharisee omits acts of hospitality.*
(3) An uninvited woman crashes the party and anoints and washes Jesus's feet.
(4) Simon demurs.
(5) Jesus tells a parable.
(6) *He contrasts the woman's behavior with the Pharisee's negligence.*
(7) Jesus pronounces the woman forgiven of her sins.

This is the story, but it is not the plot. The information in (2) —Simon's omission of acts of hospitality—is only revealed to the reader at (6). By a temporal displacement of crucial and damaging information concerning the Pharisee, the syuzhet (plot) "makes strange" Simon's behavior as well as first-century religious views concerning boundaries between "righteous" and "sinner" (Resseguie 1992, 2016, pp. 7–22).

dénouement (resolution) → **plot**.

direct presentation → **characterization**.

double entendre and **misunderstanding:** A "double entendre" or double meaning is a word or phrase that is ambiguous, usually having two meanings, and the reader/hearer must choose one meaning and reject the other. For example, *katalambanein* in the Prologue of John is a double entendre that can mean "understand" or "overcome" (John 1:5). The King James Version translates it as "comprehend": "The light shines in the darkness, and the darkness does not comprehend it". On the other hand, the New Revised Standard Version understands it in the second sense: "The light shines in the darkness, and the darkness did not overcome it". In this instance, both meanings are intended, although translators are obliged to choose one meaning over the other. Darkness is not only uncomprehending of light; it is hostile to the light (Barrett 1978, pp. 158–59). Another double entendre is found in Nicodemus' confusion over *anōthen* which means "again" or "from above" (John 3:3). Did Jesus tell Nicodemus that "no one can see the kingdom of God without being born *from above*?" or did he say that "no one can see the kingdom of God without being born *again*?". Nicodemus assumes that Jesus is talking about a physical rebirth. "How can anyone be born after having grown old? Can one enter a second time into the mother's womb and be born?" (John 3:4). Jesus, however, is speaking about a birth from above, a spiritual rebirth (John 3:5–7).

A "misunderstanding" occurs when a double entendre, an ambiguous statement, or an ambiguous metaphor, is misinterpreted. The misunderstanding is then resolved either by Jesus or the narrator. J. H. Bernard offers a simple definition: "A saying of deep import is uttered by Jesus; His hearers misunderstand it, after a fashion that seems stupid; and then He repeats the saying in a slightly different form before He explains it and draws out its lesson" (Bernard 1929, 1: cxi). A misunderstanding occurs when a hearer selects one meaning for a double entendre or ambiguous metaphor rather than another, and assumes that meaning is correct (Bultmann 1971, 135n 1). Alan Culpepper identifies three parts to a misunderstanding in the Fourth Gospel (Culpepper 1983, p. 152).

(1) Jesus makes a claim using a double entendre or an ambiguous metaphor.
(2) The hearer selects one meaning for the statement over another possible meaning. Usually the hearer selects a literal meaning when Jesus intends a figurative meaning.
(3) Jesus or the narrator clarifies the misunderstanding with an explanation.

An illustration of a misunderstanding in John is found in the story of the woman at the well in John 4, which relies on an ambiguous metaphor "living water" (*hydōr zōn*). In part 1, Jesus asks a Samaritan woman for a drink of water, but she wonders why a Jew is asking a Samaritan for a drink. Jesus responds with a statement built on the ambiguous metaphor "living water": "If you knew the gift of God, and who it is that is saying to you, 'Give me a drink,' you would have asked him, and he would have given you living water" (John 4:10). In part 2, the woman assumes that Jesus knows about a flowing stream—one possible meaning of "living water"—that will make the fetching of water easier. "Sir, you have no bucket, and the well is deep. Where do you get that living water?" (John 4:11). In part 3, Jesus explains that the living water he provides is spiritual, not literal. "Everyone who drinks of this water [from the well] will be thirsty again, but those who drink of the water that I will give them will never be thirsty" (John 4:13–14).

One of the values of analyzing John's rhetorical devices is that it teaches the implied reader how to read (or the authorial audience, see Rabinowitz 1987). Specifically, a misunderstanding teaches the implied reader to move from a reading at the surface level to a deeper level. A surface reading sees only the everyday, the quotidian, the ordinary—just as the woman at the well understood "living water" at a physical, mundane level. Yet to read and to understand at this level is insufficient. The implied author wants the reader to move from the surface to a deeper, spiritual understanding.

Other misunderstandings in John include: 2:19–22, the hearers misunderstand the meaning of the temple; 4:31–34, the disciples misunderstand the nature of Jesus's "food"; 6:32–35; 41–42, the hearers misunderstand Jesus's origins; 6:51–53, the audience misunderstands what Jesus means by bread from heaven; 7:33–36, the Jews misunderstand what Jesus means by his departure; 8:31–33, the hearers misunderstand what Jesus means by freedom; 8:51–53, the audience misunderstands Jesus's claim about those who believe in him will not die, and 8:56–58, they misunderstand the saying about Abraham.

Misunderstandings also occur in the synoptic gospels—for example, the disciples do not understand about the "loaves," for their "hearts were hardened" (Mark 6:52). However, the synoptic misunderstandings do not rise to the level of a literary device such as that found in the Fourth Gospel.

dramatic irony → irony.

dramatic method → characterization.

dramatis personae → character.

dynamic character → character.

eiron → character.

epithet → characterization.

estrangement → defamiliarization.

fabula (in Russian formalism) → defamiliarization.

figurative language → rhetoric.

figures of speech → rhetoric.

figures of thought → rhetoric.

flat character → character.

focalization: "Focalization" is a term coined by Gérard Genette [1972] (1980) that is intended to refine **point of view** and **narrative perspective**. It asks two primary questions: "Who sees?" and "Who speaks?" in a narrative (Genette [1972] 1980, p. 186; Bal 2009, p. 146). The one who sees the events and happenings of the narrative—called **focus of character**—may be the same or different from the one who tells the story—called **focus of narration**. If the narrator chooses to relate events and happenings through the perspective of a character, the character is the one who *sees* the events of a narrative, but the narrator is the one who *speaks*. In John 6:19, the disciples of Jesus see what is happening. "They saw Jesus walking on the sea and coming near the boat, and they were terrified". The narrator records the events through the perspective of the disciples, including their emotional response, but the disciples do not tell the story. In Revelation, John, the prophet, who is exiled on the island of Patmos, sees and tells the events and happenings of the narrative. (In technical terms, he is both the **focalizer**, the one who sees, and the narrator, the one who tells). Although focalization attempts to refine and replace point of view, it is not superior to the concept of point of view. *The Living Handbook of Narratology* concludes that focalization is "fraught with considerable problems" and is "hardly so much superior to point of view that the old term [point of view] can be discarded" (Niederhoff 2013a). For more on focalization see Bal (2009, pp. 145–65) and Niederhoff (2013a).

focalizer → focalization.

focus of character → focalization.

focus of narration → focalization.

foil → character.

framing device: As the term implies, "framing devices" are words, phrases, and even entire narratives that serve as brackets or bookends for individual narratives or entire books. The framing devices discussed in this glossary are **chiasmus, inclusion (*inclusio*),** and **sandwich narrative** or **intercalation**.

Freytag's Pyramid → plot.

hamartia ("error" or "mistake of judgment") → **plot**.

hubris ("pride") → **plot**.

hybrid character → character.

implicit metaphor → simile and metaphor.

implied author → reader.

implied reader → reader and reader-response criticism.

inclusion (*inclusio*): "Inclusions" are words, phrases, or concepts that bracket narratives or larger units such as a section of a book or even an entire book. This is a framing device that identifies beginnings and endings of narratives or amplifies prominent themes and concepts of a story. For example, Matt. 1:23 opens with "Emmanuel," which means "God is with us," and closes with Jesus's saying, "I am with you always" (Matt. 28:20). In the book of Revelation, God's pronouncements are bookends for the narrative: "I am the Alpha and Omega" (Rev. 1:8) and "I am the Alpha and Omega, the beginning and the end" (Rev. 21:6). Similarly, Jesus's speech brackets the book with words nearly identical to those of God: "I am the first and the last" (Rev. 1:17) and "I am the Alpha and Omega, the first and the last, the beginning and the end" (Rev. 22:13). As these examples illustrate, inclusions underscore prominent theological themes.

Individual narratives may also be bracketed by words, phrases, and concepts that help identify the structure of a narrative as well as its themes. For example, Matthew's genealogy opens and closes with references to the Messiah, David, and Abraham (Matt. 1:1; 1:17). Within the inclusion are additional brackets that divide the genealogy into three sections of fourteen generations. As a result, Jesus's birth is placed within the entire sweep of Israel's history, and the inclusion amplifies prominent christological titles of the gospel.

indirect presentation → **characterization**.

inside view → **characterization** and **point of view/narrative perspective**.

intentional fallacy → **New Criticism**.

intercalation → **sandwich narrative**.

interior monologue → **characterization** and **point of view/narrative perspective**.

intrusive narrator → **narrator**.

irony: At its root "irony" has the notion of dissembling. The word is related to an ancient Greek character in comedy called the **eiron**, who pretends to know less than he knows. He speaks in understatement to dissemble the boastful claims of a braggart called the **alazon**. Peter Childs and Roger Fowler define irony as "a mode of discourse for conveying meanings different from, and usually opposite to, the professed or ostensible ones" (Childs and Fowler 2006, p. 123). Irony's effectiveness relies on the exploitation of the distance between words and events and their contexts. D. C. Muecke identifies three basic features of irony:

(1) Irony depends on a double-layered or two-story phenomenon for success. "At the lower level is the situation as it appears to the victim of irony (where there is a victim) or as it is deceptively presented by the ironist" (Muecke 1969, p. 19). The upper level is the situation as it appears to the reader or ironist.

(2) The ironist exploits a contradiction, incongruity, or incompatibility between the two levels.

(3) Irony plays upon the innocence of a character or victim. "Either a victim is confidently unaware of the very possibility of there being an upper level or point of view that invalidates his own, or an ironist pretends not to be aware of it" (Muecke 1969, p. 20).

All irony falls into two main categories: **verbal irony**, which applies to a statement, and **situational irony**, which applies to an event (Childs and Fowler 2006, p. 123). In verbal irony a contradiction occurs between what is expressed and what is implied. The writer or speaker makes explicit one attitude or evaluation but implies a different attitude or evaluation that is often the opposite of what is expressed (Abrams and Harpham 2015, p. 186). Appreciation of verbal irony depends upon recognizing a shared disparity between what a writer says and what a writer means. Take for example, the famous dictum that opens the novel *Pride and Prejudice*. "It is a truth universally acknowledged, that a single man in possession of a good fortune, must be in want of a wife" (Austin [1813] 2001, p. 3). Jane Austin employs verbal irony to deride the nineteenth-century assumption that a single woman must be in search of a wealthy husband. In general, irony relies on understatement, paradox, puns, and other forms of wit to heighten incongruities (Childs and Fowler 2006, p. 124). In the crucifixion scene in Mark 15:29–32a, verbal irony is enhanced by clues such as "Aha" and "shaking their heads".

> Those who passed by derided him, shaking their heads and saying, "Aha! You who would destroy the temple and build it in three days, save yourself, and come down from the cross!" In the same way the chief priests, along with the scribes, were also mocking him among themselves and saying, "He saved others; he cannot save himself. Let the Messiah, the King of Israel come down from the cross now, so that we may see and believe."

The irony works on two levels. On one level the speakers do not mean what they say. When the chief priests and scribes refer to Jesus as "Messiah, the King of Israel," they say this with tongue in cheek, for it is inconceivable that the long-awaited Messiah would be rejected and killed. The religious leaders believe they are upstairs in Muecke's diagram, and from their superior vantage point they view Jesus as a fraud. But in an ironic twist the verbal irony becomes situational irony. The chief priests and scribes are now downstairs, unaware of a second level to their own words. When they taunt, "Save yourself, and come down from the cross," little do they realize that Jesus's mission is to suffer and die (Mark 8:31; 9:31; 10:33–34). Similarly, the ironists are unaware of a second level of irony in their jeer, "he saved others, he cannot save himself" (Mark 15:31). As verbal irony, their jeer mocks the absurdity of a crucified Messiah; as situational or dramatic irony it voices "one of the supreme ironies of history" which eludes the religious leaders (Taylor 1960, p. 592).

Situational irony depends for its success on an incongruity or contradiction between what a speaker says and what the author intends. Whereas in verbal irony a contradiction or incongruity—shared by both speaker and reader—exists between what is said and what is intended, in situational irony the speaker is naïve about the irony and unaware that he or she is being ironical. Only the author and reader share insight into the irony. In Muecke's two-story phenomenon, the author and reader are in a superior position upstairs while the victim of the irony, the character or speaker, is downstairs unaware of the second level. **Dramatic irony** is a form of situational irony in which the audience or reader shares knowledge with the author about present or future circumstances of which the character is ignorant.

A famed case of dramatic irony occurs in Caiaphas's remarks to the chief priests and Pharisees: "You know nothing at all! You do not understand that it is better for you to have one man die for the people than to have the whole nation destroyed" (John 11:49–50). Although Caiaphas intends no irony, his statement drips with it. In Muecke's diagram, he is downstairs unaware of a second level of meaning to his words which the narrator exploits. The high priest's solution is merely a practical response to a troublemaker: Jesus's preaching and healing pose a threat to the safety of Israel. It is better to sacrifice one person to spare the nation than to have the Romans come and destroy the temple and the nation. Caiaphas says more than he intends but not less than what the narrator intends. A second level of meaning of which Caiaphas is unaware turns his straightforward statement into dramatic irony. The preposition "for" or "in place of" (*hyper*) can also have the meaning "on behalf of". Caiaphas intends "in place of". Jesus must die in place of Israel to spare the people. But the narrator intends "on behalf of". Jesus must die on behalf of the people. Jesus's death spares the people but not in the way Caiaphas thinks. The narrator clarifies the upstairs meaning for the reader: "He did not say this on his own, but being high priest that year he prophesied that Jesus was about to die for [*hyper*] the nation, and not for the nation only, but to gather into one the dispersed children of God" (John 11:51–52). The high priest "could not suspect that Jesus would die, not in place of Israel but on behalf of the true Israel" (Brown 1966, 1:442).

The above illustrations show the value of irony: It heightens narrative claims and truths in ways that straightforward discourse cannot achieve. There is no finer example of this function of irony than the Roman soldier's salute in the gospels: "Hail, King of the Jews" (Matt. 27:29; Mark 15:18; John 19:3). With verbal irony they mock Jesus as a dismal failure and a pretend king, while dramatic irony accents the truth. The narrator and reader who are upstairs know that the acclamation rings true in ways that the soldiers could not possibly understand. Not only is Jesus the King of the Jews, the soldiers' statement and actions also confirm the paradox of his rule. He is a suffering and rejected Messiah. Standard (non-ironical) discourse could not convey the nature of Jesus's mission as effectively as the gallows humor voiced by the Roman soldiers. (On irony in the New Testament see Camery-Hoggatt 1992; Duke 1985; Smith 1996, chp. 6; Resseguie 2001, pp. 28–41; Resseguie 2005, pp. 67–75.)

kernels and **satellites:** Seymour Chatman adopted the terms from Roland Barthes (1974) to describe the logical and hierarchical connections in a plot (Chatman 1978, pp. 53–56). Kernels are major events that move the plot forward and are essential to the plot's advancement. They "are narrative moments that give rise to cruxes in the direction taken by events" (Chatman 1978, p. 53). Since kernels determine the direction of the plot, they "cannot be deleted without destroying the narrative logic" (Chatman 1978, p. 53). On the other hand, satellites are minor events that are not crucial to the logic of the plot and can be deleted without damaging the narrative. If the kernels are viewed as the skeleton of the plot, then satellites are the flesh on the bones. They fill in, elaborate, and complete the kernel but could be deleted without affecting the plot's logic.

Frank J. Matera applied the concepts of kernels and satellites to Matthew (Matera 1987, pp. 233–53). For example, the Sermon on the Mount in Matthew 5–7 is a satellite in Matera's analysis that could be eliminated without destroying the logic of the narrative. On the other hand, the inauguration of Jesus's ministry in Matt. 4:12–17 is a kernel that is essential for the movement of the plot. The difficulty with this method of analysis is identifying the kernels that are essential to plot development from the satellites that are not. Because there is no agreed upon method to distinguish the kernels from the satellites, the concept has not gained currency in New Testament narrative criticism (Kingsbury 1991, p. xv).

kinetic character → character.

MacGuffin → setting.

masterplot: Masterplots are "recurrent skeletal stories, belonging to cultures and individuals that play a powerful role in questions of identity, values, and the understanding of life" (Abbott 2008, p. 236). They explore the quest for life's meaning or build upon questions of origins: the quest for identity (Who are we?); the quest for meaning (Where are we going?); the quest for reconciliation (How do we find our way back home?); the quest to determine our destiny (Are we free agents or is our destiny determined?). For example, the masterplot of Sophocles' Oedipus narrative is a story of conflict between free will and a destiny determined by life's constraints. Oedipus seeks to find a future that is free from the constraints placed upon him by his own heritage and environment. Can he escape his fate and determine his direction in life? Or is his life determined by events and circumstances beyond his control? Oedipus learned from the Oracle at Delphi that he is fated to kill his father Laius, the king of Thebes, and marry his mother, Jocasta. He determines to avoid this destiny by never returning to Corinth, which he mistakenly believes to be his place of origin. On the road he meets an unknown man whom he kills, and then he marries his widow, which assures that fate triumphs over individual will. The man he killed was his father, Laius, and the widow he married was his mother, Jocasta (cf. Abbott 2008, pp. 195–97; Resseguie 2005, pp. 203–4).

The masterplot of the book of Revelation is a quest story of the people of God in search of the new promised land. As the Israelites of old faced obstacles and received divine protection on their exodus to the promised land, so the people of God in Revelation—the followers of the Lamb—replicate the masterplot of peril and divine solace on their journey to the new Jerusalem. The good characters of Revelation aid the people of God in their quest for a vanished Eden, while the evil characters hinder their quest. The pharaoh of Revelation is the dragon with seven heads and ten horns who pursues the woman clothed with the sun and attempts to destroy her with a flood from his mouth (Rev. 12:3, 13, 15). But she is given two wings of a great eagle to escape to the wilderness where the earth comes to her aid by swallowing the pharaoh's torrent (12:14, 16). All this is reminiscent of the Exodus masterplot: Pharaoh pursues the escaping Israelites to the Red Sea (Exodus 14–15); eagles' wings carry a persecuted people to safety in the wilderness (Exodus 19:4; cf. Deuteronomy 32:11–12); and the earth engulfs Pharaoh's army (Exodus 15:12)—just as the earth swallows the dragon's flood in Revelation. (Resseguie forthcoming (b) "Narrative Features")

Another New Testament masterplot is humankind's desire to be independent and free; yet the quest for independence can also lead to disaster and a longing to return home. In the parable of the prodigal son in Luke 15:11–24, the younger son sets out on his quest for freedom, but disaster upends his drive for independence, and he sets out on a new quest to return to the father's house.

metaphor → **simile** and **metaphor.**

mise en scène → **setting.**

misunderstanding → **double entendre** and **misunderstanding.**

mythos → **plot.**

names → **characterization.**

narratee: "Narratee", coined by Gerald Prince (1971), designates a fictive audience—the person or persons to whom the narrator addresses the narrative. The narratee *does not* exist outside the text and is reconstructed from the text proper. (See the communication box of Seymour Chatman under **reader**). For example, the narrator of Matthew creates a fictive, idealized audience—the narratee—to whom the narrative is addressed. This narratee is familiar with Jewish customs, the scriptures, and the norms and conventions of the first-century Jewish world. Most New Testament narrative critics do not distinguish the narratee from the implied reader, although Malbon separates the two (Malbon 2008, p. 33). On the role of the narratee see Wolf Schmid (2013).

narrative perspective → **point of view/narrative perspective.**

narrative criticism → **introduction** and **narratology.**

narratology: In 1969, the term "narratology" (*narratologie* in French) was coined by Tzvetan Todorov (1969). It is concerned with the theory and practice of narrative in all literary forms. In America, early New Testament narratology is called **narrative criticism** (see introduction above). In practice, New Testament narrative criticism is more concerned with the sustained interpretation of individual narratives using theory than with theory itself. On the other hand, contemporary narratology is more concerned with the development of theory than with the sustained interpretation of individual narratives (Moore 2016, pp. 33–34).

The Living Handbook of Narratology defines narratology as "a humanities discipline dedicated to the study of the logic, principles, and practices of narrative representation" (Meister 2014). The list of areas of engagement is extensive: "cognitive narratology", "critical narratology", "feminist narratology", "gender narratology", "natural narratology", "postcolonial narratology", "narrative ethics", and "rhetorical narratology" to name a few.

Cognitive narratology has only been around a little more than twenty years (Herman 2013). It focuses on the nexus of narrative and mind, including how storytellers cue the mental lives of characters and how interpreters appropriate and fill in the cues (Herman 2013). Recently, New Testament narrative critics have used cognitive narratology to broaden and deepen the description of characters in the gospels. For example, Joel Green develops the characterization of Zacchaeus in Luke 19:1–10 using cognitive narratology to show how narrative descriptors influence readers' perceptions (Green 2016). Not only does Luke rely on several character traits to describe Zacchaeus—ruler, short, rich, sinner, son of Abraham, lost; he uses spatial descriptors to thicken and enlarge the tax collector's characterization, such as up and down, in and out, and near and far. As a result, spatial notations combine with negative character traits to influence the reader's perception of the tax collector. His diminutive stature parallels his lowly status; his shortness is emblematic of his social status as an outsider even among his own townspeople. Cognitive narratology is a promising field for narrative-critical research. On New Testament narratology in Germany, see Finnern (2010, 2014).

narrator: The "narrator" is the one who tells the story to a fictive, idealized audience—the narratee. In a third-person narrative, the narrator refers to characters by name or by "he", "she", or "they".

Third-person narrators know everything that needs to be known and have privileged access to characters' thoughts, motivations, and feelings. This narrator is called **omniscient**. All gospel narrators are third-person omniscient and **intrusive narrators**: narrators that not only know everything that needs to be known and have privileged access to characters' thoughts, feelings, and motivations, but also comment on characters and events and make judgments concerning them. An omniscient, intrusive narrator moves freely from character to character, event to event, and may provide **inside views** or **asides**. For example, the third-person omniscient and intrusive narrator of Mark offers this inside view (and judgment) on Jesus's disciple: "And they [the disciples] were utterly astounded, for they did not understand about the loaves, but their hearts were hardened" (Mark 6:51b–52). A narrator may also be omniscient yet remain **un-intrusive**. He or she describes and reports but avoids commentary or judgments. New Testament narrators are **reliable narrators**—that is, their perspectives and judgments coincide with those of the implied author. An **unreliable** or **fallible narrator** is one whose perspectives and judgments are at odds with the implied author and is not found in the New Testament.

In first-person narratives, the narrator speaks as "I" or "we" and is to some degree a participant in the story. The narrator may tell his or her own story ("I" as protagonist) or someone else's story ("I" as witness, Martin 1986, p. 135). The first-person narrator infers knowledge about characters' motivations and thoughts from what they do and say, but unlike the third-person omniscient narrator, he or she cannot delve into the thoughts and motivations of others. For example, the narrator of the book of Revelation is a participant in the story and uses the first person to tell the reader what he sees in heaven: "After this *I* looked, and there in heaven a door stood open," and "*I* saw a mighty angel" (Rev. 4:1; 5:2). This stance lends authority to what the narrator says and does, although it limits his ability to comment on characters. The narrator of the Acts of the Apostles is a third-person narrator—but not always. In four sections, he adopts the first-person plural—the "we section"—to tell his story (Acts 16:10–17; 20:5–15; 21:1–18; 27:1–28:16). For example, "when [Paul] had seen the vision, *we* immediately tried to cross over to Macedonia, being convinced that God had called *us* to proclaim the good news to them" (Acts 16:10). The first person lends an air of importance to the storytelling, for now he is a participant and witness to the events and happenings. The Prologues of Luke and John also rely on first-person narration to underscore their stance as witnesses. For example, "And the Word became flesh and lived among *us*, and *we* have seen his glory" (John 1:14).

Generally, New Testament narrative critics do not identify the narrator as a separate party from the implied author—just as they do not separate the narratee from the implied reader (Culpepper 1983, pp. 16–17, 43; cf. Malbon 2008, p. 33; Malbon 2011, p. 67.). (Recently, Malbon, argues that the implied author is an identifiable party from the narrator, and the narratee is separate from the implied reader (Malbon 2008, p. 33; Malbon 2011, p. 68).)

New Criticism: "New Criticism" is a form of American (and English) literary criticism that came into vogue from the early part of the twentieth century to the late 1960s. New Critics rejected the concept that the focus of literary criticism is with the biographies of authors, or the social context of a work, or the authorial intention behind a work, or the effects of literature on the reader. New Critics popularized the term **affective fallacy**—that is, the fallacy that a poem (or literary work) can be evaluated by its effects upon the reader. They also rejected the view that author's intended aims and means in writing a literary work are relevant for interpretation, which they called the **intentional fallacy** (see Wimsatt and Beardsley 1954, pp. 3–40). Rather, New Critics contend that the proper concern of literary criticism is with the detailed analysis of a work as an independent entity or a self-sufficient object.

New Criticism is known for the practice of **close reading**, which focuses on detailed analysis of the verbal and figurative components within a work (Abrams and Harpham 2015, p. 243). New Critics pay close attention to the words on a page and analyze small units of a text and the ambiguities of words, images, and metaphors. Of the three main components of a work—

Author → Text → Reader

—New Critics focused exclusively on the text without regard for the author or the reader of a work. Close readings of biblical text bring out the subtlety and nuances of a narrative. In 1967, Dan Otto Via Jr. drew explicitly upon New Critical theory to show that the parables of Jesus are autonomous works in which form and content are inseparable (Via 1967). A few years later, the French literary critic, Jean Starobinski, provided an insightful close reading in *New Literary History* (Starobinski 1973) of the struggle with Legion (Mark 5:1–20). Robert Tannehill explored the metaphoric power, tensions, patterns, parallelisms, and paradoxes in the sayings of Jesus in his book, *The Sword of His Mouth* (Tannehill 1975). Phyllis Trible's reading of the book of Ruth is a classic close reading from a feminist perspective (Trible 1978). In 1979, Fishbane (1979) gave several close readings of narrative texts, prayers, and speeches in the Hebrew Bible. In *The Art of Biblical Narrative* (1981), Robert Alter showed the importance of repetition in biblical narratives and its affinity with repetition in short stories, novels, and poems. He opened-up a whole area of study with his analysis of **type-scenes** in the Hebrew Bible—for example, betrothal type-scenes—that drew upon type-scenes in Homer. In 1982, James L. Resseguie gave a close reading of John 9 that appeared in *Literary Interpretations of Biblical Narratives* (Resseguie 1982a). David Rhoads offered a close reading of the Syrophoenician woman in Mark (Rhoads [1994] 2004), and Outi Lehtipuu turned his attention to the parable of the rich man and Lazarus in Luke 16:19–31 (Lehtipuu 1999).

Today, narrative criticism rejects the extremes of New Criticism—for example, that an analysis of a literary work is separable from the response of the reader (cf. the affective fallacy). The development of **reader-response criticism** is partly a reaction against New Critics' rejection of the affective responses of the reader. Nevertheless, narrative criticism has benefited from the New Critical recognition of the organic unity of a text and its method of close, detailed readings of narratives. On New Criticism see Resseguie (2007).

omniscient narrator → **narrator**.

ostranenie ("making strange") → **defamiliarization**.

parallelism: "Parallelism" is the similarity in structure of a pair of words, phrases, clauses, or syntactical arrangements. For example, in Rev. 22:11:

A   Let the evildoer still do evil,

A'   and the filthy still be filthy,

… … … … … … … … … … … … … … … … … … … …

B   and the righteous still do right,

B'   and the holy still be holy.

The first two clauses (A, A') are **synonymous parallelism**, as are the last two (B, B'). The parallel clauses reiterate the same concept but use different words. Notice also that the two parts are marked off by the same adverb and verb combination: "still do"/"still be" / "still do"/"still be". And, finally, the last two clauses contrast with the first two. **Antithesis** is also a form of parallelism in which the second line or couplet contrasts with the first. John 9:39—as well as the above example—illustrates antithesis:

I came into the world for judgment

so that those who do not see (A)

may see (B),

… … … … … … … … … … … … … … … … … … …

and those who do see (B')

may become blind (A').

peripety or **peripeteia** ("reversal") → **plot.**

plot: "Plot" is an elusive term and any definition is likely to be incomplete. Yet, an understanding of plot is important to determine the structure, unity, and direction of a narrative. Plot is the designing principle, the sequence of events or incidents that make up a narrative. Events include actions (or acts) that bring about changes of state in the characters. Or events may be the actions of characters that bring about changes of state in narrative events (Chatman 1978, pp. 44–45). A character's acts are his or her physical actions, speech, thoughts, feelings, and perceptions. "What do characters think, feel, or do, and how does this bring about a change in narrative events?" is a question of plot. By and large, a character is the *subject* of acts; she or he initiates acts that bring about changes in the plot. But a plot does not consist solely of acts. It also is made up of *happenings*. As the term suggests, happenings are things that happen to a character or are events that occur in a setting. In happenings, the character is the object—not the subject—of actions; the affected, not the effector (Chatman 1978, p. 45). When we ask, "What happens to a character and why?" we are asking a question related to plot. When we ask, "What happens in a setting such as the stilling of the storm on the sea, and how does that event change the disciples' perception of Jesus?" we are developing the notion of plot. Plot and character are thus intertwined in a narrative. Henry James famously stated the inseparability: "What is character but the determination of incident? What is incident but the illustration of character?" (James [1884] 1948, p. 13).

Aristotle defined a plot (**mythos** in Greek) as a continuous sequence of events or actions with a beginning, middle, and end. "A beginning is that which does not follow necessarily from something else, but after which a further event or process naturally occurs. An end, by contrast, is that which itself naturally occurs, whether necessarily or usually, after a preceding event, but need not be followed by anything else. A middle is that which both follows a preceding event, and has further consequences" (Aristotle 1995 *Poetics* 7, 1450^b 27–31). Paul Goodman defines plot as follows: "In the beginning anything is possible; in the middle things become probable; in the ending everything is necessary" (Goodman 1954, 14). A plot is thus a unified whole. It "should be so structured that if any [part] is displaced or removed, the sense of the whole is disturbed or dislocated" (Aristotle 1995 *Poetics* 8, 1451^b 32–34).

A story, however, is not a plot. Although both story and plot have sequences of events that are linked, a plot goes further and links sequences by cause and effect. A story requires that we ask, "What happens next?" whereas a plot requires that we ask, "Why do things happen as they do?" E. M. Forster illustrates the difference between a story and a plot in the following example:

The king died and then the queen died.

The king died, and then the queen died of grief (Forster [1927] 2005, p. 86).

In the first instance, the events are strung together with no causal connection between the two. The queen could have died from an accident—falling down the stairs, for instance—or from health problems such as heart disease. But there is nothing in the brief story to suggest that the queen's death is directly related to the king's death. The only link between the two is the suggestive but inconclusive "and then". In the second instance, the same story is told with two additional words that suggest a relationship between the events. It turns the story into a plot by answering the question "why did the queen die?" Biblical plots rely on cause and effect to answer some of life's most important questions. "Where did we come from?" "Where are we going?" "What is our purpose?"

Almost all plots involve a clash of actions, ideas, points of views, desires, or values. The conflict may be physical, mental, emotional, spiritual, or moral. Plots frequently involve contests between protagonist and antagonist, or groups of good and bad characters. Conflicts may be external or internal. External conflicts include clashes with other characters, whether villains (an evil character, such as Satan) or adversaries (e.g., religious leaders) whose values, goals, or norms conflict with the protagonists. The religious authorities are often pitted against Jesus (for example, Matt. 9:14–17; Mark

2:18–22; Luke 5:33–39). Other clashes in the gospels involve battles with nature. The quelling of the tempest on the Sea of Galilee is an example of a battle with nature (Matt. 8:23–27; Mark 4:35–41; Luke 8:22–25). Still other conflicts involve battles with the supernatural such as the healing of a man possessed by demons (Matt. 8:28–34; Mark 5:1–20; Luke 8:26–39). Some clashes between Jesus and others involve conflicts with the norms and values of the dominant culture of the first century (Mark 7:1–23).

Other plot conflicts are internal—for example, decisions that a protagonist or others must make. The protagonist, Jesus, is faced with an internal conflict in the garden: he desires to have the cup of suffering taken away from him, but he also wants to follow the Father's will (Matt. 26:36–46; Mark 14:32–42; Luke 22:39–46). A character may also face a dilemma that involves two choices or actions, both of which appear undesirable. The decision may determine success with a favorable ending or failure with a tragic result. For example, the Rich Young Man faces a conflict of decision concerning his wealth (Matt. 19:16–22; Mark 10:17–22; Luke 18:18–23). Then there are conflicts within a character concerning his goals and values. The rich farmer in Luke 12:13–21 sets a goal of building larger barns, but unseen events—his impending death—determine the outcome.

Northrop Frye identifies two common plot patterns in the New Testament (Frye 1981, pp. 169–71). One pattern is a **U-shaped plot** which is the shape of a comedy. This pattern begins at the top of the U with a state of equilibrium, a period of prosperity or happiness that is disrupted by disequilibrium or disaster. Adversity, misunderstanding, or rebellion propels the plot downward to disaster or bondage. At the bottom of the U, the direction is reversed by a fortunate twist, divine deliverance, an awakening of a character to her or his tragic circumstances, or some other action or event that results in an upward turn. Aristotle referred to the reverse in fortunes as a **peripety** or **peripeteia** (Greek for "reversal," Aristotle 1995 *Poetics* 11. (A peripety can move the plot upward to success as in a comedy or downward to failure or destruction as in a tragedy). The reversal depends frequently on a recognition or discovery, which Aristotle called an **anagnorisis**—a change in the protagonist from "ignorance to knowledge" involving "matters which bear on prosperity or adversity" (Aristotle 1995 *Poetics* 11). The protagonist recognizes something of great importance that was previously hidden or unrecognized. The upward change in the U-shaped plot marks the beginning of the **dénouement** or resolution of the plot. An action is taken that ends in success, or the misunderstanding is solved, or rebellion ceases. The upward turn of the U represents movement toward a new state of equilibrium—a return home, reconciliation, new life. The top of the U is characterized by happiness or prosperity or, in biblical terms, peace, salvation, and wholeness.

An example of a U-shaped plot is the parable of the prodigal son in Luke 15:11–24. The beginning of the downward turn occurs when the younger son asks his father for his share of the property and sets out to a "distant country" (Luke 15:13). The physical setting—"a distant country"—suggests a story of alienation or rebellion, or at the very least a desire for freedom and independence. However, disaster strikes. He faces personal adversity when he squanders the property given to him by his father (Luke 15:13–14a), and then his disaster is compounded by a famine in the land (Luke 15:14b). The nadir is summarized with an economy of words: "no one gave him anything" (Luke 15:16). This is the bottom of the U-shaped plot. The peripety occurs with a recognition scene: "he came to himself" (Luke 15:17a) and "he set off and went to his father" (Luke 15:20a). The upward turn of the U-shaped plot and the dénouement occur when the father goes out to meet the son while he is "still far off" (Luke 15:20b). The clothing (best robe, sandals, ring) and grand feast represent the top of the U, a new state of equilibrium. Other U-shaped plots in the New Testament include the four gospels and the book of Revelation (Resseguie 2005, pp. 206, 213–40).

Frye's second pattern is an **inverted U-shaped** plot, which is the shape of a tragedy. The introduction of a conflict initiates the rising action or the beginning of the upward turn of the inverted U. The conflict is developed and complicated until the rising action reaches the climax of the protagonist's fortunes. This is the top. A crisis or turning point marks the reversal of the protagonist's fortunes and the beginning of the dénouement (also called **catastrophe** in tragedies). Sometimes there is a recognition scene where the protagonist discovers something of great importance that was previously unseen. The final state is disaster, adversity, and unhappiness. Frye's inverted U-shaped plot is like **Freytag's Pyramid** (Freytag 1896), which envisions a tragedy as an inverted V or pyramid. The tragedy begins with an exposition of characters, the setting, and other facts necessary to understand the plot. It is followed by a conflict and the rising action that develops and elaborates the conflict. The top of the inverted V or pyramid is the climax and the reversal of action from rising to falling. The dénouement ends in disaster.

Why analyze narratives as comedies (U-shaped plots) or tragedies (inverted U-shaped plots)? An analysis of the parable of the ten bridesmaids in Matt. 25:1–13 will illustrate. The parable is a tragedy for the five foolish bridesmaids. The exposition introduces the setting—a marriage feast—and the characters—five wise maidens who bring extra flasks of oil and five foolish bridesmaids who bring no additional oil. The conflict occurs when "the bridegroom was delayed" (Matt. 25:5a). A crisis—the sudden arrival of the bridegroom at midnight—then marks the turning point in the fortunes of the five foolish attendants. Since the foolish have brought insufficient oil for their lamps, the falling action is a series of frantic attempts to reverse the downward turn to disaster. They ask the wise to share their oil, but they decline. And then they rush to the market to buy more oil. But this only complicates their dilemma, for they are late for the party and the door is locked. Their recognition scene comes too late to make a correction in their tragic flaw (**hamartia** in Greek, meaning "error" or "mistake of judgment"). Although they plead with the bridegroom to open the door, they are met with the same sort of indifference that they demonstrated in their lack of preparation for the wedding: "Truly, I tell you, I do not know you" (Matt. 25:12).

This illustrates the importance of plot analysis. Tragedies and comedies develop and elaborate anagnorisis (recognition), peripety (reversal), and hamartia or fatal flaw. Recognition scenes illuminate something of great importance that was hitherto unknown to the protagonist or to a character. The recognition scene for the Prodigal Son is the realization that his present state of servitude in a far land does not compare with the pleasant condition of his father's hired hands; therefore, he sets about to reverse the downward turn of the U. The recognition scene of the five foolish bridesmaids comes too late to reverse their fate. However this does not preclude the reader from benefitting from their decisions. The reader can ask "What was their hamartia or fatal flaw that sealed their fate?". Often hamartia is rooted in **hubris**—"pride" or "overwhelming self-confidence"—that leads a character to assume that he or she is in full control of a situation. The five bridesmaid's assumption is a classic illustration of hubris or foolishness. Peripety is the turning point in a plot when the arc of the U either moves upward (as in comedy) or downward (as in tragedy). The reader benefits from the choices the protagonist or group of characters make when faced with a crisis. On plot, see also **fabula** and **syuzhet** and **masterplot** in this glossary. On recognition scenes in John, see Larsen (2008).

point of view/narrative perspective: Point of view "signifies the way a story gets told" and elaborates the relationship between the storyteller and the story (Abrams and Harpham 2015, p. 300). Some narrative critics prefer the concept of **focalization**. Point of view focuses on the way the author presents the reader with the constitutive features of a narrative: characters, dialogue, actions, setting, and events. Narrative perspective is a complex and controversial concept, and the literary critic Susan Sniader Lanser suggests why: "Unlike such textual elements as character, plot, or imagery, point of view is essentially a *relationship* rather than a concrete entity. As it tends to evade stabilization into the language of 'things', it has been difficult to grasp and codify" (Lanser 1981, p. 13, emphasis Lanser).

The Russian literary critic, Boris Uspensky, identifies five planes on which point of view is expressed in a work: (1) spatial, (2) temporal, (3) psychological, (4) phraseological, and (5) ideological (Uspensky 1973). Each plane represents an observable position that the implied author or narrator takes in relationship to the textual world. The spatial plane describes the stance in space that the narrator takes in relation to the text. For example, the narrator may offer a "bird's-eye" perspective on characters and events that results in distancing the reader from individual characters and actions. Alternately, the narrator may adopt the spatial stance of a character and move with that character throughout the narration, observing what the character says and does (Uspensky 1973, pp. 58–59). Further, the narrator may adopt the point of view of an observer within a scene, avoiding the perspective of any one character. In this instance, the point of view is that of the narrator and not of the character. For example, the narrator may describe the guests at a banquet scene and move from one character to another as if she or he were also a guest at the table. Finally, the narrator may simply be an invisible, roving presence as in a moving camera and montage—present but invisible (Resseguie 2016, p. 83).

An example of Uspensky's spatial point of view can be seen in the spatial (and temporal) stance of the third person, omniscient and intrusive narrator in John 2:13–22. After Jesus says, "destroy this temple, and in three days I will raise it up" (John 2:19), the hearers naturally assume he is talking about the temple complex that had been under construction for forty-six years. The narrator intervenes to clarify the misunderstanding: "But he [Jesus] was speaking of the temple of his body" (John 2:21). Then he continues: "After he was raised from the dead, his disciples remembered that he had said this; and they believed the scripture and the word that Jesus had spoken" (John 2:22). In this instance, the spatial position of the narrator is as an omniscient and intrusive presence that corrects the misperception of the hearers. Additionally, the narrator adopts **posterior narration** to clarify Jesus's saying—that is, a post-resurrection perspective on events and happenings.

Temporal point of view refers to (1) the pace of narration and (2) the temporal distance between the moment of telling and the actual events (Lanser 1981, p. 198). The temporal distance of the narrator in the Fourth Gospel is a post-resurrection point of view or posterior narration, which is illustrated in the example above (John 2:20–2). Temporal pace focuses on the acceleration of narrative storytelling or the slowing down of narrative pace. With narrative retardation (slowing down the pace of narration), events and happenings are foregrounded, which forces the reader to notice what is important. For example, the narrative pace in John moves from rapid narration in the first two and half years of Jesus's ministry (chapters 1–12) to a snail's pace in the last half, which depicts Jesus's last twenty-four hours (chapters 13–19). The retarded pace magnifies the passion so that as Jesus is "lifted up" in his ordeal leading to the cross (cf. John 3:14; 8:28; 12:32), the narrator "lifts up" the events with narration that elongates and amplifies their significance (Resseguie 2001, p. 187).

Psychological point of view focuses on behaviors. Uspensky and Lanser describe two ways human behavior may be observed by the narrator (Uspensky 1973, p. 83; Lanser 1981, p. 207). If the narrator takes the point of view of an outside observer, then the storyteller is restricted to what can be observed objectively. This stance corresponds to a camera that records the behavior of a person without access to internal consciousness. On the other hand, the narrator may set aside the perspective of an objective observer and record the feelings, thoughts, and motivations of a character. A third possibility is that the psychological point of view may be described from the perspective of a character. For example, an **interior monologue** reveals the unspoken thoughts and lays bare a character's perspective for the reader to evaluate. This aspect of point of view also allows the implied reader to identify conflicts and opposing points of view. A character's point of view that goes against the norms, beliefs, and worldview of the narrator creates distance between the character and the reader, while a character's perspective that agrees with the narrator's stance creates affinity.

Phraseological point of view focuses on the narrator's discourse and characters' speech. If the narrator speaks in his or her own voice, she or he expresses a point of view—however subtle. The narrator may use the idiosyncrasy of a character's speech to express the narrative's point of view. Alternately, the narrator's speech can seamlessly merge with a character's speech, or vice versa. In this instance, the narrator has taken the character's point of view as his own, or the narrator has imbued the character's speech with his own point of view. For example, John 3:13–21 is "a classic instance of the blending of the narrator with Jesus' voice" (Culpepper 1983, p. 42). Does the narrator speak in his own voice or is this Jesus's voice? The narrator's phraseological point of view also shapes the reader's response to a character. For example, Judas's actions are judged harshly in John 12:6: "He said this not because he cared about the poor but because he was a thief; he kept he common purse and used to steal what was put into it." The narrator's point of view has sealed the reader's judgment concerning Judas's nefarious reputation.

Ideological point of view is not only "the most basic aspect of point of view" but also the "least accessible to formalization, for its analysis relies, to a degree, on intuitive understanding" (Uspensky 1973, p. 8). It focuses on the norms, values, beliefs, and general worldview of the implied author, narrator, or characters. An ideological perspective may be stated outright—what Susan Lanser calls "explicit ideology"—or it may be embedded at "deep-structural" levels of the text (Lanser 1981, pp. 216–17). The ideological point of view of the Fourth Gospel is an example of explicit ideology. "The Word became flesh [*sarx*] and lived among us, and we have seen his glory [*doxa*], the glory as of a father's only son, full of grace and truth" (John 1:14). With astuteness beyond the ordinary, Rudolf Bultmann summarizes John's ideology: "The δόξα is not to be seen *alongside* the σάρξ, nor *through* the σάρξ as through a window; it is to be seen in the σάρξ and nowhere else. If man wishes to see the δόξα, then it is on the σάρξ that he must concentrate his attention without allowing himself to fall victim to appearances" (Bultmann 1971, p. 63, emphasis Bultmann). Some characters in the Fourth Gospel—the crowds and the religious leaders, for example—miss the glory and see Jesus's flesh alone. They stumble over his words, misconstrue his actions as misguided, and conclude that he is lawless. Others—the Samaritan woman, the man born blind, Mary of Magdala, the beloved disciple, and Thomas, for example—see the glory in the flesh, the otherworldly in the ordinary. If a character/reader falls victim to appearances and misconstrues Jesus's actions as antagonistic, then he or she becomes blinded to the *doxa* in the *sarx*. On the other hand, if a character/reader glimpses the glory in the flesh, the supranatural in the natural or the ordinary, then she or he comes to believe that "Jesus is the Messiah, the Son of God" (John 20:31; Resseguie 2013a, pp. 93–95; see also Sheridan 2016, p. 215). On point of view see Burkhard Niederhoff (2013b), Gary Yamasaki (2007), and Resseguie (Resseguie 1982b, 2001, 2005, pp. 167–96).

posterior narration → **point of view/narrative perspective.**

primacy and recency effect: The material that occurs first in a plot and affects the reader initially is known as the" primacy effect," while what follows is called the "recency effect". The order of events in a plot creates expectations in the reader (the primacy effect) that are fulfilled, modified, or even shattered by what comes later in the narrative (the recency effect; Perry 1979, pp. 35–64, 311–61). Three types of primacy/recency effects have practical and theoretical implications for the reading of New Testament literature (Sternberg 1978, pp. 90–158).

(1) A primacy effect can be developed, elongated, and reinforced by the recency effect.
(2) A recency effect can undermine, shatter, or in some other way subvert the primacy effect.
(3) A recency effect can modify, exploit, or revise the primacy effect.

An example from the book of Revelation illustrates a primacy effect that is reinforced in a counterintuitive way by what comes afterwards. In Rev. 5, John hears the voice of an elder announce the appearance of an animal of conquest that is worthy to open a mysterious scroll: "See, the Lion of the tribe of Judah, the Root of David, has conquered, so that he can open the scroll and its seven seals" (Rev. 5:5). Although this is what John *hears*, it is not what he *sees*. "Then I saw between the throne and the four living creatures and among the elders a Lamb standing as if it had been slaughtered, having seven horns and seven eyes, which are the seven spirits of God sent out into all the earth" (Rev. 5:6). Is the primacy (what John hears in Rev. 5:5) reinforced by the recency effect (what John sees in Rev. 5:6)? Is it undermined by the recency or is the primacy effect revised and modified by the recency effect? In this instance, the primacy effect is not overturned by what follows, although it is fulfilled in a surprising way. Jesus is indeed the Lion of Judah who is the descendent of the root of David (Koester 2014, pp. 375–76, 385). Yet the primacy/recency effects force the reader to reconcile the expectation of a lion's appearance on the one hand with the appearance of a slaughtered yet risen lamb on the other. The recency effect adds a counterintuitive message to the primacy. The conquering might of

God's Messiah is found in a slaughtered lamb that is risen (Boesak 1987, pp. 56–57; Resseguie 2009, pp. 118–19).

A second example establishes a primacy effect that is clarified and elongated by what comes later. In Rev. 7:4, John *hears* the number of those who were sealed: one hundred and forty-four thousand, twelve thousand from each of the twelve tribes of Israel. The one hundred and forty-four thousand is a symbolic number of completeness, representing all of God's Israel. But what John *sees* is different from what he hears: "After this I looked, and there was a great multitude that no one could count from every nation, from all tribes and peoples and languages, standing before the throne and before the Lamb, robed in white, with palm branches in their hands" (Rev. 7:9). The recency effect reinterprets and expands what John hears in Rev. 7:4–8. God's Israel is the symbolic one hundred and forty-four thousand from the twelve tribes of Israel (primacy effect); but that number is not limited to the twelve tribes of Israel. It includes a countless throng from every nation and tribe and people and language on earth (recency effect; Resseguie 2009, p. 138).

A third example illustrates a primacy effect that is overturned by the recency. In Revelation 13:11, John sees a beast arise from the earth that has "two horns like a lamb" (13:11a). But the expectation of a lamblike creature is immediately thwarted when the beast opens its mouth and speaks "like a dragon" (13:11b). Although the primacy effect raises the expectation of an unthreatening animal like a lamb, the recency effect proves the lie of this assumption. The beast is a fraud, a poseur, a wolf in sheep's clothing (cf. Matt. 7:15), for when it speaks, its discourse reveals its identity. It is the progeny of the "great dragon" (cf. Rev. 12:9). (See also Mark 10:29–30 under **defamiliarization** above. The primacy effect is overturned by the addition of "with persecutions"—the recency effect.)

protagonist → character.

reader: Who is the reader of a narrative? Who is the author? And what is the role of the flesh and blood reader? All narratives have parties within and outside the text. The following communication diagram by Seymour Chatman identifies the author outside the text from the author within. Chatman also recognizes that there is a reader outside the text—a real, flesh and blood reader—that is not the same as the reader within the text (Chatman 1978, p. 151).

Narrative Text

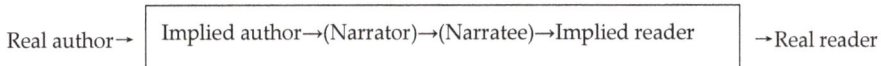

Real author→ | Implied author→(Narrator)→(Narratee)→Implied reader | →Real reader

The above diagram shows the parties external and intrinsic to a narrative. The real author and the real reader are extrinsic and accidental to narratives. On the other hand, the implied author, narrator, narratee, and implied reader are immanent to narratives. In Chatman's view the narrator and narratee are optional parties and thus the parentheses above. All parties within the narrative are reconstructed from the text itself and do not exist as entities apart from the text.

The real author creates a second self or persona called the **implied author** (Wayne Booth's term) that is within the narrative. The implied author is not the real author but the author's second self that builds the narrative structure. The narrative critic analyzes the choices and directives of the implied author—such as his or her style, the commentary on characters, and the *Weltanschauung* (worldview) of the implied author. For example, the writer of the book of Revelation—John the prophet on the Island of Patmos—creates a second self, the implied author (who is also the narrator) that tells the story to the implied reader. The **implied reader** of Revelation is not an actual flesh and blood reader; this reader is a fictive, idealized reader of the first-century that is in the implied author's mind when he creates the narrative.

Narrative critics focus on the implied reader and the way he or she reads the narrative. Whereas flesh and blood readers allow biases, socio-cultural instincts, and accumulated experiences to influence their reading the story, the implied reader understands and interprets the narrative in the manner the implied author intends. The real reader who adopts the role of the implied reader knows the conventions of the implied author of the first century and assembles the message according to the author's design. This implied reader knows koine Greek, recognizes the implied author's historical and socio-cultural stance, understands references to earlier works, and accepts the implied author's worldview. The actual reader, however, may resist—even reject outright—the implied author's worldview, but as an implied reader she or he accepts the author-in-the-text's worldview.

On the role of the real reader as a "resisting reader" see Reinhartz (2001, pp. 81–98). See also the short introduction to feminist criticism by Janice Capel Anderson in *Mark and Method* (2008).

reader-response criticism: "Reader-response criticism" pays close attention to the actions of the reader and focuses on what the text *does* to the reader (Resseguie 1984, 2016). Any literary work has three main components—

$$\boxed{\text{Author} \rightarrow \text{Text} \rightarrow \text{Reader}}$$

This criticism gives the reader an essential role in the production of textual meaning. An examination of the text in and of itself is replaced by an analysis of the reading process: a sequential reading of the text with the reader's ongoing responses. The literary critic Stanley Fish describes the temporal, sequential approach in this way: "The concept is simply the rigorous and disinterested asking of the question, what does the word, phrase, sentence, paragraph, chapter, novel, play, poem *do*? And the execution involves an analysis of the developing responses of the reader in relation to the words as they succeed one another in time" (Fish 1980, pp. 26–27, emphasis Fish).

Some reader-response critics give more interpretative authority to actual flesh and blood readers than others. At one end of the spectrum are Gérard Genette [1972] (1980) and Prince (1973) who focus on the responses of the *reader in the text*. The reader is inscribed within the text and responds the way the implied author expects. The role of a flesh and blood reader is to identify the responses of the reader in the text and respond in the same way. At the other end of the spectrum is the subjective approach of Norman Holland (1975a, 1975b) and David Bleich (1975) who give the actual reader dominance *over the text*. Holland's and Bleich's readers are flesh and blood readers that determine the meaning of the literary work through their responses to the text. A third approach sees the reader as one who interacts *with the text*. This reader is neither confined within the text nor entirely free to produce textual meaning. Rather the reader is an actual reader that has limits placed on him or her in the production of textual meaning. Wolfgang Iser (1971, 1972, 1974, 1978) calls this reader an "implied reader"—one who interacts in a dialectical fashion with the text. Textual meaning is a result of this of reader-text interaction.

Several New Testament critics adopt the insights of Wolfgang Iser in their analyses of New Testament narratives (Culpepper 1983; Scott 1989; Roth 1997; Darr 1992, 1998; Fowler 1991; Fowler 2008, pp. 70–74; Howell 1990; Kurz 1993; Powell 2001; Resseguie 1984, 2016). Two of Iser's critical assumptions are generally accepted by narrative and reader-response critics (Resseguie 1984; Resseguie 2016, pp. 8–12). The first concerns the role of the reader in the production of textual meaning. The reader is active—not passive—and contributes to the text's meaning by filling in information that is implied but not written. The implied sections of a text are called "gaps," areas of "indeterminacy", or "blanks," and the assumption is that every text has gaps that the reader completes in the reading process. Iser calls the gap-filling by the reader the "realization" (*Konkretisation*) of the work. Thus, an important distinction is made between the "text" written by the author and the "work" realized by the reader. "The work is more than the text, for the text only takes on life when it is realized, and furthermore the realization is by no means independent of the individual disposition of the reader—though this in turn is acted upon by the different patterns of the text. The convergence of text and reader brings the literary work into existence" (Iser 1974, pp. 274–75). Although the work is the realization of the text by the reader, he or she is somewhat limited in the production of meaning. Iser uses the image of two people gazing at the stars to illustrate how the reader contributes to textual meaning. "Both [may] be looking at the same collection of stars, but one will see the image of a plough, and the other will make out a dipper. The 'stars' in a literary text are fixed, the lines that join them are variable" (Iser 1974, p. 282). The Iserian reader selects and organizes the parts of a text, fills in gaps, and develops an interpretation, but the written portions of the text place limits on the reader's participation in the formation of the work. Although this reader is called an "implied reader" (*impliziter Leser* or "implicit reader") in the English translations of Iser's works, he or she is different from Wayne Booth's and Seymour Chatman's "implied reader" (see **reader** above). Whereas Booth's and Chatman's reader is a property of the text and assembles the text in the way the "implied author" expects, the Iserian reader is an intermediary between the real reader and the ideal reader, filling in the gaps in his or her own way and assembling textual meaning according to the parameters set by the implied author. Although the implied reader is a function of the real reader's mind, he or she is called into being by an authorial text that asks to be read in a certain way (Iser 1978, pp. 27–38).

A second critical assumption concerns the maneuvers of a reader as she or he realizes the literary work. Iser paid close attention to the process of reading, which is one of anticipation of what lies ahead, frustration of unfulfilled expectations, retrospection, and reconceptualization of new expectations. The reader approaches the text with a "repertoire" that consists "of all the familiar territory within the text. This may be in the form of references to earlier works, or to social and historical norms, or to the whole culture from which the text has emerged" (Iser 1978, p. 69). But this familiar repertoire is made to seem strange by textual strategies that disorient the reader and forces her or him to modify expectations and to reconceptualize new information. The textual strategy of readerly disorientation is called **defamiliarization** (Iser 1974, p. 87), which encourages the reader to anticipate outcomes, only to have expectations frustrated and revised. Familiar elements of the reader's repertoire are backgrounded or foregrounded, diminished or highlighted, trivialized or magnified, so that a "strategic over magnification, trivialization, or even annihilation" of the familiar occurs. The reading process is a continual revision of expectations and the formation of new expectations. "We look forward, we look back, we decide, we change our decisions, we form expectations, we are shocked by their nonfulfillment, we question, we muse, we accept, we reject; this is the dynamic process of recreation" (Iser 1974, p. 288).

Iser is criticized for unproblematically distinguishing between the determinate and indeterminate parts of a text. How does the reader know that she or he has correctly identified the gaps and has filled them in to the satisfaction of the implied author? Also problematic is how the real reader avoids imposing his or her disposition and socio-cultural stance upon the final product? Nevertheless, Iser's theory of the reading process—anticipation, frustration, retrospection, and reconstruction—is a viable theory of the temporal reading process.

Recently, narrative critics have recognized the importance of the reader as an active participant in the production of textual meaning. For example, Powell (1990, p. 21; Powell 2001, p. 63) and Resseguie (2016) have merged narrative-critical approaches with reader-oriented criticism to form readings that are focused not only on the literary text itself; they also consider the essential role the reader plays in the production of the work. Powell regards narrative criticism as a "subset or variety of reader-response criticism," (Powell 2001, p. 63), and, more recently, he speaks of "reader-oriented narrative criticism" (Powell 2011, pp. 36–42). The third edition of Rhoads et al.'s *Mark as Story* (Rhoads et al. 2012) also moved towards a reader-oriented or audience-oriented narrative criticism with a discussion of the "ideal audience" (Rhoads et al. 2012, pp. 138–44) and an epilogue on "Reading as a Dialogue: The Ethics of Reading" (Rhoads et al. 2012, pp. 153–56).

On reading strategies see **primacy** and **recency effect** in this glossary. Important surveys of reader-response criticism are Jane P. Tompkins (1980), Suleiman and Crossman (1980), and Steven Mailloux (1982). Gerald Prince offers a critique of the Iserian reader in his article "Reader" in *The Living Handbook of Narratology* (Prince 2013). See also "Reader-Response Criticism" in *The Postmodern*

Bible (Castelli et al. 1995, pp. 20–69) and Moore (1989) for critiques of reader-oriented approaches to biblical literature.

reliable narrator → **characterization** and **narrator.**

repetition → **sequence of action.**

rhetoric (figurative language): "Rhetoric" is the art of persuasion. It breathes life into a narrative and influences how the reader feels and thinks about what the implied author says. Rhetoric is an integral part of every mode of expression and is the means by which the implied author convinces the implied reader of the narrative's point of view, norms, beliefs, values, and worldview. The narrative critic is interested in the rhetorical devices (figurative language) and techniques that an implied author uses to persuade the reader to make a proper interpretation of a work—that is, the informed conclusions that the implied author wants the reader to make. The rhetorical devices discussed in this glossary are (1) **figures of speech** and (2) **figures of thought**.

   Figures of speech or rhetorical figures (also called **schemes** from the Greek word for "form") depart from customary or standard usage of language by the order and pattern of words and phrases. Although figures of speech use words or phrases in their customary or literal manner, they achieve special effects by the arrangement of words, phrases, clauses, and syntactical forms. For example, "the sabbath was made for humankind, and not humankind for the sabbath" (Mark 2:27) is a figure of speech that achieves special effects by the arrangement of words in a reverse pattern, which is called a chiasmus (sabbath/humankind//humankind/sabbath). In this glossary **anaphora**, **antithesis**, **chiasmus**, **parallelism**, **rhetorical question**, and **sequence of action (repetition)** are explained.

   Figures of thought (also called **tropes** meaning "turns" of phrases) are words or phrases that depart from customary or standard ways of using the language. This rhetorical feature is different from figures of speech. Whereas figures of speech use language in the customary, standard, or literal way, figures of thought use words and phrases in a nonliteral way. Verbal irony is an example. When the soldiers at the crucifixion salute Jesus as "King of the Jews," (Matt. 27:29; Mark 15:18; John 19:3), they do not mean what they say. But the implied reader enjoys the irony—for what they say is precisely what the implied author intends. In this glossary, **double entendre** and **misunderstanding, simile** and **metaphor**, and **verbal irony** are discussed. [Note: rhetoric is restricted to figurative language in this glossary. However, it is an expansive and multifaceted concept. The reader should consult James Phelan (2005a, 2005b) for a discussion of rhetoric.]

rhetorical figures → **rhetoric.**

rhetorical question: A "rhetorical question" is a statement in the form of a question that does not expect a reply but is stated to achieve greater persuasive power than a direct statement. The answer to a rhetorical question is usually obvious and is the only one available. For example, when the Pharisees complain about the plucking of grain by Jesus's disciples on a sabbath, Jesus resorts to rhetorical questions to dismantle their complaint.

> Have you not read what David did when he and his companions were hungry? He entered the house of God and ate the bread of the Presence, which it was not lawful for him or his companions to eat, but only for the priests. Or have you not read in the law that on the sabbath the priests in the temple break the sabbath and yet are guiltless? (Matt. 12:3–5)

A rhetorical question states the obvious and, in this instance, draws upon two portions of the Torah to undermine the Pharisees' objection.

round character → **character.**

Russian formalism → **defamiliarization.**

sandwich narrative (intercalation): A "sandwich narrative" is a framing device in which one narrative is tucked inside another narrative. The embedded or intercalated narrative (B) interrupts the framing narrative (A, A′), which resumes after the embedded narrative ends. For example, Mark splits a narrative in half to nestle a second narrative within the framing narrative (Kermode 1979, pp. 128–34; Edwards 1989; Shepherd 1995; Resseguie 2005, pp. 54–55; Rhoads et al. 2012, pp. 51–52). The framing narrative may comment on the embedded narrative by either comparison or contrast, or the embedded narrative may comment on the framing narrative.

A famed example of a framing narrative and its embedded narrative is the cursing and withering of the fig tree and the cleansing of the temple in Mark. Whereas Matthew has the cursing and withering as a single event that happens after the cleansing of the temple (Matt. 21:18–19), Mark separates the cursing from the withering and uses it to frame the cleansing of the temple:

A   Cursing of the Fig Tree (Mark 11:12–14)

B   Cleansing of the Temple (Mark 11:15–19)

A′   Withering of the Fig Tree (Mark 11:20–21)

The framing narrative (A, A′) provides a commentary on the embedded narrative (B). Other intercalations in Mark include: (1) a narrative about Jesus's family (3:20–21, 31–35) frames an accusation that he is demon possessed (3:22–30); (2) a story about Jairus and his daughter (5:21–24; 35–43) frames the story of a woman with a hemorrhage (5:25–34); (3) a story about the sending and return of the Twelve (6:7–13, 30–32) frames the narrative of the death of John the Baptist (6:14–29); (4) a story of conspiracy and intrigue (14:1–2, 10–11) frames a story of the anointing of Jesus at Bethany (14:3–9), and (5) the story of Peter's denial (14:53–54, 66–72) frames Jesus's trial before the Sanhedrin (14:55–65).

scheme → rhetoric (figurative language).

sequence of action (repetition): "Sequence of action" is a form of repetition that relies on actions in numerical series (of two and three, for example) to create emphasis. Rhoads, Dewey, and Michie refer to the repetition of twos in Mark as **two-step progression** (Rhoads et al. 2012, pp. 49–51). Although the second step appears to repeat the first, it adds new information that clarifies or amplifies the first step. For example, Mark uses two-steps to clarify the setting when the crowds came to Jesus for healing: "that evening, at sundown" (Mark 1:32). The second step—"at sundown"—explains that the Sabbath was over, and people could travel to Jesus for healing without violating sabbath laws (Rhoads et al. 2012, p. 49). The poor widow who put two copper coins in the treasury "put in everything she had, all she had to live on" (Mark 12:44). The second step clarifies the first. Not only did she put all she had into the treasury at that moment; she put everything she had to live on as an offering. On series of two in Mark see Neirynck (1988).

A series of three may indicate that an action is complete, finished (Resseguie 2005, p. 49). There may be an intensification of an action from one occurrence to the next, with the third in a series representing a climax. In Matthew's account of Peter's denial each occurrence is progressively intensified. In the first denial, Peter denies knowing what the servant-girl is talking about when he is questioned (Matt. 26:70). In the second, his denial is more forceful with an oath sworn: "I do not know the man" (Matt. 26:72). In the third, his denial is complete. He invokes a curse on himself as well as taking an oath (Matt. 26:74). The three steps leave no doubt that he has completely abandoned Jesus.

Other threes are important. In the Garden of Gethsemane, the disciples are found to be asleep three times during a time of trial (Mark 14:37, 40, 41). Jesus asks Peter three times if he loves him (John 21:15–17). Three temptations of Jesus are found in Matthew and Luke (Matt. 4:1–11; Luke 4:1–13). Three predictions of Jesus's passion are found in the Synoptic Gospels (Mark 8:31–33; 9:30–32; 10:32–34, and parallels). In the Fourth Gospel, Pilate declares three times that he finds "no case against [Jesus]" (John 18:38b; 19:4, 6). In Acts, Peter is commanded to eat three times (Acts 10:13, 15, 16). In the book of Revelation, sequences of threes describe God's action and being. God's eternity is underscored with threes: "who is and who was and who is to come" (Rev. 1:4). Threes describe God's work as Creator: "who created heaven and what is in it, the earth and what is in it, and the sea and what is in it" (Rev. 10:6).

setting: "Setting" is the background of a narrative—the historical, physical, socio-cultural, religious, economic, and temporal circumstances in which the action of the narrative occurs. Setting contributes to the mood of a narrative (Chatman 1978, p. 141), or enlarges the traits of a character, or enhances the development of a plot and its conflicts. The historical setting of the New Testament is the Roman occupation of the first century Mediterranean world. Physical settings include topographical landscape (desert or wilderness; river; lake; sea; mountain; road or way); architectural landscape (temple; house; synagogue; marketplace; garden; sheepfold; tomb; well; praetorium; cities); and geographical landscape (Judea; Samaria; Galilee; "the other side" in Mark 5:1). Socio-cultural settings include meals, rich, poor, "sinners", leaders, tax collectors, pharisees, sadducees, priests, unclean (lepers), women, children, disabled (lame, crippled, blind), soldiers, centurions. Religious settings include special days and feasts (Sabbath, Passover, Tabernacles).

The desert or wilderness is the "fierce landscape" of solace and peril (Lane 1998). The harsh, feral setting of the desert is a place of testing that reveals one's resolve (Resseguie 2004, pp. 12–16; Resseguie 2005, pp. 95–97). For example, Jesus's loyalties are tested in the unreceptive landscape of the desert. Will he follow a false god and receive "the kingdoms of the world and [their] splendor" (Matt. 4:8, Luke 4:5–6)? Or will he remain faithful to the Lord God? Yet this unreceptive terrain is also a place of solace and divine succor ("the angels waited on him," Mark 1:13). The desert or wilderness is also in-between landscape; it is neither here, nor there. It is liminal space. This significance is derived from the Israelites' experience in the desert during their exodus out of Egypt. On the one hand, they are no longer slaves in Egypt; on the other, they are not yet free in the promised land. They are in-between captivity and freedom, between enslavement and a new life. As in-between space, the desert setting plays an important part in the plot of the book of Revelation. In Revelation 12, a woman clothed with the sun, the moon under her feet, and a crown of twelve stars is pursued or persecuted by the great dragon (Rev. 12:1, 13). But she is given two wings of a great eagle and flees to the desert where she receives divine solace during the in-between times (one thousand two hundred sixty days or a time, and times, and half a time; see below under temporal settings). The persecuted woman and her children are images of the Christian community (Rev. 12:17); the "great dragon" or Satan is the bloodthirsty pharaoh of Revelation who seeks to destroy the Christian community; and the desert or wilderness is a symbolic place of solace and divine protection for the Christian community during the time between Christ's exaltation and his return at the end of times (Resseguie 2009, pp. 171, 175–76).

Props—sometimes called **mise en scène**—may take on a significance of their own, enlarging the traits of characters, adding important details to the plot, and signaling transitions in a character's social and spiritual life. In the gospels, props include a water jar, purification water jars, clothing, perfumed spices, charcoal fire, a judge's bench, an untorn net, sop, and so forth. For example, a charcoal fire (*anthrakia*), which occurs only twice in the New Testament, is the setting for both Peter's denial of Jesus (John 18:18) and his restoration at the Sea of Tiberias (John 21:9). The reader is to recall both settings when analyzing Peter's characterization.

Clothing marks transitions in one's social or spiritual life. In Luke 15:22, the prodigal son receives the best robe, sandals for his feet, and a ring—emblematic of his transition from alienation to new life. Clothing also symbolizes a demoniac's transition from bondage and enslavement by evil powers to new life. Before his exorcism the demoniac in Luke is stark naked like an animal; afterwards he receives once more his humanity and puts on clothes.

For a long time he had worn *no clothes* (Luke 8: 27).

They found the man from whom the demons had gone sitting at the feet of Jesus, *clothed*, and in his right mind (Luke 8: 35).

Clothing reveals the inner landscape of a character—her or his values, commitments, inclinations, motivations, and desires. An interesting example is a man who arrives at a wedding feast without a formal wedding garment (Matt. 22:11–14). When he arrives, the king is incredulous because of his negligence: "Friend, how did you get in here without a wedding robe?" (Matt. 22:12). By arriving at the wedding in his work clothes rather than a wedding robe, he flouts conventions. The king then has him bound hand and foot and cast into outer darkness. Clothing or its lack is important to the plot of this parable, for it is an outward sign that reveals the guest's true colors. A festal occasion requires a festal garment; but the invitee breaks with the norms and conventions of the day and appears in soiled work clothes (Bauckham 1996, p. 485; Olmstead 2003, p. 126). "For any such occasion guests would be expected to wear clothes that were both longer than those worn by ordinary working people on working days and also newly washed" (Bauckham 1996, p. 485). In the parable, clothing announces the desires and inclinations of this guest, he does not want to be there. Although he is present at the party, he is absent in other ways. Since this is not the party for him, the king fulfills his wishes and sends him on his way to another party, one in outer darkness, where the guests celebrate with the weeping and gnashing of teeth (Resseguie 2005, p. 106).

An abandoned water jar (*hydria*) would appear to be "a narratively unnecessary detail" that readers could easily skip over (Schneiders 1999, p. 192). Yet the prop raises questions about why the narrator records something so minor. The abandoned jar occurs in the story of the Samaritan woman who encounters Jesus at Jacob's well: "Then the woman left her water jar and went back to the city" (John 4:28). Could it be that she left the water jar for Jesus to draw water? Or did she leave the bucket behind because she intended to return to the well with the villagers? (O'Day 1986, p. 75). Or perhaps she was in such a hurry to tell the villagers about Jesus that she simply forgot the jar? Or does the water jar have symbolic significance? If symbolic, does it symbolize the woman's freedom from "her entire oppression" (Schottroff 1998, pp. 160, 174). Schottroff argues that she is no longer in bondage with the man she is living with and no longer bound by the tasks that woman normally do in that society, such as fetching water. Or is the symbolism to be found in the equivalent action of the male disciples who abandon their fishing nets? (Schneiders 1999, p. 192). Like the disciples, she abandons her past to follow Jesus; water jars and fishing nets are no longer needed for this new adventure. Perhaps, the symbolism is to be found in the kind of water she has now found. The woman leaves the water jar behind because it is worthless for "living water" (Brown 1966, p. 173; Lee 1994, pp. 84–85; Koester 2003, pp. 190–91; Culpepper 1983, p. 194; Boers 1988, pp. 182–83). Whatever the explanation, the abandoned water jar is the type of prop that keeps the reader engaged in the narrative and searching for answers.

Another type of prop is a **MacGuffin**, a term popularized by Alfred Hitchcock, although the term precedes Hitchcock's usage of it (Harmon 2012, p. 283). It is an object, event, or character that serves as a motivator for the plot (Chatman 1978, p. 140). Although the MacGuffin may be insignificant, even a gimmick, it is necessary to move the plot forward (Harmon 2012, p. 283) and, although it is frequently mysterious and unexplained, it is something the characters care about. For example, the falcon statuette in the movie, *The Maltese Falcon* (1941), is an object that the characters pursue in earnest, becoming a device that moves the action forward to its dénouement. In the film, *Raiders of the Lost Arc* (1981), the protagonist, Indiana Jones, is in pursuit of a MacGuffin—the ark of the covenant—that the antagonists (the Nazis) are also in search of. In the parable of the guest who arrives without a wedding robe (Matt. 22:11–14 above), the wedding gown is a MacGuffin that is important for the plot. Yet it is never explained why it is essential for the guest to have a special robe or even why the guest's oversight should result in such drastic consequences, but clearly it is something the characters care about or should care about. In Revelation 10, a mighty angel holds a MacGuffin in his hand—an opened scroll—that is important for the plot's dénouement. The scroll is a mysterious and unexplained object that John cares about for he devours its contents, which are sweet as honey in his mouth but bitter in his stomach (Rev. 10:10). With the last trumpet plague (Rev. 9), the plot of Revelation has come to a complete standstill. But the MacGuffin-scroll moves the plot forward. Whereas the plagues were ineffective in persuading the stolid to abandon their wicked ways (Rev. 9:20–21), the MacGuffin-scroll advances the plot to its dénouement. The suffering and prophetic witness of the Christian community now accomplishes what the plagues alone were unable to effect. Their actions persuade the recalcitrant to give glory to God (Resseguie forthcoming (b) Narrative Features"; Koester 2014, p. 505; Mounce 1998, p. 210; Charles 1920, 1:260; Mazzaferri 1989, pp. 267–69).

Temporal settings are either chronological or typological (Powell 1990, pp. 72–74). Chronological references refer to the time an action takes place: the disciples are to take up their cross "daily" (Luke 9:23); a rich man feasts "every day" (Luke 16:19); the Beroeans examine the scriptures "every day" (Acts 17:11). In Mark 13:18, the disciples are to pray that the end-time tribulation not occur in winter. Matthew, however, includes another temporal setting that he considers important: "Pray that your flight may not be in winter or *on a sabbath*" (Matt. 24:20). The small detail gives the reader a glimpse into Matthew's social setting.

Typological settings, on the other hand, indicate the kind of time in which an action takes place and are often symbolic. In John, a nighttime setting is more than background atmosphere; it is saturated with meaning. Darkness may symbolize opacity or represent a character's abandonment of the light for darkness. Nicodemus comes to Jesus "by night," (John 3:2), which describes not only the time of day but also Nicodemus' lack of understanding. "It was night" when Judas leaves the Last Supper to hand Jesus over to the authorities (John 13:30). The nighttime setting is symbolic: he goes out at night to join the powers of darkness in their cabal against Jesus. In Revelation 20, the millennium is a kind of time—not the actual length of time. The symbolic one thousand years is a Satan-free period in which the saints reign. The kind of time is expressed by several other temporal settings in Revelation: (1) a time, and times, and half a time (=three and a half times or years, Rev. 12:14); (2) one thousand two hundred and sixty days (=three and a half years, Rev. 11:3; 12:6); (3) forty-two months (=three and a half years or forty-two months of thirty days, Rev. 11:2; 13:5); and (4) three and a half days (Rev. 11:9, 11). The temporal notations are numerical ciphers for the "in-between times"—that is, the period between Jesus's ascension and exaltation and his return at the end of time (Koester 2014, p. 498). This kind of time is a period of peril and solace: intense but limited persecution on the one hand, and divine protection on the other (Resseguie forthcoming (b) "Narrative Features").

showing (in narrative) → **characterization.**

simile and **metaphor:** Similes compare two distinctly different things with the use of "like" or "as." The parable of the leaven in Matt. 13:33 is a simile. "The kingdom of heaven is *like* yeast that a woman took and mixed in three measures of flour, till it was leavened". On the other hand, a metaphor does not state explicitly a comparison between two distinctly different things. Rather it ascribes an action or quality of one thing to a second by way of identity. Jesus's statements "I am the bread of life" and "I am the light of the world" are metaphors that ascribe two different qualities (light and bread) to Jesus by way of identity.

I. A. Richards uses the concepts of **tenor** and **vehicle** to analyze metaphors (Richards 1936, pp. 119–27). The tenor is the subject of the comparison and the vehicle is the image. To phrase it differently, the vehicle is the image that illumines the tenor—the subject of the metaphor. The vehicle and tenor make up the metaphor, and the reader must identify the comparison that exists between the two parts. The following saying from Matthew illustrates the importance of Richards' concepts. "Wherever the corpse is, there the vultures will gather" (Matt. 24:28). The tenor is not specified and can only be gleaned from the context itself. Nevertheless, the vehicle—the imagery of vultures and carcasses—should be analyzed before identifying the tenor. When one sees vultures circling above, a carcass is certain to be found below. The **implicit metaphor**—a metaphor that does not specify the tenor—is solved by an examination of the context in Matthew 24. The tenor is the coming of the Son of Man again. In the end times false messiahs and false prophets will appear that will "produce great signs and omens, to lead [people] astray" (Matt. 24:24). Some will be swayed by counterfeit messiahs and prophets' appearance that claim that the Messiah has appeared in secret—for example, in the wilderness or in inner rooms (Matt. 24:26). The question the metaphor addresses is: Will the Son of

Man's appearance be in secret or will it be unmistakable? The vehicle (vultures and carcasses) suggests that the coming of the Son of Man will be as apparent as birds of prey circling in the sky announces a carcass below. Matthew reinforces this comparison with a simile: "For as the lightning comes from the east and flashes as far as the west, so will be the coming of the Son of Man" (Matt. 24:27).

situational irony → **irony.**

static character → **character.**

stock character → **character.**

story and **discourse**: "Story and discourse" are terms used by Seymour Chatman to describe the necessary components of a narrative: the *what* and the *how*. The story or the *what* is its content such as actions, happenings, characters, and setting. The discourse or the *how* is "the means by which the content is communicated" (Chatman 1978, p. 19). Narrative critics generally ask the same questions as Chatman: (1) *What* is the narrative about? and (2) *How* is the story told or how is its content communicated? The four gospels—Matthew, Mark, Luke, and John—illustrate the importance of analyzing story and discourse. Although there is considerable overlap in the narrative content of the gospels (the story), the way the stories are told (the discourse) is distinctive to each writer (Malbon 2008, p. 32).

stream of consciousness → **character** (**interior monologue**).

synonymous parallelism → **parallelism.**

syuzhet (in **Russian formalism**) → **defamiliarization.**

telling (in narrative) → characterization.

trope → **rhetoric.**

two-step progression → **sequence of action.**

type-scene: A "type-scene" is a recurrent motif that is recognized by the reader as conventional. Robert Alter drew upon Homer to develop the concept of type-scenes in biblical literature. They are common stories that are "dependent on the manipulation of a fixed constellation of pre-determined motifs" (Alter 1981, p. 51). For example, betrothal scenes in the Hebrew Bible have the following recurrent motifs:

(1) A future bridegroom travels to a foreign land.

(2) He encounters a girl or girls at a well.

(3) The girl(s) rush home to bring news of the stranger's arrival.

(4) A betrothal is concluded between the stranger and the girl, often involving a meal (Alter 1981, p. 52).

The variations in the betrothal type-scenes add to the artistry of individual scenes and draw attention to important words, motifs, themes, and characters. Examples of betrothal type-scenes in the Hebrew Bible are: the encounter between Abraham's servant and Rebekah (Genesis 24:10–61); Jacob's encounter at the well with Rachel (Genesis 29:1–20); Moses and Zipporah (Exodus 2:15b–21); and the book of Ruth.

In John 4, Jesus's encounter with the woman at the well is a betrothal type-scene, though a betrothal of a very different kind—"not in marriage but in worship (4:21–24) and in mission (4:35–42)" (Black 2001, p. 17). Other type-scenes include the annunciation of a hero's birth (Alter 1983); trial/temptation in the wilderness; danger and rescue on the sea; healing miracles; exorcisms; meal scenes; and recognition type-scenes (Resseguie 2005, pp. 53–54; Rhoads et al. 2012, p. 51).

The most extensive study of type-scenes in the New Testament is found in Kasper Bro Larsen's monograph, *Recognizing the Stranger* (2008), which explores recognition (**anagnorisis**) scenes in the Fourth Gospel. Like Alter, Larsen draws upon Homer's *Odyssey* for his analysis of type-scenes—especially the famous bath-scene in which Eurycleia, Odysseus' childhood nurse, gives him a bath and recognizes the boar-hunt scar on his thigh from early days (Homer 2017, Book 19). Although Odysseus attempts to conceal his identity from Penelope, his beloved, and Eurycleia, the secret is revealed in this moment of tearful recognition. Larsen identifies five "typical moves" found in recognition scenes (Larsen 2008, pp. 63, 219–20).

(1) The meeting.
(2) Cognitive resistance in which doubts are raised or requests of proof are made.
(3) A token of recognition is displayed.
(4) The moment of recognition.
(5) Attendant reactions and physical (re-)union.

Larsen notes that not all moves are present in every recognition scene, and, like Alter, he concludes that variations in type-scenes amplify themes and motifs of individual narratives. Some of the recognition scenes that Larsen develops are: the Samaritan woman (John 4), the man born blind (John 9), Peter's denial (John 18:15–18, 25–27), Mary Magdalene (John 20:11–18), and Thomas (John 20:26–29).

un-intrusive narrator → **narrator.**

unreliable narrator → **characterization** and **narrator.**

unspoken soliloquy → **character.**

U-shaped plot or **inverted U-shaped plot** → **plot.**

vehicle and **tenor** → **simile** and **metaphor.**

verbal irony → **irony.**

verbal thread: "Verbal threads" are repeated words or phrases that may link together episodes and draw the reader's attention to disparate narratives. For example, the word for "charcoal fire" (*anthrakia*) occurs only twice in the New Testament, both times in the Fourth Gospel (John 18:18; 21:9). When Peter enters the high priest's courtyard, he joins the posse that just arrested Jesus, and warms himself by the charcoal fire (John 18:18). The memorable setting is the backdrop for his threefold denial of Jesus. The second occurrence of *anthrakia* occurs in John 21:9 when Jesus invites the disciples to eat a meal of bread and fish, cooked on a charcoal fire. Shortly after this scene, Peter professes his love for Jesus three times. The verbal thread ties together two separate events involving the same characters, Jesus and Peter, and encourages the reader to ponder the connection between the events (Resseguie 2005, pp. 42–45).

walk-on → **character.**

Funding: This research received no external funding.

Conflicts of Interest: The author declares no conflict of interest.

References

Abbott, H. Porter. 2008. *The Cambridge Introduction to Narrative*, 2nd ed. Cambridge Introductions to Literature. Cambridge: Cambridge University Press.

Abrams, Meyer H., and Geoffrey Galt Harpham. 2015. *A Glossary of Literary Terms*, 11th ed. Stamford: Cengage Learning.

Alter, Robert. 1981. *The Art of Biblical Narrative*. New York: Basic Books.

Alter, Robert. 1983. How Convention Helps Us Read: The Case of the Bible's Annunciation Type-Scenes. *Prooftexts* 3: 115–30.

Anderson, Janice Capel. 1983. Matthew, Gender and Reading. *Semeia* 28: 3–28.

Anderson, Janice Capel, and Stephen D. Moore. 2008. *Mark and Method: New Approaches in Biblical Studies*, 2nd ed. Minneapolis: Fortress Press.

Aristotle. 1995. *Poetics*. Loeb Classical Library 199. Edited and translated by Stephen Halliwell. Cambridge: Harvard University Press.

Arp, Thomas R., and Greg Johnson. 2017. *Perrine's Story and Structure*, 15th ed. Boston: Wadsworth Cengage Learning.

Austin, Jane. 2001. *Pride and Prejudice*, 3rd ed. Edited by Donald Gray. New York: W. W. Norton. First published 1813.

Bakhtin, Mikhail. 1984. *Problems of Dostoevsky's Poetics*. Theory and History of Literature. Edited and translated by Caryl Emerson. Minneapolis: University of Minnesota Press, vol. 8.

Bal, Mieke. 2009. *Narratology: Introduction to the Theory of Narrative*, 3rd ed. Translated by Christine van Boheeman. Toronto: University of Toronto Press.

Barr, David L. 1998. *Tales of the End: A Narrative Commentary on the Book of Revelation*. Santa Rosa: Polebridge Press.

Barr, David L. 2016. Narrative Technique in the Book of Revelation. In *Oxford Handbook of Biblical Narrative*. Edited by Danna Nolan Fewell. Oxford: Oxford University Press, pp. 376–88.

Barrett, C. K. 1978. *The Gospel According to St. John: An Introduction with Commentary and Notes on the Greek Text*, 2nd ed. Westminster: Philadelphia.

Barthes, Roland. 1974. *S/Z: An Essay*. Translated by Richard Miller. New York: Hill and Wang.

Bauckham, Richard. 1996. The Parable of the Royal Wedding Feast (Matthew 22:1–14) and the Parable of the Lame Man and the Blind Man (*Apocryphon of Ezekiel*). *Journal of Biblical Literature* 115: 471–88. [CrossRef]

Bernard, J. H. 1929. *A Critical and Exegetical Commentary on the Gospel according to St. John*. 2 vols. New York: Scribner's.

Black, C. Clifton. 2001. *The Rhetoric of the Gospel: Theological Artistry in the Gospels and Acts*. St. Louis: Chalice.

Bleich, David. 1975. *Readers and Feelings: An Introduction to Subjective Criticism*. Urbana: National Council of Teachers of English.

Boers, Hendrikus. 1988. *Neither on This Mountain nor in Jerusalem: A Study of John 4*. Society of Biblical Literature Monograph Series 35. Atlanta: Scholars Press.

Boesak, Allan A. 1987. *Comfort and Protest: Reflections on the Apocalypse of John of Patmos*. Philadelphia: Westminster Press.

Booth, Wayne C. 1983. *The Rhetoric of Fiction*, 2nd ed. Chicago: University of Chicago Press.

Brown, Raymond E. 1966. *The Gospel according to John I–XII*. Anchor Yale Bible 29. New Haven: Yale University Press.

Bultmann, Rudolf. 1971. *The Gospel of John: A Commentary*. Translated by G. R. Beasley-Murray. Philadelphia: Westminster.

Camery-Hoggatt, Jerry. 1992. *Irony in Mark's Gospel: Text and Subtext*. Society for New Testament Studies Monograph Series 72. Cambridge: Cambridge University Press.

Carter, Warren. 2004. *Matthew: Storyteller, Interpreter, Evangelist*, rev. ed. Grand Rapids: Baker Academic.

Castelli, Elizabeth A., Stephen D. Moore, Gary A. Phillips, and Regina M. Schwartz, eds. 1995. Reader-Response Criticism. In *The Postmodern Bible*. The Bible and Culture Collective. New Haven: Yale University Press, pp. 20–69.

Charles, R. H. 1920. *A Critical and Exegetical Commentary on the Revelation of St. John*. 2 vols. International Critical Commentary. New York: Scribner's.

Chatman, Seymour. 1978. *Story and Discourse: Narrative Structure in Fiction and Film*. Ithaca: Cornell University Press.

Childs, Peter, and Roger Fowler. 2006. *The Routledge Dictionary of Literary Terms*. London: Routledge.

Coleridge, Samuel Taylor. 1983. *Biographia Literaria or Biographical Sketches of My Literary Life and Opinions*. Bollingen Series 75; Edited by James Engell and W. Jackson Bate. Princeton: Princeton University Press. First published 1817.

Culpepper, R. Alan. 1983. *Anatomy of the Fourth Gospel: A Study in Literary Design*. Philadelphia: Fortress Press.

Darr, John A. 1992. *On Character Building: The Reader and the Rhetoric of Characterization in Luke-Acts*. Literary Currents in Biblical Interpretation. Louisville: Westminster John Knox Press.

Darr, John A. 1998. *Herod the Fox: Audience Criticism and Lukan Characterization*. Journal for the Study of the New Testament Supplement Series 163. Sheffield: Sheffield Academic Press.

Dawsey, James M. 1986. What's in a Name: Characterization in Luke. *Biblical Theology Bulletin* 16: 143–47. [CrossRef]

Dicken, Frank E. 2014. *Herod as a Composite Character in Luke-Acts*. Wissenschaftliche Untersuchungen zum Neuen Testament II 375. Tübingen: Mohr Siebeck.

Dicken, Frank E., and Julia A. Snyder, eds. 2016. *Characters and Characterization in Luke-Acts*. Library of New Testament Studies 548. London: Bloomsbury T & T Clark.

Dinkler, Michal Beth. 2013. *Silent Statements: Narrative Representations of Speech and Silence in the Gospel of Luke*. Beihefte zur Zeitschrift für die neutestamentliche Wissenschaft 191. Berlin: De Gruyter.

Dinkler, Michal Beth. 2015. 'The Thoughts of Many Hearts Shall be Revealed': Listening in on Lukan Interior Monologues. *Journal of Biblical Literature* 134: 373–99.

Dinkler, Michal Beth. 2017. Building Character on the Road to Emmaus: Lukan Characterization in Contemporary Literary Perspective. *Journal of Biblical Literature* 136: 687–706. [CrossRef]

Docherty, Thomas. 1983. *Reading (Absent) Character: Towards a Theory of Characterization in Fiction*. Oxford: Clarendon.

Duke, Paul. 1985. *Irony in the Fourth Gospel*. Atlanta: John Knox Press.

Edwards, James R. 1989. Markan Sandwiches: The Significance of Interpolations in Markan Narratives. *Novum Testamentum* 31: 193–216.

Elliot, Scott S. 2011. *Reconfiguring Mark's Jesus: Narrative Criticism after Poststructuralism*. The Bible in the Modern World 41. Sheffield: Sheffield Phoenix Press.

Elliott, J.K. 1972. Κηφᾶς: Σίμων Πέτρος: ὁ Πέτρος: An Examination of New Testament Usage. *Novum Testamentum* 14: 241–56.

Finnern, Sönke. 2010. *Narratologie und Biblische Exegese: Eine integrative Methode der Erzählanalyse und ihr Ertrag am Beispiel von Matthäus 28*. Wissenschaftliche Untersuchungen zum Neuen Testament 285. Tübingen: Mohr Siebeck.

Finnern, Sönke. 2014. Narration in Religious Discourse: The Example of Christianity. In *The Living Handbook of Narratology*. Edited by Peter Hühn, Jan Christoph Meister, John Pier and Wolf Schmid. Hamburg: Hamburg University. Available online: http://www.lhn.uni-hamburg.de/article/narration-religious-discourse-example-christianity (accessed on 18 March 2019).

Fish, Stanley E. 1980. *Is There a Text in This Class? The Authority of Interpretative Communities*. Cambridge: Harvard University Press.

Fishbane, Michael. 1979. *Text and Texture: Close Readings of Selected Biblical Texts*. New York: Schocken Books.

Forster, Edward M. 2005. *Aspects of the Novel*. New York: Penguin Books. First published 1927.

Fowler, Robert M. 1991. *Let the Reader Understand: Reader-Response Criticism and the Gospel of Mark*. Minneapolis: Fortress Press.

Fowler, Robert M. 2008. Reader-Response Criticism: Figuring Mark's Reader. In *Mark and Method: Approaches in Biblical Studies*, 2nd ed. Edited by Janice Capel Anderson and Stephen D. Moore. Minneapolis: Fortress, pp. 59–93.

Freytag, Gustav. 1896. *Freytag's Technique of the Drama: An Exposition of Dramatic Composition and Art*, 2nd ed. Translated by Elias J. MacEvan. Chicago: S. G. Briggs and Company.

Frye, Northrop. 1981. *The Great Code: The Bible and Literature*. New York: Harcourt Brace Jovanovich.

Genette, Gérard. 1980. *Narrative Discourse: An Essay in Method*. Translated by Jane E. Lewin. Ithaca: Cornell University Press. First published 1972.

Gombrich, E. H. 1961. *Art and Illusion: A Study in the Psychology of Pictorial Representation*, 2nd ed. revised. Bollingen Series 35. Princeton: Princeton University Press.

Goodman, Paul. 1954. *The Structure of Literature*. Chicago: University of Chicago Press.

Green, Joel B. 2016. A Cognitive Narratological Approach to the Characterization(s) of Zacchaeus. In *Characters and Characterization in Luke-Acts*. Library of New Testament Studies 548. Edited by Frank E. Dicken and Julia A. Snyder. London: Bloomsbury T & T Clark, pp. 109–20.

Harmon, William. 2012. *A Handbook to Literature*, Twelfth Edition ed. Boston: Longman.

Herman, David. 2013. Cognitive Narratology. In *The Living Handbook of Narratology*. Edited by Peter Hühn, Jan Christoph Meister, John Pier and Wolf Schmid. Hamburg: Hamburg University. Available online: http://www.lhn.uni-hamburg.de/article/cognitive-narratology-revised-version-uploaded-22-september-2013 (accessed on 18 March 2019).

Hochman, Baruch. 1985. *Character in Literature*. Ithaca: Cornell University Press.

Holland, Norman N. 1975a. *5 Readers Reading*. New Haven: Yale University Press.

Holland, Norman N. 1975b. Unity Identity Text Self. *Publications of the Modern Language Association* 90: 813–22. [CrossRef]

Homer. 2017. *The Odyssey*. Translated by Emily Wilson. New York: W. W. Norton & Company.

Hongisto, Leif. 2010. *Experiencing the Apocalypse at the Limits of Alterity*. Biblical Interpretation Series 102. Leiden: Brill.

Horsley, Richard A. 2001. *Hearing the Whole Story: The Politics of Plot in Mark's Gospel*. Louisville: Westminster John Knox.

Howell, David B. 1990. *Matthew's Inclusive Story: A Study of the Narrative Rhetoric of the First Gospel*. Journal for the Study of New Testament Supplement Series 42. Sheffield: JSOT Press.

Hunt, Steven A., D. Francois Tolmie, and Ruben Zimmermann, eds. 2013. *Character Studies in the Fourth Gospel: Narrative Approaches to Seventy Figures in John*. Wissenschaftliche Untersuchungen zum Neuen Testament 314. Tübingen: Mohr Siebeck; reprint. Grand Rapids, MI: Eerdmans, 2016.

Iser, Wolfgang. 1971. Indeterminacy and the Reader's Response in Prose Fiction. In *Aspects of Narrative*. Edited by J. Hillis Miller. New York: Columbia University Press, pp. 1–45.

Iser, Wolfgang. 1972. The Reading Process: A Phenomenological Approach. *New Literary History: A Journal of Theory and Interpretation* 3: 279–99. [CrossRef]

Iser, Wolfgang. 1974. *The Implied Reader: Patterns of Communication in Prose Fiction from Bunyan to Beckett*. Baltimore: Johns Hopkins University Press.

Iser, Wolfgang. 1978. *The Act of Reading: A Theory of Aesthetic Response*. Baltimore: Johns Hopkins University Press.

James, Henry. 1948. The Art of Fiction. In *The Art of Fiction and Other Essays by Henry James*. Edited by Morris Roberts. New York: Oxford University Press, pp. 3–23. First published 1884.

Kermode, Frank. 1979. *The Genesis of Secrecy: On the Interpretation of Narrative*. The Charles Elliot Norton Lectures 35. Cambridge: Harvard University Press.

Kingsbury, Jack Dean. 1991. *Matthew: Structure, Christology, Kingdom*. Minneapolis: Fortress Press.

Koester, Craig R. 2003. *Symbolism in the Fourth Gospel: Meaning, Mystery, Community*, 2nd ed. Minneapolis: Fortress Press.

Koester, Craig R. 2014. *Revelation*. Anchor Yale Bible 38A. New Haven: Yale University Press.

Kurz, William S. 1993. *Reading Luke-Acts: Dynamics of Biblical Narrative*. Louisville: Westminster John Knox Press.

Lane, Belden C. 1998. *The Solace of Fierce Landscapes: Exploring Desert and Mountain Spirituality*. New York: Oxford University Press.

Lanser, Susan Sniader. 1981. *The Narrative Act: Point of View in Prose Fiction*. Princeton: Princeton University Press.

Larsen, Kasper Bro. 2008. *Recognizing the Stranger: Recognition Scenes in the Gospel of John*. Biblical Interpretation Series 93. Leiden: Brill.

Lee, Dorothy A. 1994. *The Symbolic Narratives of the Fourth Gospel: The Interplay of Form and Function*. Journal for the Study of the New Testament Supplement Series 95. Sheffield: JSOT Press.

Lehtipuu, Outi. 1999. Characterization and Persuasion: The Rich Man and the Poor Man in Luke 16, 19–31. In *Characterization in the Gospels: Reconceiving Narrative Criticism*. Journal for the Study of the New Testament Supplement Series 184; Edited by David Rhoads and Kari Syreeni. Sheffield: Sheffield Academic Press, pp. 73–105.

Mailloux, Steven. 1982. *Interpretive Conventions: The Reader in the Study of American Fiction*. Ithaca: Cornell University Press.

Malbon, Elizabeth Struthers. 1983. Fallible Followers: Women and Men in the Gospel of Mark. *Semeia* 28: 29–48.

Malbon, Elizabeth Struthers. 2000. *In the Company of Jesus: Characters in Mark's Gospel*. Louisville: Westminster John Knox Press.

Malbon, Elizabeth Struthers. 2008. Narrative Criticism: How Does the Story Mean? In *Mark & Method: New Approaches in Biblical Studies*, 2nd ed. Edited by Janice Capel Anderson and Stephen D. Moore. Minneapolis: Fortress Press, pp. 29–57.

Malbon, Elizabeth Struthers. 2009. *Mark's Jesus: Characterization as Narrative Christology*. Waco: Baylor University Press.

Malbon, Elizabeth Struthers. 2011. Characters in Mark's Story: Changing Perspectives on the Narrative Process. In *Mark as Story: Retrospect and Prospect*. Resources for Biblical Study 65. Edited by Kelly R. Iverson and Christopher W. Skinner. Atlanta: Society of Biblical Literature, pp. 45–69.

Marguerat, Daniel, and Yvan Bourquin. 1999. *How to Read Bible Stories: An Introduction to Narrative Criticism*. London: SCM Press.

Martin, Wallace. 1986. *Recent Theories of Narrative*. Ithaca: Cornell University Press.

Matera, Frank J. 1987. The Plot of Matthew's Gospel. *Catholic Biblical Quarterly* 49: 233–53.

Mazzaferri, Frederick David. 1989. *The Genre of the Book of Revelation from a Source-Critical Perspective*. Beiheft zur Zeitschrift für die neutestamentliche Wissenschaft und die Kunde der älteren Kirche 54. Berlin: de Gruyter.

Meister, Jan Christoph. 2014. Narratology. In *The Living Handbook of Narratology*. Edited by Peter Hühn, Jan Christoph Meister, John Pier and Wolf Schmid. Hamburg: Hamburg University. Available online: http://www.lhn.uni-hamburg.de/article/narratology (accessed on 18 March 2019).

Moore, Stephen D. 1989. *Literary Criticism and the Gospels: The Theoretical Challenge*. New Haven: Yale University Press.

Moore, Stephen D. 2016. Biblical Narrative Analysis from the New Criticism to the New Narratology. In *The Oxford Handbook of Biblical Narrative*. Edited by Danna Nolan Fewell. New York: Oxford University Press, pp. 27–50.

Mounce, Robert H. 1998. *The Book of Revelation*, rev. ed. New International Commentary on the New Testament. Grand Rapids: Eerdmans.

Muecke, D. C. 1969. *The Compass of Irony*. London: Methuen.

Neirynck, Frans. 1988. *Duality in Mark: Contributions to the Study of the Markan Redaction*, rev. ed. Bibliotheca Ephemeridum Theologicarum Lovaniensium 31. Louvain: Louvain University Press.

Niederhoff, Burkhard. 2013a. Focalization. In *The Living Handbook of Narratology*. Edited by Peter Hühn, Jan Christoph Meister, John Pier and Wolf Schmid. Hamburg: Hamburg University. Available online: http://www.lhn.uni-hamburg.de/article/focalization (accessed on 18 March 2019).

Niederhoff, Burkhard. 2013b. Perspective—Point of View. In *The Living Handbook of Narratology*. Edited by Peter Hühn, Jan Christoph Meister, John Pier and Wolf Schmid. Hamburg: Hamburg University. Available online: http://www.lhn.uni-hamburg.de/article/perspective----point-view (accessed on 18 March 2019).

O'Day, Gail. 1986. *Revelation in the Fourth Gospel: Narrative Mode and Theological Claims*. Philadelphia: Fortress Press.

Olmstead, Wesley G. 2003. *Matthew's Trilogy of Parables: The Nation, the Nations, and the Reader in Matthew 21:28–22:14*. Society for New Testament Studies Monograph Series 127. Cambridge: Cambridge University Press.

Perry, Menakhem. 1979. Literary Dynamics: How the Order of a Text Creates Its Meanings. *Poetics Today* 1: 35–64, 311–61. [CrossRef]

Phelan, James. 2005a. *Living to Tell about It: A Rhetoric and Ethics of Character Narration*. Ithaca: Cornell University Press.

Phelan, James. 2005b. Rhetorical Narratology. In *Routledge Encyclopedia of Narrative Theory*. Edited by David Herman, Manfred Jahn and Marie-Laure Ryan. London: Routledge, pp. 500–4.

Powell, Mark Allan. 1990. *What is Narrative Criticism?* Guides to Biblical Scholarship, New Testament Series. Minneapolis: Fortress Press.

Powell, Mark Allan. 2001. *Chasing the Eastern Star: Adventures in Biblical Reader-Response Criticism*. Louisville: Westminster John Knox Press.

Powell, Mark Allan. 2011. Narrative Criticism: The Emergence of a Prominent Reading Strategy. In *Mark as Story: Retrospect and Prospect*. Resources for Biblical Study 65. Edited by Kelly R. Iverson and Christopher W. Skinner. Atlanta: Society of Biblical Literature, pp. 19–43.

Prince, Gerald. 1971. Notes toward a Characterization of Fictional Narratees. *Genre* 4: 100–5.

Prince, Gerald. 1973. Introduction to the Study of the Narratee. *Poétique* 14: 177–96.

Prince, Gerald. 2013. Reader. In *The Living Handbook of Narratology*. Edited by Peter Hühn, Jan Christoph Meister, John Pier and Wolf Schmid. Hamburg: Hamburg University. Available online: http://www.lhn.uni-hamburg.de/article/reader (accessed on 18 March 2019).

Rabinowitz, Peter J. 1987. *Before Reading: Narrative Conventions and the Politics of Interpretation*. Ithaca: Cornell University Press.

Reinhartz, Adele. 2001. *Befriending the Beloved Disciple: A Jewish Reading of the Gospel of John*. New York: Continuum.

Resseguie, James L. 1982a. John 9: A Literary-Critical Analysis. In *Literary Interpretations of Biblical Narratives*. Edited by Kenneth R. R. Gros Louis. Nashville: Abingdon Press, vol. 2, pp. 295–303; reprinted in *The Gospel of John as Literature: An Anthology of Twentieth-Century Literature*, 1993, pp. 115–22.

Resseguie, James L. 1982b. Point of View in the Central Section of the Gospel of Luke (9:51–19:44). *Journal of the Evangelical Theological Society* 25: 41–47.

Resseguie, James L. 1984. Reader-Response Criticism and the Synoptic Gospels. *Journal of the American Academy of Religion* 52: 307–24. [CrossRef]

Resseguie, James L. 1988. Defamiliarization in the Gospels. *Mosaic: A Journal for the Interdisciplinary Study of Literature* 21: 25–35. [CrossRef]

Resseguie, James L. 1990. Defamiliarization and the Gospels. *Biblical Theology Bulletin* 20: 147–53. [CrossRef]

Resseguie, James L. 1991. Automatization and Defamiliarization in Luke 7:36–50. *Journal of Literature and Theology* 5: 137–50. [CrossRef]

Resseguie, James L. 1992. Luke 7:36–50. *Interpretation: A Journal of Bible and Theology* 46: 285–90. [CrossRef]

Resseguie, James L. 1998. *Revelation Unsealed: A Narrative Critical Approach to John's Apocalypse*. Biblical Interpretation Series 32; Leiden: Brill.

Resseguie, James L. 2000. Literature, New Testament. In *Eerdmans Dictionary of the Bible*. Edited by David Noel Freedman. Grand Rapids: Eerdmans, pp. 815–17.

Resseguie, James L. 2001. *The Strange Gospel: Narrative Design and Point of View in John*. Biblical Interpretation Series 56. Leiden: Brill.

Resseguie, James L. 2004. *Spiritual Landscape: Images of the Spiritual Life in the Gospel of Luke*. Peabody: Hendrickson.

Resseguie, James L. 2005. *Narrative Criticism of the New Testament: An Introduction*. Grand Rapids: Baker Academic.

Resseguie, James L. 2007. Formalist/New Critical Interpretation. In *Dictionary of Biblical Criticism and Interpretation*. Edited by Stanley E. Porter. New York: Routledge, pp. 114–17.

Resseguie, James L. 2009. *The Revelation of John: A Narrative Commentary*. Grand Rapids: Baker Academic.

Resseguie, James L. 2013a. The Beloved Disciple: The Ideal Point of View. In *Character Studies in the Fourth Gospel: Narrative Approaches to Seventy Figures in John*. Wissenschaftliche Untersuchungen zum Neuen Testament 314. Edited by Steven A. Hunt, D. Francois Tolmie and Ruben Zimmermann. Tübingen: Mohr Siebeck, pp. 537–49; reprint, Grand Rapids, MI: Eerdmans, 2016, pp. 537–49.

Resseguie, James L. 2013b. A Narrative-Critical Approach to the Fourth Gospel. In *Characters and Characterization in the Gospel of John*. Library of New Testament Studies 461. Edited by Christopher W. Skinner. London: Bloomsbury T & T Clark, pp. 3–17.

Resseguie, James L. 2016. The Woman Who Crashed Simon's Party: A Reader-Response Approach to Luke 7:36–50. In *Characters and Characterization in Luke-Acts*. Library of New Testament Studies 548. Edited by Frank E. Dicken and Julia A. Snyder. London: Bloomsbury T & T Clark, pp. 7–22.

Resseguie, James L. Forthcoming (a). Narrative Criticism/Narratology. In *Encyclopedia of the Bible and Its Reception*. Edited by Christine Helmer, Stephen L. Mackenzie, Thomas Chr Romer, Jen Schroter, Barry Dov Walfish and Eric Ziolkowski. Berlin: de Gruyter.

Resseguie, James L. Forthcoming (b). Narrative Features of the Book of Revelation. In *Oxford Handbook of the Book of Revelation*. Edited by Craig R. Koester. New York: Oxford University Press.

Rhoads, David. 2004. Jesus and The Syrophoenician Woman in Mark: A Narrative-Critical Study. *Journal of the American Academy of Religion* 62: 343–75; reprinted in *Reading Mark*, pp. 63–94. First published 1994. [CrossRef]

Rhoads, David. 1982. Narrative Criticism and the Gospel of Mark. *Journal of the American Academy of Religion* 50: 411–34. [CrossRef]

Rhoads, David. 2004. *Reading Mark: Engaging the Gospel*. Minneapolis: Fortress Press.

Rhoads, David, and Donald Michie. 1982. *Mark as Story: An Introduction to the Narrative of a Gospel*. Minneapolis: Fortress Press.

Rhoads, David, and Kari Syreeni, eds. 1999. *Characterization in the Gospels: Reconceiving Narrative Criticism*. Journal for the Study of the New Testament Supplement Series 184. Sheffield: Sheffield Academic Press.

Rhoads, David, Joanna Dewey, and Donald Michie. 2012. *Mark as Story: An Introduction to the Narrative of a Gospel*, 3rd ed. Minneapolis: Fortress Press.

Richards, I. A. 1936. *The Philosophy of Rhetoric*. New York: Oxford University Press.

Rimmon-Kenan, Shlomith. 2002. *Narrative Fiction: Contemporary Poetics (New Accents)*, 2nd ed. London: Routledge.

Roth, S. John. 1997. *The Blind, the Lame and the Poor: Character Types in Luke-Acts*. Journal for the Study of the New Testament Supplement Series 144. Sheffield: Sheffield Academic Press.

Schmid, Wolf. 2013. Narratee. In *The Living Handbook of Narratology*. Edited by Peter Hühn, Jan Christoph Meister, John Pier and Wolf Schmid. Hamburg: Hamburg University. Available online: http://www.lhn.uni-hamburg.de/article/narratee (accessed on 18 March 2019).

Schneiders, Sandra M. 1999. *The Revelatory Text: Interpreting the New Testament as Sacred Scripture*, 2nd ed. Collegeville: The Liturgical Press.

Scholes, Robert, James Phelan, and Robert Kellogg. 2006. *The Nature of Narrative*. Fortieth Anniversary Edition Revised and Expanded. New York: Oxford University Press.

Schottroff, Luise. 1998. The Samaritan Woman and the Notion of Sexuality in the Fourth Gospel. In *What is John: Literary and Social Readings of the Fourth Gospel*. Edited by Fernando Segovia. Atlanta: Scholars Press, vol. 2, pp. 157–81.

Scott, Bernard Brandon. 1989. *Hear Then the Parable: A Commentary on the Parables of Jesus*. Minneapolis: Fortress Press.

Sellew, Phillip. 1992. Interior Monologue as a Narrative Device in the Parables of Jesus. *Journal of Biblical Literature* 111: 239–53. [CrossRef]

Sheeley, Steven M. 1992. *Narrative Asides in Luke-Acts*. Journal for the Study of the New Testament Supplement Series 72. Sheffield: JSOT Press.

Shen, Dan. 2013. Unreliability. In *The Living Handbook of Narratology*. Edited by Peter Hühn, Jan Christoph Meister, John Pier and Wolf Schmid. Hamburg: Hamburg University. Available online: http://www.lhn.uni-hamburg.de/article/unreliability (accessed on 18 March 2019).

Shepherd, Tom. 1995. The Narrative Function of Markan Intercalation. *New Testament Studies* 41: 522–40. [CrossRef]

Sheridan, Ruth. 2016. Persuasion. In *How John Works: Storytelling in the Fourth Gospel*. Edited by Douglas Estes and Ruth Sheridan. Atlanta: SBL Press, pp. 205–23.

Shklovsky, Victor. 2012. Art as Technique. In *Russian Formalist Criticism: Four Essays*, 2nd ed. Translated by Lee T. Lemon, and Marion J. Reis. Lincoln: University of Nebraska Press, pp. 3–24. First published 1917.

Skinner, Christopher W., ed. 2013. *Characters and Characterization in the Gospel of John*. Library of New Testament Studies 461. London: Bloomsbury T & T Clark.

Skinner, Christopher W., and Matthew Ryan Hauge, eds. 2014. *Character Studies and the Gospel of Mark*. Library of New Testament Studies 483. London: Bloomsbury T & T Clark.

Smith, Stephen H. 1996. *A Lion with Wings: A Narrative-Critical Approach to Mark's Gospel*. The Biblical Seminar 38. Sheffield: Sheffield Academic Press.

Starobinski, Jean. 1973. The Struggle with Legion: A Literary Analysis of Mark 5:1–20. *New Literary History: A Journal of Theory and Interpretation* 4: 331–56. [CrossRef]

Sternberg, Meir. 1978. *Expositional Modes and Temporal Ordering in Fiction*. Baltimore: Johns Hopkins University Press.

Suleiman, Susan R., and Inge Crossman, eds. 1980. *The Reader in the Text: Essays on Audience and Interpretation*. Princeton: Princeton University Press.

Tannehill, Robert. 1975. *The Sword of His Mouth: Forceful and Imaginative Language in Synoptic Sayings*. Semeia Supplements. Philadelphia: Fortress Press.

Taylor, Vincent. 1960. *The Gospel according to St. Mark*, 2nd ed. London: Macmillan.

Todorov, Tzvetan. 1969. *Grammaire du Décaméron*. The Hague: Moulton.

Tolmie, D. Francois. 1999. *Narratology and Biblical Narratives: A Practical Guide*. San Francisco: International Scholars Publications.

Tompkins, Jane P., ed. 1980. *Reader-Response Criticism: From Formalism to Post-Structuralism*. Baltimore: Johns Hopkins University Press.

Trible, Phyllis. 1978. *God and the Rhetoric of Sexuality*. Overtures to Biblical Theology. Philadelphia: Fortress Press.

Tull, Patricia K. 2013. Narrative Criticism and Narrative Hermeneutics. In *The Oxford Encyclopedia of Biblical Interpretation*. Edited by Stephen L. McKenzie. New York: Oxford University Press, vol. 2, pp. 37–46.

Uspensky, Boris. 1973. *A Poetics of Composition: The Structure of the Artistic Text and Typology of Compositional Form*. Translated by Valentina Zavarin, and Susan Wittig. Berkeley: University of California Press.

Via, Dan Otto, Jr. 1967. *The Parables: Their Literary and Existential Dimension*. Philadelphia: Fortress Press.

Whitenton, Michael R. 2016. The Dissembler of John 3: A Cognitive and Rhetorical Approach to the Characterization of Nicodemus. *Journal of Biblical Literature* 135: 141–58.

Wimsatt, W. K., Jr., and Monroe C. Beardsley. 1954. *The Verbal Icon: Studies in the Meaning of Poetry*. Lexington: University Press of Kentucky.

Yamasaki, Gary. 2007. *Watching a Biblical Narrative: Point of View in Biblical Exegesis*. London: T & T Clark.

religions

MDPI

Article

Paul, Timothy, and the Respectability Politics of Race: A Womanist Inter(con)textual Reading of Acts 16:1–5

Mitzi J. Smith

Ashland Theological Seminary, Southfield, MI 48075, USA; msmith19@ashland.edu

Received: 10 February 2019; Accepted: 10 March 2019; Published: 13 March 2019

check for
updates

Abstract: In this paper, I interpret the story of the Apostle Paul's circumcision of Timothy in the New Testament text The Acts of the Apostles (16:1–5) from a womanist perspective. My approach is intersectional and inter(con)textual. I construct a hermeneutical dialogue between African American women's experiences of race/racism, respectability politics, and the Acts' narrative. In conversation with critical race theorists Naomi Zack, Barbara and Karen Fields, and black feminist E. Frances White, I discuss the intersection of race/racism, gender, geopolitical Diasporic space, and the burden and failure of respectability politics. Respectability politics claim that when non-white people adopt and exhibit certain proper behaviors, the reward will be respect, acceptance, and equality in the white dominated society, thereby ameliorating or overcoming race/racism. Race and racism are modern constructions that I employ heuristically and metaphorically as analytical categories for discussing the rhetorical distinctions made between Jews and Greeks/Gentiles, Timothy's bi-racial status, and to facilitate comparative dialogue between Acts and African American women's experiences with race and racism. I argue that Paul engages in respectability politics by compelling Timothy to be circumcised because of his Greek father and despite the Jerusalem Council's decision that Gentile believers will not be required to be circumcised.

Keywords: New Testament; womanist; Acts; Paul; Timothy; race; respectability; interpretation; intercontextuality; racism; Diaspora politics

1. Introduction

In the New Testament canonical text, The Acts of the Apostles, the Apostle Paul has Timothy circumcised so that he can join Paul's evangelistic team in the Diaspora (16:1–5). In this paper, I read that story from a womanist perspective. More specifically, I interpret the narrative through the framework of and in conversation with respectability politics, race/racism, and black women's experiences. A womanist perspective prioritizes the historical and contemporary concerns, traditions, and experiences of black women as a starting point and as an interpretive lens for reading biblical and other sacred texts and contexts. My approach is a womanist inter(con)textual reading of Acts 6:1–5, in that I construct a dialogue between African American women's experience of respectability politics and the biblical story. A womanist perspective takes seriously the intersectionality of gender, race, and class, since most non-white women experience the world as poor or middle-class women and are simultaneously impacted by sexism, racism, and elitism or classism. In my analysis of Acts 6:1–5, the term *race* heuristically refers to the dichotomous biracial[1] categorization of peoples as two kinds (*genos*) of people (*ethnē*), as in Jew or Greek/Gentile, as either one or the other, but never both.[2]

---

[1] The racialized biracial system of the U.S. divides peoples into two primary categories: One is either white or non-white. This is manifested in the U.S. census forms.

[2] Denise K. Buell (2002, 2005) has argued that, in the second through early third centuries CE, being a Christian was regarded as a universal or new race in the *Shepherd of Hermas*, Clement of Alexandria, and Origen. Love Sechrest (2010) asserts that

Of course the term *race* as a modern social construct "stands for the conception or the doctrine that nature produced humankind in distinct groups, each defined by inborn traits that its members share and that differentiate them from the members of other distinct groups of the same kind but of unequal rank" (Fields and Fields 2014, p. 16). Racism is also a social construct based upon the concept of *race*, but the difference between the two, as Fields and Fields argue, is that, while race is a construct like the "the evil eye," racism is like genocide (ibid., p. 129). I also employ *race* metaphorically to talk about the distinctions and relationship constructed between Jews and Greeks/Gentiles in Acts, particularly between Paul and Timothy in Acts 6:1–5. A metaphor makes an implicit, implied, or hidden comparison between two things that are somewhat unrelated, but which share some common characteristics. Race/racism in the modern sense is historically and ideologically distant and different from the rhetorical construction of Jew and Gentile in Acts, but we can find points of comparison or common characteristics. For example, in the modern social construction of people as "white" or "black"/non-white, one is never fluidly both, and white people are considered superior to and/or they dominate non-white peoples. Similarly, in Acts, one is either a Jew or Gentile, but not both. The Jewish leadership and apostles dominate over the Gentile believers in that the former make the crucial decision about outsiders and insiders, how people become insiders and on what basis; the Jews are the dominant race in Acts (of course Rome is the overarching hegemony).

Using the works of critical race theorists Naomi Zack, Barbara and Karen Fields, and black feminist E. Frances White, I deploy race and the burden and failure of respectability politics as a framework for reading and in dialogue with Timothy's circumcision. Respectability politics is the notion that if a member of a subordinated, marginalized, or oppressed group exhibits acceptable and submissive behaviors, is socially compliant in her appearance and ways of being (e.g., attire, hair style, language, voice, sexuality, marital status, and so on), achieves some measure of success regardless of any systemic obstacles, and according to the standards of the dominant culture, she will be accepted by the dominant group; she will be treated justly and equally and will earn access to the same privileges and protected rights enjoyed by the dominant group. In Acts, Paul, as a member of the dominant race, succumbs to and imposes the burden of respectability on Timothy when he has him circumcised *after* the Jerusalem Council had ruled, under the leadership of James, the brother of Jesus, that the burden of circumcision should not be hoisted on the backs of Gentile believers. Often the superior, dominant group regard other people as possessing some perennial problematic difference that can never fully be overcome in this life (or in the afterlife with its segregated heaven, as some whites believe(d)). The contextually superior and dominant group is the privileged race and the other subordinated race is compelled to submit to the will and rules of the dominant group, especially if they expect to experience any degree of inclusion or access to resources and privileges. Respectability is inherent in and defined in relation to the dominant race and is often a fetish of the subordinated race. Thus, this paper begins with a discussion of respectability politics, African American women, and Timothy. Second, I examine the problem of race and bi-racial identity in Acts and in the U.S. The hyphenated form *bi-racial* refers to people who, because of known, observable mixed parentage, are (self-) identified as bi-racial. Without the hyphen, *biracial* refers to the dichotomous construction of peoples as either one race or another and never both. "Races do not exist in the sense in which reasonable people persist in speaking as if they did [scientifically]. If races do not exist, then mixed races do not exist either," but because of their common usage in the U.S., it is necessary to both mention and use them in our quest to comprehend significant human behaviors (Zack 1993, pp. 70–71). Third, I address geopolitical Diaspora space, the circumcision of Timothy, and respectability. The intersection of race, gender and Diaspora politics compel the cutting of Timothy's flesh, as an act of respectability. Finally, I discuss the relationship between problematic flesh, exceptionalism, and the myth of acceptance in Acts and

---

Paul understood himself as a Christian, which can be understood as a third race within the context of Second Temple Judaism; Paul no longer saw himself as a Jew. In my view, this is not the case in Acts (or in Paul's writings) where the Jesus movement is still a sect within Judaism with Jewish leaders who do not cease to be Jewish or to call the shots.

in the U.S. concerning African American women. Respectability is carved in the flesh of exceptional racialized non-white and non-Jewish women, men, and their children, but it never achieves human equality and never satiates the genocidal monster of racism.

2. Respectability Politics, African American Women, and Timothy

Respectability politics has been imposed upon and employed by enslaved and free black and brown people as a means to ameliorate racial and gender violence and oppression, or to facilitate assimilation into or acceptance by the dominant culture. Some enslaved Africans in the American South believed that by becoming Christians, their enslavers would treat them more humanely and perhaps emancipate them (Raboteau 1978; Smith and Jayachitra 2014). In the last part of the 19th and first half of the 20th century, African American educator, spokeswoman, and author of *A Voice From the South*, Dr. Anna Julia Cooper (1988), placed the burden for the uplift of the "Negro" race on the shoulders of elite educated black women[3]: "Now the fundamental agency under God in the regeneration, the re-training of the race, as well as the ground work and starting point of its progress upward, must be the *black woman*," and to do so she must be educated and reflect "true womanhood" (p. 28, Cooper's emphasis). A black woman was labeled "unrespectable" if she was positioned outside the "protection" of womanhood (White 2001, p. 33). She should achieve a high level of education *and* be somebody's good, domesticated wife. Cooper (1988) believed that educated and passionate women—empathetic intellectual thinkers—were what the world needed, but education should never interfere with marriage (pp. 50, 65–68). An "earnest, well-trained, Christian young woman, as a teacher, as a home-maker, as a wife, mother, or silent influence even, is as potent a missionary agency among our people as is the theologian"; an "elevated and trained womanhood" would purify the Negro race from within (ibid., pp. 29, 79). Cooper articulated black womanhood within the framework of white women's Victorian womanhood (although not without critique). Thus, assimilation to ideal Christian womanhood (the achievement of respectability and consequently inclusion and/or equality) would uplift the black race through the ideal black woman; like white Victorian womanhood, her views were elitist and reinforced distinctive notions of conduct respectable for men and women, respectively.[4]

Thus, African Americans practiced politics of respectability long before it was theoretically conceptualized. Evelyn Brooks Higginbotham (1994) coined the term "politics of respectability" in her book *Righteous Discontent*, where she analyzed the activities of the Women's Convention of the Black Baptist Church (1880–1920) and its focus on individual behaviors like cleanliness, thrift, proper manners, sexual purity, and temperance as means by which black women could uplift the black race. Higginbotham states that "African American women were particularly likely to use respectability and to be judged by it" (ibid., p. 213). It was important to act and appear respectable and educated in public, especially when one had to traverse the white world where one worked or conducted business. In this 21st century, notable elite (and middle class) members of the black community, like Bill Cosby and President Obama, have criticized black children for how they behave and dress and publicly chastised black parents for how they and their children are perceived by the dominant society. Such perceived failure to adhere to respectability politics is grounds for blaming those children and their parents (especially single mothers) for most of what has gone wrong in their lives and communities; the impact of systemic racism and concomitant poverty is minimized. As Paisley Harris (2003) posits, the "politics of respectability undermined the rigidly scientific nature of racial categories, but generally tended to reinforce status distinctions within the African American community. These distinctions were about class, but they were defined primarily in behavioral not economic terms. By linking worthiness for respect to sexual propriety, behavioral decorum, and neatness, respectability served a gatekeeping function, establishing a behavioral "entrance fee," to the right to respect and the right to

---

[3] Cooper earned a master's degree from Oberlin College in 1887 and defended her Ph.D. at the University of Paris in 1925.
[4] See Alridge (2007).

full citizenship," and the protection of black people's rights, if white people are so inclined (p. 213). But E. Francis White (2001) argues that, rather than acquiesce to respectability politics, black women are required to make their boundaries as expansive and elastic or flexible as possible (p. 16). Black women should resist submission to respectability politics.

We find no evidence of resistance in Acts when Timothy is compelled by Paul to acquiesce to the demands of the Diaspora "Jews," and to bear the marks of his assimilation in his flesh. Differently, William Jennings (2017) asserts that Timothy, the mulatto child, chose to be circumcised, although it was "Paul's design" (p. 154). But, nothing in the narrative implies that Timothy chose to submit to circumcision. We have no idea about Timothy's age; how old or young he was. We do know that before Paul arrives and expresses his desire for Timothy to accompany him and consequentially be circumcised, it had not occurred to Timothy's believing mother or to Timothy himself that he should submit to circumcision. One can be compelled to do something one would not ordinarily do in order to fit in or to obtain the benefits, privileges, or position that others enjoy. Thus, one acquiesces to gain acceptance, privileges, and human dignity otherwise denied in a racialized world. Circumcision becomes an option when Timothy is offered the opportunity and privilege of becoming one of Paul's co-laborers.

It seems hypocritical that Paul should take Timothy on the mission to deliver the Jerusalem Council's decision to the *ekklēsiai* (assemblies, often translated as churches) that the Gentile believers should not be asked to undergo circumcision, after having Timothy circumcised contrary to the decree of that very Council. The Jerusalem Council decided that Gentile believers should only be asked to abstain from eating meats improperly killed or prepared and meats offered to idols (Acts 15:19–29; cf. Gal 2:1–10). James Baldwin (1991) has harsh words for Paul and his impact on Christianity and white Christians: "[White Christians] have forgotten that the religion that is now identified with their virtue and their power ... came out of a rocky piece of ground in what is now known as the Middle East before color was invented and that in order for the Christian church to be established, Christ had to be put to death, by Rome and that the real architect of the Christian church was not the disreputable, sunbaked Hebrew who gave it his name, but the mercilessly fanatical and self-righteous St. Paul" (p. 44).

3. Race, Bi-Racial Identity, and Respectability

It was because of "the Jews" who insisted on the circumcision of Gentile believers that the Jerusalem Council was convened and Paul and Barnabas were sent to appear before it (Acts 15:1–6; cf. Gal 1:18–2:1–10). Gentiles are not Jews; Jews are not Gentiles. It is a matter of race. When we talk about race, we are also talking about racism, since race functions in the service of racism. Racism is political; it concerns how people, communities and societies act and institutions function on the basis of race—policies and laws are enacted, rights are recognized/denied and protected/violated, and resources/benefits are provided or withheld on the basis of race. "*Racism* is first and foremost a social practice, which means that it is an action and a rationale for action, or both at once. *Racism* always takes for granted the objective reality of *race*" (Fields and Fields 2014, p. 17; emphasis author's). Race is not biological and has no scientific or genetic basis (ibid., p. 8). Paul wants to make Timothy one of his co-laborers, but Paul is concerned about the Jews in the Diaspora where Paul has been sent to preach the gospel of God's grace. Thus, Paul decides that Timothy should be circumcised because of his father's race—he is Greek (*Hellenos*) and not Jewish. But Timothy's mother is a Jewish woman (*gynaikos Ioudaias*) of faith (*pistes*); she is a believer or member of the Jesus movement. She is anonymous in Acts. Commentators only marginally mention Timothy's mother, if at all. She is silent and silenced, as are many other women in Acts (Reimer 1995; Smith 2011). Perhaps her silence reflects her impotency to intervene; potency is gendered. The anonymity of Timothy's mother in Acts highlights the insignificance of her presence and her voice.

If non-white people, particularly black and brown people, can be convinced that their silence and acceptable behaviors, including language, dress, and a smile, are the ticket into the center, then race/racism can continue unmolested. Those who do not act deaf, dumb and blind will bear the blame for any and all rejection and failures of the system to treat black people fairly or with equity and/or to protect them or their rights. Respectability politics demands a level of complicity with the system and the silence of those who try to acquiesce to the system's demands and to assimilate to the dominant culture. As Audre Lorde (1984) asserts our silence immobilizes us and our silence will not save us (pp. 11, 44). The silence of black women and our communities will not save us, our children, or the generations that follow. A child's suffering is a mother's suffering. Black women are generally well-liked, as long as they suffer in relative silence: Do not demonstrate anger; do not challenge dominant authority; do not ask too many questions; and certainly do not accuse well-meaning white people of being or acting racist.

The Deutero-Pauline text of Second Timothy identifies Timothy's grandmother as Lois, and his mother as Eunice, both of whom were known as women of faith (1:5). Timothy is a believer like his mother, but he is his father's son first and foremost and the latter is neither a believer nor Jewish. No mention is made of Timothy's father in 1 or 2 Timothy. Perhaps, Timothy's father was an absentee father. Paul describes Timothy as one whose concern for others is unparalleled. The relationship between Paul and Timothy is as a child (*teknon*) to a father (*patri*) in the Deutero-Pauline texts; Timothy slaved (*edouleusen*) with Paul for the gospel and apparently submitted to Paul as his superior in order to serve Paul in the Gospel (Phil 2:22; cf. Rom 16:21; 1 Cor 4:17; 1 Tim 1:2, 18; 6:20; 2 Tim 1:2, 3:10). Indeed, according to Acts, Timothy submitted to circumcision, as a son would (or an enslaved man) to a Jewish father.

Eunice's Jewishness is insufficient and Timothy's father's Greekness is a problem that can only be surmounted by the cutting of the young man's flesh, by circumcision. Eric Baretto (2010) argues differently that Luke (and Paul) never resolves the matter of Timothy's "irreducibly mixed ethnic identity"; Timothy was both Greek and Jewish (p. 63). But when racial-ethnic identity is bifurcated as in Jew and Gentile/Greek in Acts and in Paul's writings, even when Gentiles become believers, hybridity is never an option. Claims to be Jew *and* Gentile, bi-racial, as in modern racialized societies, reify the ideology of race and racial purity. Because of the mixing of diverse peoples throughout human history, most all peoples are hybrid. Bi-racial claims usually imply that one is equally white and non-white or Jew and Gentile. Which veins carry white blood and which non-white blood? Which parts of Timothy are Jewish and which parts are Gentile? Perhaps Paul has a phallic solution in Timothy's case. Racial purity is a myth of the social construction of race. Race is not biological or genetic and racial purity is an ideological charade that allows dominant groups to subordinate and dehumanize others for their own benefit and purposes.

In 1977 the U.S. federal government identified the following basic racial/ethnic categories: American Indian or Alaskan Native; Asian or Pacific Island; Black; Hispanic (regardless of race); and White. One could select American Indian or Asian; Hispanics could identify as White or Black, but all persons with any origins in Africa were "black racial groups" (Ferrante and Browne 2001, pp. 135–40). In 1997, twenty years later, the U.S. Office of Management and Budget (OMB) asserted that no one could report belonging to more than one race or as being "multiracial," and in the same year changed the "Black" category to "Black or African American," leaving the definition unchanged (Ferrante and Browne 2001, pp. 139–41).[5] The U.S. Census required that citizens choose between White and other categories; the only category associated with ethnicity was Hispanic. In essence, if a people are not identified as White, they are considered non-White (i.e., Black/African American, Asian, Native Indian, or non-White Hispanic). Paul Knepper (2001) states that throughout American legal history, state and federal governments were inclined to enforce a narrow definition of "White" and a broad definition of "Black" and opposed attempts to blur "racial distinctions with a greater

---

[5] The OMB also allowed for the use of terms like "Negro" or "Haitian."

delineation of racial lines" (p. 130).[6] Instead, the U.S. has sometimes identified subcategories for "Black" persons. For example, in the 1854 California Supreme Court case, *People v. Hall*, a white man named George Hall appealed his murder conviction on the grounds that the witness against him was not white; a "Negro" or "Indian" could not legally testify against a white man. Not wanting to leave the question of race in doubt, the Court ruled that "white," by its very definition, ex vi termini (by the force of the boundary or by implication), excludes black, yellow, and any other color; a "black person" should be understood as "everyone who is not of white blood" (ibid., p. 131). In the 1896 U.S. Supreme Court case of *Plessy v. Ferguson*, the plaintiff, Homer Plessy, represented the Citizen's Committee to Test the Constitution of the Separate Car Law, a group of multiracial New Orleanians. Louisiana's Railway Accommodations Act of 1890 provided "equal but separate" accommodations for white and "colored races," wherein it was a misdemeanor for conductors to violate the seating law. Plessy, who appeared to be white, argued that since he was seven-eighths Caucasian and one-eighth African, and the "colored" part was *not* discernable, he deserved the legal status of white citizens (emphasis mine). But Justice Brown sided with Louisiana's law: The state has the power to decide a person's race and the railway conductor by extension has the power to determine a person's race and who should sit where, without assuming any risk (ibid.). Throughout the Jim Crow period, the courts decided upon issues of racial identity. Even white people mistaken for and thus treated as black brought cases to prove that they were white, which usually resulted in more rigid definitions of whiteness. One drop of African blood excluded a person from being identified as white and made him black, better known as the "one-drop rule". Under Tennessee law, all "Negroes, mulattoes, mestizos, and their descendants" with any African blood coursing in their veins were considered colored or non-white people (ibid., pp. 131–32). It did not matter if the African blood came from the father or the mother.

Both Jewish and Greek society were patrilineal in that the racial-ethnic status of the children was determined by the father's race. Shaye Cohen (1985) asserts that in biblical times since Israelite society was patrilineal and not matrilineal, offspring between an Israelite and a non-Israelite was determined patrilineally; the father's status would determine the children's ethnicity or social status. First century Jewish writers like Philo, the Apostle Paul, and Josephus show no familiarity with the matrilineal principle and it is unclear whether Luke is familiar with it in Acts 16 (p. 28). Later, in the mid-second century CE, we find matrilineal marriage in the Mishnah, which states that marriage between an Israelite woman and a Gentile man produces offspring that are considered Jews of impaired status (*mamzer*) (ibid., p. 19).[7] Thus in first century CE Judaism, Timothy would be considered a Gentile, despite having a Jewish mother.

The mother's racial–religious status does not count and in a patriarchal household where the father/patriarch is Greek apparently male children are not circumcised, at least not in this case—a fact that seems to be known by Paul based on the racial–religious status of Timothy's parents (Acts 16:3). In a racialized society, few would identify Timothy as *bi-racial*; the dominant group in a *biracial* society would view Timothy as Greek/Gentile, associating him with the subordinated race. Claims of *bi-racial* or multi-racial identity are disruptive and political. Brian Bantum (2010) asserts that "interracial bodies ... perform a disruption they themselves do not fully understand or live into ... their presence is political even if they are not" (p. 50).

---

[6] During the colonial period, lawmakers constructed an ideology of race and enacted laws to enforce it; mutually exclusive categories of race were used to sustain the distinction between enslaved and enslaver. For example, in 1664 the Maryland Colonial Assembly enacted laws to clarify persons identified as "Negro." The law stated that all Negroes and the enslaved already in the province and those later imported shall be enslaved in perpetuity (durante vita). However, previously, like other servants, "black" persons had the opportunity to be freed (Knepper 2001, p. 130; see Giddings 1984).

[7] Cohen (1985) argues for parallels between Roman laws about marriage between non-Roman citizens and Roman citizens as possibly influential on the development of the matrilineal principle in rabbinic literature.

4. Geopolitical Diaspora, Circumcision, and Respectability

It was because of "the Jews," or the circumcisers in Judea, that the Jerusalem Council was convened to decide on what basis the Gentile believers would be accepted into the Jewish Jesus movement (15:1–6). Timothy, and perhaps at least his mother, are living in Lystra in the Diaspora, which is thirty miles northwest of Derbe in the region of Galatia (16:1). Timothy is already a disciple when Paul decides he should undergo adult circumcision. Thus, Timothy has likely experienced both water baptism and Spirit baptism because neither are required and both are insufficient in light of Paul's anxieties about "the Jews" in Lystra and Iconium, all of whom know that Timothy's father is Greek (6:3), the "gaze" of "the Jews" in the Diaspora. Similarly, black people who embraced respectability politics were very conscious of the "white gaze," adopting a different code of conduct and language (especially for their children) when in the presence of white people, dissimilar from their behaviors in the private space of their homes and neighborhoods. "Respectability became an issue at the juncture of public and private" space (Higginbotham 1994, p. 213).

Paul treats Timothy like his child/son when he has him circumcised and later in the ministry, but what Paul is most concerned about is how Timothy is perceived by "the Jews" in the geopolitical space of Diaspora. It is perhaps both the fact that Timothy's father is not a believer *and* is Greek that could cause trouble for Timothy among "the Jews" in Lystra, Iconium, and throughout the Diaspora (cf. 14:1–2). When "Gentiles and Jews" of Iconium pursued Paul beyond Iconium, Paul fled to Derbe and Lystra in the region of Lycaonia, where the Lycaonians (mis)identify Paul and Barnabas as the Greek gods Hermes and Zeus, respectively, after Paul heals a man who had been born unable to walk (14:5–18). The Jews from Antioch and Iconium stoned Paul and left him for dead outside the city; his disciples rescued him, and they fled to Derbe (14:19–20).

Timothy's good reputation among the brothers or believers in his hometown counts less than the possible hostility of "the Jews" toward him (and Paul) in the Diaspora. Richard Pervo (2009) argues that the act of circumcising Timothy (whether Paul did it himself, we cannot know), "serves the Lucan program of 'Jews first,' and demonstrates Paul's loyalty to the traditional faith," but Paul's insistence that Timothy be circumcised makes him vulnerable to the charge Paul makes against Peter in Gal 2:14 (p. 388). Benny Tat-Siong Liew (2004) asserts that, not only does Acts have "an ethnicity problem," Paul, as portrayed in Acts, has one too. Liew notes that "Acts contains many references to the community's successful mission to Gentiles, but the work of mission and evangelism is restricted to Jews (Palestinian and Hellenistic . . . This ethnic monopoly (a kind of 'glass ceiling' for Gentile Christ-followers? [perhaps] may explain why [Luke's] Paul circumcises Timothy" (p. 422). Timothy likely became a believer prior to the Jerusalem Council's decision that Gentile believers should not be made to submit to circumcision. Did Paul not view the Council's decision as retroactive?

As the most influential Diaspora evangelist that the Antioch *ekklēsia* commissioned in Acts (Paul seems to arise to the same status as Barnabas who vouched for and mentored him, Acts 9:26–27, 13:1–3, 15:36–41), Paul had the authority and influence to place the burden of circumcision on Timothy, despite the Jerusalem Council's decree, and he did. Paul's bias and fears superseded the just decision of the Council not to place the burden of circumcision on the Gentiles (cf. 1 Cor 16:10).

We might argue that Paul is a good person. He has sacrificed his well-being to take the gospel to the Gentiles; he meant no harm. But he still operates from a position of racial bias and as the one with the authority and power, his bias is oppressive, harmful, consequential, and impacts Timothy's quality of life. Sometimes white people know that the pound of flesh that other white people demand of non-white bodies is unjust and overly burdensome, but they are silent and thus complicit in racism. Whitney Alese (2018) writes that respectability politics imply that the racism I encounter is my fault.

Paul's desire that a *circumcised* Timothy labor with him in the Diaspora is more important than the physical impact on Timothy as an adult. Jewish males are normally circumcised on the eighth day of their birth, as was Paul (Phil 3:5); adult circumcision can be debilitating or fatal and perhaps more so if the circumcised male adult is required to travel immediately after the procedure (cf. Gen 34:25–31, after the rape of Dinah, the men of Shechem agree to be circumcised; the men are slaughtered while they were still in pain on the third day after their circumcision). It is likely that the recovery time in the first century CE was greater than in modern times with advanced medicine and health care—an adult circumcision now takes about an hour to perform (compared with 2–3 minutes for an infant) and recovery time is 2–3 weeks. While the churches are strengthened as Paul and his traveling companions spread the news of the Jerusalem Council's decision, Timothy, the Greek son, has been compelled to submit to the cutting of his flesh and thus is very likely ailing and weak (6:4–5). This recovery time may account for Timothy's absence when Paul and Silas arrive in Macedonia and where they are jailed and accused of being Jews who are troubling the city; Timothy is not with Paul and Silas when they are arrested in Philippi of Macedonia (Acts 16:19–24). Timothy mysteriously reappears in Berea where Paul and Silas preach the Gospel after being set free from the Philippian jail (17:10–14; cf. 18:5, 19:22, 20:4).

According to Paul's letter to the Galatians, he never compelled his traveling companion Titus to be circumcised, even though he was a Greek (Gal 2:3). In his own writings, Paul is consistent in his view that Gentiles do not need to be circumcised; the Pauline writings also have no single "theology of circumcision" (see Livesey 2010). Perhaps Paul's insistence on Timothy's circumcision is part of Luke's construction of "the Jews" as the arch-enemy of the Pauline mission and of those who co-labor with him (see Smith 2011); "the Jews" would be as antagonistic toward Timothy and more so if they knew his father was Greek and that he was uncircumcised; the Jesus movement, as noted, is still a Jewish movement or a sect/party within Judaism, as the Jewish leaders articulate when they visit Paul under house arrest in Rome (Acts 28:17–22). Perhaps by persuading Timothy to submit to circumcision, Paul can present Timothy as respectable to "the Jews" and therefore as less of a target of their hostilities. Another possibility is that Luke attempts to show that Paul never really regarded the Jerusalem council as authoritative over his Diaspora ministry, as Paul states in his own writings (Gal 1:11–2:10).

It is also possible that Paul viewed Timothy as such an asset to his ministry that he wanted to ensure Timothy would not be hindered as his co-laborer in the Diaspora, despite that Paul himself, a circumcised Jewish male, had been forced to flee from place to place by "the Jews" and hostile mixed mobs that "the Jews" incited (9:23–25, 13:50–51, 14:6, 19–20, 17:13–14, 18:6). It does appear in Acts that Timothy is able to travel from region to region unmolested, either with or without Paul, unlike the way that non-white immigrants have been restricted from crossing U.S. borders. But Timothy had to become a Jewish man or like a Jewish man in order to move freely unmolested in the Diaspora.

The U.S. has a history of restricting the movement of non-white peoples wanting to immigrate into the country and non-white immigrants carry the burden of respectability as they are expected to behave better and work harder at menial jobs for less wages than the average white U.S. citizen, or they bear the risk of being called aliens, thugs, and thieves, being deported, and/or having their children snatched from them in their homes, at school, and/or at the U.S. border. The U.S. government asserts that it is not respectable for non-white mothers to risk their lives to seek asylum for their children and a better life away from unspeakable violence and poverty. President Donald Trump has referred to non-white asylum seekers as "stone cold criminals."[8] As of June 2018, Trump's immigration ban consisted of primarily non-white Muslim countries: Iran, Libya, Somalia, Syria, Yemen, North Korea, and Venezuela. The U.S. Immigration of Act of 1917 and 1920 prohibited and restricted, respectively, immigration from Asia and the Pacific Islands; the 1920 Act reduced the numbers of immigrants accepted into the U.S. from Southern and Eastern Europe (Knepper 2001, p. 132). In the 1922 federal court decision in *Ozawa v. U.S.* the court ruled that, based on the understanding of the "average man," there is an "unmistakable and profound difference between" Japanese people and white people and thus Takao Ozawa, who had been born in Japan but lived in California for twenty years, was not considered a "free white person" and thus was ineligible for naturalization (ibid., pp. 132–33). Knepper writes that "[t]he judiciary has refused to recognize the multiple and overlapping ancestry of the American people, but it has consistently upheld efforts to separate black from white" (ibid., p. 133).

---

8   Jansen and Gomez (2018).

5. Problematic Flesh, Exceptionalism, and the Myth of Acceptance

As mentioned above, according to Galatians, Paul did not insist that Titus, a Greek, be circumcised. Perhaps Paul viewed Timothy as exceptional; they certainly had an incomparable relationship as Paul's authentic and disputed letters attest. African Americans generally recognize that the problem with respectability politics is that they often appeal to the "exceptional Negro" or to Du Bois's "Talented Tenth" (Du Bois 1989) and not to African Americans in general (O'Neal 2018, p. 28). As Marsha Darling (2011) argues in her essay "The Personal is Always Political," African American and other non-white communities have always conceived and nurtured "bright, ambitious, high-achieving black American women and men, girls and boys," and too many "never made their mark as professionals, not because they lack motivation and smarts, but because racial bigotry and discrimination and disdain for women and girls slammed and jammed shut opportunity's doors" (p. 231).

Respectability politics has driven black women (men and children) to seek to be pure and acceptable by other people's standards, particularly the dominant white culture and to be blemish free, even as the dominant white culture nudges the yardstick forward to ensure that black people never measure up or the goal is placed out of reach for the masses of non-white people—only the exceptional black people achieve. When desperate, the white majority will simply change the rules. We saw this with President Barack Obama's candidacy and presidency, manifested in the birtherism movement that propagated the mendacious notion that Obama was not a citizen of the U.S. because he had not been born in the U.S. When the Republican-controlled Senate and House blocked President Obama's March 2016 nomination of Chief Judge Merrick Garland to replace Supreme Court Justice Antonin Scalia, they argued that, since President Obama was in his final year in office, he had no right to replace Scalia. Thus the nomination remained before the Senate for 293 days, the longest nomination process in U.S. history; Garland's nomination expired on 3 January 2017, with the end of the 114th Congress. Obama was treated as if he was no longer the President in his last year in office. Of course, it was a ploy to allow the incoming President (Donald Trump) to fill Scalia's seat with an ultra-conservative nominee. Non-white people will never measure up if the standard is to *be* white in a racialized society dominated by whiteness, undergirded by an ideology of white supremacy and entitlement.

In their quest for racial respectability and human dignity, some black people with extremely light skin, straight hair, and other features associated with whiteness attempted to pass as white—to be more than exceptional, namely to be white; it is called "passing."[9] As Bantum (2010) argues: "[T]he ability of some folks to pass implies how racial purity and notions of fixed identity require peoples to adhere or live into racial (and cultural) ideals" (p. 46). The "tragic mulatto" is the black person who, because she looks white, is rejected by the black community, but is also regarded as black and rejected by the white community because of her black blood, even if one drop (the kind that can only be detected when her parents are known to be black), is coursing through her veins. The classic film *Imitation of Life* is the story of the "tragic mulatto" and her struggle for inclusion into the white community because she looks (and feels) white; she attempts to *pass* as white. In the 1959 version of *Imitation of Life*, Sara Jane's parents are both considered black or Negro, but her father was a very fair skinned "Negro" who looked "practically white" and was likely so-called mixed race himself. Sara Jane favors her father and wants to pass as white, which she constantly attempts to do, but her mother always intervenes, showing up at her elementary school and at the club where she obtains a job as a chorus girl far from home. Even as a young child, Sara Jane was made to feel different and to know what it meant to be treated like a Black person. When Susie, Sara Jane's little white playmate and daughter of the white woman Laura Meredith (Lana Turner), for whom Annie Johnson (Juanita Moore) serves as a live-in maid, asks Annie, also known as "mammie," what color Jesus was, Sara Jane responds that "he was white like me." Sara Jane refused to attend the "Negro" church and "Negro" schools, to date "Negro" boys, to play with Susie's "black" doll, and to let anyone know that her mother was a "mammie." As a

---

[9]   See Nella Larsen (2000) and James Weldon Johnson (1994).

teenager, Sara Jane enters into a relationship with a white boy, who assumes she is white. When he discovers through town gossip that Sara Jane is black, he beats her, leaving her bloody and curled up like a dog in an alley on a dreary rainy night; it seemed like nature or God was crying with her, for her or both. It is never enough to look white, to be the exceptional black person, one must *be white* to enter into the white world as an equal. Sara Jane is determined to have the jobs, connections, and respect that the white folks whom she resembles are given and have opportunities to achieve because they are white. Sara Jane is willing to disown her mammie-mother to *be white*. Finally, in desperation to live as she looks, she disowns her mother, asking her that if she ever sees her on the street to act like she does not know her; her worn-out and broken-hearted mother agrees to honor Sara Jane's wishes. Mammie returns home where she resides in Ms. Laura's house and dies of a broken heart.

Respectability politics require that marginalized and minoritized women and men, particularly African American women, be exceptional; that they view themselves and are seen by the "elite" within their own community, as well as by the dominant white group, as set apart or different from the rest of their people/community. But the exceptional "Negro" is still a "Negro" to the dominant white group! Alice Walker's (1979) first definition of the term *womanist* describes the black woman in her short story "Coming Apart" as a womanist, which is "a feminist only more common." My own experiences as an African American woman are more common to black women and the black community; mine are not exceptional. I offer my personal experience with the idea and expectation of the "exceptional Negro," which is quite common, even if anecdotal. In my former life, as Paul would say, I was a legal secretary—I trained to be a good one, one of the best, sometimes the best at typing or shorthand in my high school class and among the top four in the region. When I landed my first job as a legal secretary in Columbus, Ohio for a sole practitioner and his law clerk, the law clerk thought it good to inform me one day that I was the first black girl they had ever hired; they presumed that all black women were slower than white women. Then he said, "But you are the fastest secretary we have ever had." I remember first being shocked and then being unimpressed. I had a number of high school classmates, black and white, who were professional and excellent at typing, shorthand, and other office skills. I thought about all the black women who never got an interview, simply because they were black and presumed to be too slow. However, possessing the skills that the law clerk thought were so superior did not keep them from paying me well below market rate, I soon found out. And my being on time and never absent for almost two years straight did not keep them from stating in my presence that black people are always late; I guess I was considered the exception. Being the exceptional "Negro" means that you cannot make mistakes, or your mistakes are attributed to an innate deficiency and not to a bad day—it is inherent in what the dominant group thinks of black people. I remember turning in a paper on time in my doctoral program, even though it was incomplete; in my anxiety, I presumed it was better that the paper was turned in on time, regardless of how unfinished it was. The white male professor wrote on my paper that I should know how to do analysis by now (I knew I had not finished writing the paper). He felt that was the only scenario that could account for my unfinished paper. I was hurt, but I knew my truth.

Paul regards Timothy as exceptional, but even the exceptional have a price to pay for inclusion. The price of inclusion is steep for Timothy and for black women—sometimes life threatening, death dealing, and it definitely can be traumatizing. The circumcision of Timothy was no microaggression. I don't know how old Timothy was but he was far from being an eight-day-old baby. The respectable behaviors that the dominant white group requires of non-white people to be accepted, to be included, or that the non-white people require of their own, are futile. It is not the behaviors of non-white people per se that are the problem for the dominant culture, it is our non-white flesh and what that flesh represents in a racialized society—that part of us that we cannot change no matter how well-behaved we act. As White (2001) asserts, "race remains immutable in the minds of most Americans" (p. 19). And racism, grounded on the ideology of race, demands a pound of black or brown flesh, but never envisions equality or parity.

Respectability was a principal basis upon which African Americans asserted their equal status and citizenship during the Progressive era. Defined more broadly, respectability continued to be a significant basis for claiming rights throughout the civil rights era and beyond, but it also potentially promoted exclusionary gatekeeping by linking claims of rights to certain behaviors and potentially limited the impact and effectiveness of black antiracism scholarship (White 2001). Most of the world never heard Serena Williams, the GOAT (greatest of all time), talk about the racial injustices and microaggressions she experienced as a strong capable black woman throughout her tennis career. Even now it is not respectable for Serena to claim that she felt cheated and to have the audacity to be angry and to stand up for herself while steeping in that anger. Black women have a right to be angry without being accused of whining, of being immature, or showing poor sportswomanship. Angry black women are often intelligent, capable individuals, who are forced to spend too much of our time dealing with rudeness, insults, and doubts about our capabilities from white (and some non-white and male) colleagues; black women are "[n]ot whiners, not complainers—just living a different reality" (Tillman 2011, p. 95). Serena is an example of how hard black women can work and how much they can achieve and still be accused of cheating or not measuring up—of being deficient. When black women (and men and their children) bend the rules of black respectability, they are no longer the exceptional "Negro." This reality is universal for black women. In her essay "Being Black and Female in the Academy," Linda Tillman (2011) argues that "the assumption that one can be promoted and tenured, promoted to full professor, and become a distinguished scholar and a respected leader if one just simply works hard is often a myth when applied to black faculty ... the norms of the academy do not allow for a critical mass of accomplished black female scholars ... only one or two black females are allowed to excel during any given period of time. More than a few intelligent black women in the academy is contradictory to the traditional roles that have been assigned to us" (pp. 91, 96). Tillman further asserts that she learned that the academy expected her not to act "too black" and not to "talk back" or to believe that she really belonged in academia. In fact, "no amount of publications, conference presentations, committee appointments, or awards will ever make others respect us or our work," she states (ibid., pp. 96, 105). Respectability politics reinforce the idea that black people will never measure up and that the majority of African Americans are inferior and will never fit in, but there are always exceptions.

Prior to that moment at the U.S. Open Championships in New York in 2018 where Serena expressed her anger publicly, many white folks who previously supported her turned against her on twitter and Facebook posts, calling her behavior unacceptable and announcing that Serena has been replaced, in their hearts, by Naomi Osaka, the somewhat shy and composed twenty-year-old young woman, whose Haitian identity many of those same white people conveniently forget to acknowledge. Osaka, according to the white dominant account, is the first Japanese player to win a Grand Slam single title. Naomi is still finding her own voice, but she will know, if she does not already, that respectability politics that demand our silence on issues of race/racism will not shield her/us from racism, that inclusion is at a cost to self and community and is not to be confused with equality and equity. Neither a politics of respectability nor a politics of inclusion will dismantle racism, sexism, classism, heterosexism, and other forms of oppression. What non-white peoples need from white allies is active engagement in dismantling, brick-by-brick, the "big houses" that slavery built and the structures that racism maintains and fortifies. From my own experience, and based on the stories of other African American women, well-behaved non-white women, those deemed worthy of acceptance and inclusion and those most acceptable once included, are black women who conduct themselves above reproach and teach their children to do likewise; they imitate ideals and ideas of white womanhood and culture, seeking to blend in and not to stand out; and they do not complain, or complain very little, at least not about systemic racism and the microaggressions that non-white people endure. But non-white women (men and their children) know, experientially and statistically, that inclusion—whether it be acceptance in a doctoral program or into a seminary or divinity school where one might be the only black female professor—usually means that African American women

Religions **2019**, *10*, 190

and men are expected to bare the burdens of systemic racism in silence and without naming the racism that one experiences.

Funding: This research received no external funding.

Conflicts of Interest: The author declares no conflict of interest.

References

Alridge, Derrick P. 2007. Of Victorianism, Civilizationism, and progressivism: The Educational Ideals of Anna Julia Cooper and W.E.B. Du Bois, 1891–1940. *History of Education Quarterly* 47: 416–46. [CrossRef]

Alese, Whitney. 2018. 7 Reasons Why respectability Politics are BS (Medium.com). Available online: https://medium.com/@TheReclaimed/7-reasons-why-respectability-politics-are-bs-1c97041ccfe2 (accessed on 31 January 2019).

Baldwin, James. 1991. *The Fire Next Time*. New York: Vintage.

Bantum, Brian. 2010. *Mulatto Messiah. A Theology of Race and Christian Hybridity*. Waco: Baylor University Press.

Baretto, Eric. 2010. *Ethnic Negotiations: The Function of Race and Ethnicity in Acts 16*. WUNT 2/276. Tübingen: Mohr Siebeck.

Buell, Denise Kimber. 2002. Race and Universalism in Early Christianity. *Journal of Early Christian Studies* 10: 429–48. [CrossRef]

Buell, Denise Kimber. 2005. *Why this New Race? Ethnic Reasoning in Early Christianity*. New York: Columbia University Press.

Cohen, Shaye J. D. 1985. The Origins of the Matrilineal Principle in Rabbinic Law. *AJS Review* 10: 19–53. [CrossRef]

Cooper, Anna Julia. 1988. *A Voice from the South*. New York: Oxford University Pres.

Darling, Marsha J. Tyson. 2011. The Personal is Always Political: Reflections on Creating Habitable Space in Academia. In *The Black Professoriat. Negotiating the Habitable Space in the Academy*. Edited by Sandra Jackson and Richard Greggory Johnson III. New York: Peter Lang, pp. 228–46.

Du Bois, William Edward Burghardt. 1989. *The Souls of Black Folk*. New York: Bantam.

Ferrante, Joan, and Princer Browne Jr. 2001. *The Construction of Race and Ethnicity in the United States*, 2nd ed. Upper Saddle River: Prentice-Hall.

Fields, Barbara, and Karen Fields. 2014. *Racecraft. The Soul of Inequality in American Life*. New York: Verso.

Giddings, Paula. 1984. *Where and When I Enter. The Impact of Black Women on Race and Sex in America*. New York: William Morrow.

Harris, Paisley J. 2003. Gatekeeping and remaking: The politics of respectability in African American women's history and black feminism. *Journal of Women's History* 15: 212–20. [CrossRef]

Higginbotham, Evelyn Brooks. 1994. *Righteous Discontent. The Women's Movement in the Black Baptist Church, 1880–1920*. Cambridge: Harvard University Press.

Jansen, Bart, and Alan Gomez. 2018. President Trump Calls Caravan of Immigrants 'Stone Cold Criminals. *USA Today*, December 6. Available online: https://www.usatoday.com/story/news/2018/11/26/president-trump-migrant-caravan-criminals/2112846002/ (accessed on 2 February 2019).

Jennings, Willie James. 2017. *Acts. Belief. A Theological Commentary on the Bible*. Louisville: Westminster John Knox.

Johnson, James Weldon. 1994. *Autobiography of an Ex-Coloured Man*. New York: Vintage.

Larsen, Nella. 2000. *Passing*. New York: Modern Library.

Liew, Benny Tat-Siong. 2004. Acts of the Apostles. In *Global Bible Commentary*. Nashville: Abingdon, pp. 419–28.

Livesey, Nina E. 2010. *Circumcision as a Malleable Symbol*. Wissenschaftliche. Untersuchungen zum Neuen Testament 2. Reihe 295. Tübingen: Mohr Siebeck.

Lorde, Audre. 1984. *Sister Outsider*. Freedom: Crossing.

Knepper, Paul. 2001. Historical origins of the prohibition of multiracial legal identity in the states and the nation. In *The Construction of Race and Ethnicity in the United States*, 2nd ed. Edited by Joan Ferrant and Prince Browne Jr. Upper Saddle River: Prentice-Hall, pp. 129–34.

O'Neal, Traci D. 2018. *The Exceptional Negro. Racism, White Privilege and the Lie of Respectability Politics*. Atlanta: iCart Media.

Pervo, Richard I. 2009. *Acts*. Hermeneia: A Critical and Historical Commentary on the Bible. Minneapolis: Fortress.

Raboteau, Albert J. 1978. *Slave Religion: The 'Invisible Institution' in the Antebellum South*. New York: Oxford University Press.

Reimer, Ivoni Richter. 1995. *Women in the Acts of the Apostles. A Feminist Liberation Perspective*. Minneapolis: Fortress.

Sechrest, Love. 2010. *A Former Jew. Paul and the Dialectics of Race*. New York: T&T Clark.

Smith, Mitzi J. 2011. *The Literary Construction of the other in the Acts of the Apostles: Charismatic others, 'the Jews', and Women*. Eugene: Wipf and Stock.

Smith, Mitzi J., and Lalitha Jayachitra. 2014. *Teaching All Nations: Interrogating the Great Commission*. Minneapolis: Fortress.

Tillman, Linda. 2011. Sometimes I've Felt Like a Motherless Child: Being Black and Female in the Academy. In *The Black Professoriat. Negotiating the Habitable Space in the Academy*. Edited by Sandra Jackson and Richard Greggory Johnson III. New York: Peter Lang, pp. 91–107.

Walker, Alice. 1979. *Coming Apart*. New York: Bantam.

White, E. Francis. 2001. *Dark Continent of Our Bodies: Black Feminism and the Politics of Respectability*. Philadelphia: Temple University Press.

Zack, Naomi. 1993. *Race and Mixed Race*. Philadelphia: Temple University Press.

MDPI

St. Alban-Anlage 66

4052 Basel

Switzerland

Tel. +41 61 683 77 34

Fax +41 61 302 89 18

www.mdpi.com

Religions Editorial Office

E-mail: religions@mdpi.com

www.mdpi.com/journal/religions